THE FORTITUDE, FAITH AND FOIBLES OF THE PEEVERS OF COMMANDA

# In the Land of the White Pine

THELMA JAMES

Best Regards Thelma

STONE'S THROW PUBLICATIONS

ISBN 978-0-9921040-2-3

Edited by Ruth Walker
Cover design by Sue Reynolds
Cover and Text Design: Sue Reynolds and James Dewar

Published by Stone's Throw Publications
13240 Mast Rd., Port Perry, Ontario, Canada L9L 1B5.
www.stonesthrowps.ca

Printed and bound in Canada

1 2 3 4 5 6 7 8 9 10

In 1836 John Peever and his pregnant wife, Ellen Farmer Peever, left County Kerry, Ireland and emigrated to The Canadas, leaving two small children behind in their homeland.

These are the stories of the struggles and victories of John and Ellen Farmer Peever, and their descendants.

James and Annie Peever 1954

James and Annie Peever and Grown Children 1956

(Inset) Preston and Mervyn

EARLY PARRY SOUND DISTRICT

Nipissing Road
Pickerel Hills Road
Great North Road
Poor Mans' Road

Townships and additional towns added to Everett Kirtons' Nov., 1962 map by F. Presley.

# ~Acknowledgements~

Thank you first of all to my editor Ruth E. Walker for her wise guidance and kind encouragement while writing my first book. Thanks to James Dewar of Stone's Throw Publications for his advice and assistance in launching my book and thanks to Sue Reynolds of Piquant Press for her lovely book cover design. Fond gratitude is due to my daughter Lorraine James Jones and my granddaughter Dannielle Prince, both teachers, for carefully proofreading this book and to my son Larry James for assisting this technologically challenged writer.

I am extremely grateful that my late parents James and Annie Peever were storytellers, providing windows into a bygone era and thankful that my brothers and sisters inherited their storytelling talent. My brothers Rea, Carl, Preston, Gerald, Lloyd, Howard, Mervyn and Archie, and my sisters Lillian, Edna and June all loved to get together to share their memories of events and circumstances that challenged and shaped their lives, although our sister-in-laws often groaned at hearing another of their husband's hunting stories.

While writing this book, I often tied up my siblings' phone lines checking and recheck facts from the past.

I especially want to thank my late brother Howard's former wife Wilma Clark for use of some information and events about their ministry mentioned in her book Arctic Challenge. Special thanks to my sister-in-law Joyce for sharing with us poignant events of Mervyn's passing. I also want to thank Archie's wife Kathy, my sister-in-law for giving me insights into the tasks and challenges of being a minister's wife, of sharing her husband with others and working alongside him as an equal partner in ministry.

Lloyd's wife Eunice, my sister-in-law gave clear example s of the responsibilities that farmer's wives still carry today. I respectfully thank each of them for their contribution to the stories in my book.

I am indebted to Douglas, son of the late John Albert Peever (Uncle Ab), for sharing his account of his father's lonely journey on the Moccassin Trail, transporting the family's household goods to Peevers' new home in Commanda in 1886. John Albert died in 1937. His story might have been lost.

Warm thanks to Lisa (Schermer) Fry, family friend, former neighbour and school teacher, and Commanda Museum Board member, for sharing memories and information about Commanda, surrounding settlements and especially for the history of Trinity Lutheran Church.

Thanks to the family of Everet Kirton who gave me permission to use Everet's 1962 Early Parry Sound District map, adapted with permission by Fred Presley to show some additional township names, boundaries and towns.

I enjoyed time spent with Fred Presley and his wife, Bertha (Anderson) Presley, my cousin when they visited from Ottawa, poring over old maps. I appreciated Fred's expertise in cartography, for sharing his adapted map of Early Parry Sound District and for his time and skill in the reproducing the old Peever Fortune photograph.

Peever researcher Lois (Peever) Nuth has been a valuable source of information for family records and early Peever settlement in Canada. I thank her for her time and marvel at her precise record keeping.

Thanks to Laurie Dobbs, parish secretary of St. Johns Alsace. A special thanks to my former schoolmate Gladys Piper, of Powassan. As St. John's Alsace Church historian she gave me extensive information about the lives and challenges of people who long ago settled in Alsace and created the history of the church and the community. And thanks to United Church of Canada's archivist, Ms. Mathews for her information regarding the historical dates of the Commanda United Church.

Finally, thank you to my husband and photographer Arthur James for reproducing in his own darkroom, old family pictures used in this book, including a 1928 photograph of the old Commanda School that he enlarge to an 8x10 copy and donated to the Commanda Museum. In addition, I thank him for taking the 1954 portrait of my parents, the 1956 group photograph of my family and photographs of the 2010 Ireland Peever Reunion that are used in this book.

# ~Table of Contents~

# ~The Founding of a Canadian Dynasty: The John and Ellen Peever Story~

What prompts people to pack up their belongings and move to a new land? The reasons are as varied as the individuals who emigrate. But one thing is known: people who immigrate to new countries are risk-takers and innovators who dare to chart a new course for their lives. John and Ellen Farmer Peever are believed to be the second of the Peever Diaspora out of Ireland to settle in Canada (John's uncle James is thought to be the first, arriving between1827-1834.) John and Ellen left their home in Ballyseedy, near Tralee, County Kerry in 1836, between the birth of their second and third child. They left behind their two children, Robert, born February 1834 and John, born May1835, with Ellen's parents. Oral history tells of Ellen's brother John Farmer following them to Canada three years later, bringing their two little boys. Their anxious grandmother Farmer sent along schoolbooks to ensure the boys learned their letters and numbers.

John and Ellen arrived in Quebec City on the ship Dockfour that sailed out of Cork, on June 6, 1836. Quebec City was the entry point for immigrants headed for Upper Canada. Shipping companies were not required by the government to keep their passenger manifests until 1865. However, the Chief Emigrant Agent Anthony B. Hawke kept all his emigrant records. They are filed in the Ontario Archives.

When the Peevers landed, their travelling was not over. Immigrants landing in Quebec City, destined for Upper Canada, had to take a steamboat up the St. Lawrence River to Montreal. The cost was five to ten shillings per person, including their luggage. From Montreal they had to travel by horse or oxen-drawn stage. In the Peevers' case, they needed to reach the Ottawa River and had to take another steamboat up the Ottawa River and overland again by stage to their destination in Huntley Township.

The Peevers' homeland in Tralee is on the southwestern tip of Ireland. It sits at the end of Tralee Bay, on the north side, at the base of the Dingle Peninsula that juts out like a thumb from the mainland. The town of Inch forms the south shore base of that 'thumb'. It was from this magical corner of Ireland that the couple set out when John was barely 21, and already the father of two young children.

Birth records in the Republic of Ireland are difficult to trace as most government records were destroyed in the Irish uprising against the English in 1916. But the method of their destruction is an interesting symbol for both the ingenuity and cheek of the rebels.

Records were used to block bullets from coming through the windows of besieged government buildings (according to Jimmy Curshman, an Irish historian speaking at a meeting of the Oshawa, Ontario Historical Society April 6, 1999). The government later canvassed parish records and doctors and lawyers offices to compile, as close as possible, an historical census of the population.

John Peever, born February 24, 1815, is believed to be the grandson of David (Anne) Peevers, son of John Peevers, born 1797 and buried 1839 in Killorglin, just a few miles from Tralee, and his wife Eliza O'Neill Peevers. John's siblings were William, Deborah, Thomas, Dorothy and James and Anne. This information is provided thanks to Peevers researcher Kevin Weatherall of New Zealand. The Tralee Parish Records show the baptismal dates of all his younger siblings. Church records also show that from the eighteenth century onward, the O'Neills and Peevers continued to intermarry.

When the Peevers arrived in Canada immigration authorities dropped the "s" from the spelling of their name and henceforth the name changed to Peever for all their Canadian descendants.

Oral history told by our father, James T. W. Peever, states that his grandfather John was the eldest son of the family and left Ireland because he fell out of favour with his father. William Farmer Peever, John's, son knew this. William F. passed the story on to his children. Records do show that John breached custom at age eighteen by going off to London, England to marry Ellen Farmer, daughter of John Farmer of nearby Farmer's Bridge. She, a woman three years older than him, and married by a Church of England Curate no less!

The previously quoted 1823 Irish Householders Index (Griffith Valuation) lists all the Peevers in County Kerry as Methodists. The Methodists had split from the Church of Ireland. Some Peevers in Ireland remained Church of Ireland and some Methodist. In Canada, John's sons – Richard, William F. and James – maintained their Wesleyan Methodist roots when, after their father's death, they travelled from their father's settlement of Fitzroy Harbour, north to the Parry Sound District.

As a family name, Farmer is uncommon in Ireland. Jimmy Curshman informed me that the name was likely to have been McScollog in the old Irish but changed to Farmer by the English overlords. The Canadian 1871 census of Fitzroy Township lists a John Farmer, who is six years older than John Peever, living in the same household. John Farmer's religion is listed as Church of England. He was the brother of Ellen Peever. In the census, John Peevers' occupation is listed as farmer while John Farmer's is listed as plasterer. The Farmer family continues to live in Farmers Bridge, a hamlet just a few miles from Balleyseedy, four miles from Tralee. The Farmers still work in the building trade.

Why John and Ellen chose to settle in Fitzroy Harbour in Fitzroy Township, on the Ottawa River is not known. *The Carlton County Atlas of 1879* states:

> *This is the most north-westerly portion of the County of Carlton, and is bounded on the north-west by the Ottawa River, on the north-east by Huntley, and on the south-west by the county of Lanark. It presents a great diversity of soil and surface—ranging in the one case from the most level to the roughest and most broken, and in the other, from that of little value or almost utter worthlessness to a quality of superior excellence.*
>
> *The early settlement of Fitzroy was due to Charles Shirreff, from Leith, near Edinburgh, Scotland, and its early history was very intimately identified with that family.*

Mr. Shirreff, a man of means, emigrated from Scotland in 1817 and settled in about 1818-1819 at the "Chats' on the Ottawa river. He accepted a 3,000-acre grant of land by the authorities, who were eager to settle the region as they planned to build the Rideau Canal as an east-west means of transport and commerce. According to the 1871 Atlas, no other settlers came to the township until 1823. By 1830 Shirreff had built a gristmill, sawmill and a general store. The Chats is about 10 miles up the Ottawa River from Fitzroy Harbour, where John Peever and his family settled to raise their growing family, eventually numbering twelve children.

United Empire Loyalists were given grants of land in Fitzroy Township by the military as rewards for their loyalty to the British Crown but the Township was still very sparsely populated when the Peever family arrived. John, no doubt, had read newspaper advertisements in Ireland offering land and knew that his uncle James had settled in Huntley Township. When they landed, that is where John and Ellen headed. But within two years, Fitzroy Township opened up for settlers. John and Ellen moved to claim the dream of all Irish – to own their own land. The 1871 census shows that the majority of immigrants to Fitzroy Township were Irish.

The 1871 Fitzroy township map shows the John Peever farm abutting the farms of Styles, Carr and, nearby, the Bradley farm. John and Ellen Peever's sons married their neighbours' daughters. James married Annie Styles, William F. married Maria (pronounced Mariah in the Old Irish tongue) Carr and Richard married Alice Bradley. All three couples migrated north and settled in the Parry Sound district.

John and Ellen's farm was obviously sufficiently fertile to feed their twelve children but the land surrounding their immediate area might not have been, as some of their offspring, who, like their own father, were also possessed of wanderlust.

Several of them headed for the United States of America and four of them, including our grandfather, travelled to Northern Ontario, taking advantage of the *Free Land Act of 1868*.

Unaware of the government's hidden agenda to lure labourers to the forest industry, William F.'s decision to take advantage of free land being offered was to be a rigorous adventure for himself and for Peever generations to come.

# ~Carving Out a Homestead in Commanda~

*Grandma Peever had the bluest eyes! Her eyes were the colour of the sky on a clear day.*

When she laughed, her eyes danced, but her eyes also knew tears of loneliness. Separated by miles of wilderness from family and friends in the Ottawa Valley, Grandma Maria ached with loneliness.

As women have done for centuries, Maria, who could neither read nor write, followed her husband and the dream that drew him to new land and the promise of prosperity. Both William and Maria were the children of Irish immigrants who'd settled in the Ottawa Valley in the early 1800s. John's parents John and Ellen (Farmer) Peever and Maria's parents, William and Margaret (Laroth) Carr were fortunate to have immigrated about ten years before the Great Potato Famine of 1847 that swept through Ireland. The Potato Famine caused starvation and death in Ireland and it brought waves of destitute Irish immigrants to land on Canadian shores.

Most of the sons of John and Ellen were satisfied to take up farming close to the homestead of their parents in the Ottawa Valley, but William F. at the age of forty-seven chose to uproot his wife and family to grasp at adventure and a new opportunity. The dream was triggered by the Canadian government's enactment of the *Free Land Act of 1868*.

At the urging of lumber barons for manpower to harvest the white pine forests, politicians responded. In Europe and in the rest of Canada, the government advertised that grants of good farmland were available for the taking. All that was required of settlers was a commitment to build a homestead and clear fifteen acres of land within five years. William F.

Peever and two of his brothers, Richard and James heeded the call and settled in the Parry Sound District.

In the early spring of 1896, Maria Carr Peever said goodbye to her parents and neighbours and with her husband, left the Ottawa Valley farming community of Fitzroy Harbour, Upper Canada where she'd been born. Transported by a teamster driving horses and sleigh, they followed rudimentary roads. The 'moccasin road' that the pioneers followed had originally been a series of trails blazed by Indians and voyageurs. Maria, William and ten of their twelve children made the journey to their new home by that historic route. Susan, the youngest, was not yet born and their third eldest, John Albert, was commissioned to follow later. En route, they used frozen rivers and lakes as thoroughfares. Along the way, they rested at rustic inns called "stopping places." The inns provided shelter but the travellers had to supply food for themselves and for their horses.

The route led north, up the Ottawa and Mattawa Rivers, across Trout Lake and La Vasse River, across Lake Nippissing and the South River. Finally, the Peever family took the route now known as the Old Barrett Road, exiting south of the present town of Powassan, coming out at the top of the big hill on the east side of the village of Trout Creek.

As the children grew restless from the tedious journey, the teamster helped to distract them. "I'll show you how to make alder whistles," said the teamster. He had transported the family by horse and sleigh on that long, uncomfortable journey. The teamster now entertained nine-year-old Jim and his brothers and sisters by showing them how to make whistles from slender sticks of green alders that grew along creek banks. Cutting a stick about four inches long, the teamster explained, "Alder whistles can only be made in early spring when the bark is easily loosened from the stick. You must be careful to gently beat the stick on all sides against a hard surface then test the bark to see if it has loosened from the wood. When it is loose, carefully slip the bark off the stick," he instructed. "Now cut notches along the stick and shave off a little wood between the notches for the notes to come out and then shape a mouthpiece at the end. Next slip the bark back on the stick, notch the bark, and you've got your whistle," the teamster said.

The children were enthralled and delighted with their new instruments.

James T. W. (Jim) Peever handed down the skill of making alder whistles (which sound like 'Pan Flutes') to his children and grandchildren.

The strong and capable teamster impressed him.

To Jim's young mind, the job of a teamster was important and exciting. "When I grow up, I'm going to be a teamster," he announced to his parents.

I remember my father telling us this story. "We were nearly there when the weather suddenly turned warm," he said. "Beyond the village of Trout Creek, as we neared Black Creek, we heard a loud grinding sound. Large chunks of ice were jammed against the pilings of the bridge. The dark water surged around the ice jam and over the bridge." He continued, "The Black Creek Bridge was impassable so we had to spend most of that last miserable week of the journey, camped in the door yard of a farm family."

Dense forest shaded the partly snow-covered trail that lead to Commanda. The sleigh runners squeaked and ground over rocks and mud protruding through the snow. At the general store, the Peever family stopped to buy provisions before continuing the last two miles northwest beyond Commanda to their allotted piece of wilderness.

"Wanna fight?" A boy near Jim's age, sitting on the front steps of the Commanda general store, issued the challenge.

"Sure!" Jim answered. The two wrestled and rolled around in the dirt until Jim's mother came out of the store.

"Faith, will you look at yourself! You look like a ragamuffin covered in dirt. You're not bringing that dirt into the sleigh," exclaimed Maria in dismay. She whacked Jim's back and the seat of his pants while Jim busily dusted off his chest and knees. Jim clambered onto the sleigh with a secret grin on his face. He'd made a new friend.

John Albert Peever (Ab), 21 years old, the second son of Maria and William, set out for Commanda about two weeks after the family's arrival. Ab's son Douglas, who was more than eighty years old when I interviewed him about the story of his father travelling the 'Moccasin Road' related, "My dad set off with the Peever's own team of horses and sleigh loaded with the 'flitting' - the family's household goods and feed for the horses. He and the team of horses rested at 'stopping places' along the way. "

"Not long after the Peever family arrived in Commanda, my dad married my mother, Emily Tennant, daughter of another pioneer family. He cleared the land and settled on the shore of Commanda Lake, about five miles northwest of Commanda."

Uncle Ab, a big jovial man, died of a heart attack in 1937, at the age of fifty-eight when his youngest daughter Alma was fifteen years old. A grandson and namesake, John Peever, son of Hugh, lives on Ab's old homestead in the settlement of Carr – now incorporated into the village of Restoule.

By the mid 1800s the Parry Sound district had recently been surveyed. Roads and railways were being built. A railroad was planned to be built, linking the busy port of Parry Sound with the mines of Cobalt and Chapleau. Settlers expected that the rail line would follow the route of the Nippissing Road and would bring commerce to towns along the way. Instead, in 1883 the plan changed. The railway would run west, skirting the north shore of Lake Nippissing, making its stop at North Bay instead of at the thriving port of Nippissing. Even so, Commanda, which was then a centre of commerce at the junction of the Nippissing and Rousseau Roads, appeared to hold promise as a good place to settle. In 1896, when the Peevers arrived, Commanda already boasted a general store, sawmill, a furniture and casket factory, two churches – one Methodist and one Presbyterian – a log schoolhouse and a hotel. Commanda is one of the few settlements on the Old Nippissing Road that, in later years, didn't become a ghost town.

"Why do you want to weep?" our grandfather William F. once asked his wife, Maria. She had been crying and he couldn't understand why. "Look at this beautiful valley and see the deer feeding in the clearing. You couldn't see that sight where we came from," he exulted.

His joy was for the land that was his as far as his eyes could see. He had no sense of the social isolation that his wife and most pioneering women experienced. Other than at church, women rarely saw each other but their men-folk rarely experienced the same isolation. The men found camaraderie while working in lumber camps or engaged in selling farm products. As for Grandpa William, he took his fine stallion to service the mares of the farms in the area. When the railway station at Trout Creek was established, he hauled his beef and pork by horse and wagon twelve miles to the station. The meat was shipped north up the Ontario Northland Railway line to feed workmen building the railroad or to feed men in logging camps. He spent the nights at the local hotel spinning yarns and exchanging 'man talk' about the prowess of his stallion or telling the latest news he'd picked up from local farmers or from the cook at a lumber camp.

Grandpa William built his sturdy home of squared pine logs, chinked with mortar. At the base of a sunny hill facing west, he dug a well and a root cellar for winter storage of vegetables. Grandma Maria laid out her garden with vegetables and herbs, such as caraway and pungent horseradish and herbs for medicinal purposes. She grew rhubarb and red currant bushes. Hardy plum trees and fruit-bearing hawthorn trees bordered her garden. At the corner of the log house grew a rose bush producing large fragrant pink roses.

Grandpa William, however, made a fatal mistake. Behind the house on the hillside he built the barn and animal pens. In 1906, at the age of sixty-four, the feisty, strong-willed patriarch took ill of a typhus-like fever and died. The well, on the downward slope from the barn, was the suspected source of contamination. His death certificate lists typhoid fever as the cause of death.

William F. Peever was a broad shouldered, full-bearded man with high bridged nose and cheekbones. In 1925, his portrait hung on the wall of his eldest son William Alexander Peever in Kelso, a village now incorporated into Iroquois Falls.

Jim's eldest son William Rea Peever tells the story of visiting 'Uncle Willie' that year and witnessing a neighbour ask "why have you got a picture of King George (V) on your wall?"

Uncle Willie responded, "That's not King George. That's a picture of my late father."

Church records show that William F. served as Sunday School Superintendent for the Methodist Church throughout his lifetime. In 1925, however, the Methodist Church and the Presbyterian Church amalgamated, forming the United Church of Canada. The Presbyterian Church was purchased and moved by the German-speaking Lutheran settlers to about 200 yards north from its original site at the brink of Carr's Hill on the south side of the "Old Nippissing Road". To this day, it still serves their descendants, although the services are now in English.

# ~Grandma Peever~

"I'll tell you what I remember about Grandma Peever, which isn't much," said Rea in his serious matter-of-fact way. He was responding to his sister Edna's question about Grandma Peever, while visiting in her home in Powassan. As he cast his mind back in time, his words seemed to take on the form of the child that he was then.

"I was only about eight years old when she died. They say she was small but I didn't seem to realize that, when I was small. I remember her singing hymns. One hymn she sang was *Wash Me in the Blood of the Lamb and I Will Be Whiter than Snow*. That puzzled me, for of course, we did our own butchering and I knew what blood looked like. I said, 'Grandma, if you were washed in lamb's blood, you wouldn't be white, you'd be red.' She had quite a time explaining to me the meaning of that hymn."

"Our grandma was a great housekeeper, I believe," stated Rea. "Carl and I used to spend the night with her when her youngest son, our Uncle Bob, was away. I was surprised to see that she swept the floor before breakfast. I said, 'Grandma why don't you have breakfast first?' She answered, 'Oh, I couldn't sit down to breakfast when the floor is all dirty like this!'"

Farmers, in those days, didn't remove their boots before entering the house; keeping the floor swept and clean was a constant chore.

"I remember that Grandma had farm animals," Rea recalled. "There were chickens and sheep and some cows. She had a garden too. Near the house, Grandma also had a root cellar, which was dug into the side of a hill. One day in the winter, I went with her to the root cellar. We took a lantern with us because it was dark inside. She opened an outer door, which she closed after us to keep the cold air outside. Beyond the inner door there were bins of carrots, parsnips and potatoes. Grandma filled a pail with vegetables from the bins."

"Grandma wore her dresses long, almost to the floor. I remember asking her, 'Grandma, why do you wear your dresses so long?'

She laughed and said, 'Well, I couldn't wear my dresses short like a young girl!'

"Another memory I have is of going over to visit Grandma while Aunt Susie was staying with her. The scene puzzled me so that it stuck in my memory. During the Great War our dad's sister Aunt Susie and her eldest children, Crystal and Melville (Buddy), stayed with Grandma while her husband Uncle Alex (Smith) was overseas." Rea recalls, "After he had returned from the war, I remember seeing Uncle Alex pacing the floor. I asked, 'What's he doing that for?'

"'Oh, Uncle Alex is feeling tough." Grandma answered.

"I didn't know what that meant," commented Rea. "Years later, I met one of the men from his unit who told me that Alex would often come striding into camp after a long march, carrying the pack of one of his less sturdy comrades as well as his own pack."

Alex was in fact, experiencing what is known today as post-traumatic stress disorder from the horrors and carnage of the First World War.

Carl, who'd driven from New Liskeard for the same family gathering, is a year younger than Rea. He added his memories of Grandma Peever. Carl recalls hearing Grandma saying to him when he was little, "You have blue eyes just like me." She was pleased because Carl was the first grandchild to have her distinctive, sky-blue eyes.

Carl recounted this story: "When I was about six, Grandma was old and not well, so I was sent to stay with her. One night, as she tucked me into bed, Grandma heard me heaving a great sigh and she asked me what was wrong. I told her that I hoped she didn't die because I didn't want to go home alone in the dark to tell Ma and Pa. Grandma just hugged me and laughed.

"When Grandma died, it was in the spring," related Carl. "Uncle Bob (Robert Allan Peever) was clearing land to grow turnips. He was tearing out charred stumps that he'd burned and was piling them out of the way so he could sow seed in the cleared land. When he returned to the homestead, he found Grandma lying on the floor. She had died on her knees scrubbing the floor. Bob came running to the house to get Ma and Pa. He was all black from soot. They all ran across the road to the homestead. Rea and I cried because we had been left at home."

Rea recalled, "I remember the funeral. It seemed to have been held at the house. There were lots of buggies and several cars."

Our grandmother Maria Carr Peever, died on April 26, 1924, at age seventy-four. According to her death certificate she died of "apoplexy". She was buried in the Commanda Cemetery. The cemetery occupies land that was donated by our father James T. W. Peever, to the community for that purpose.

Grandma Peever's rose bush flourished for years after the old log house sagged in one corner and finally fell from neglect. The rose bush survived by being transplanted, many years later, to the garden of grand-daughter Edna Peever Holtforster in Powassan. Rea was born in 1915 and Carl in 1916. They were eighty-two and eighty-three respectively, when they told this story. The two, who grew up as close as twins and enjoyed every opportunity to be together, were separated when Carl died suddenly from a massive stroke the next year, 1998.

Rea passed away in his sleep in 2002, at the age of eighty-seven.

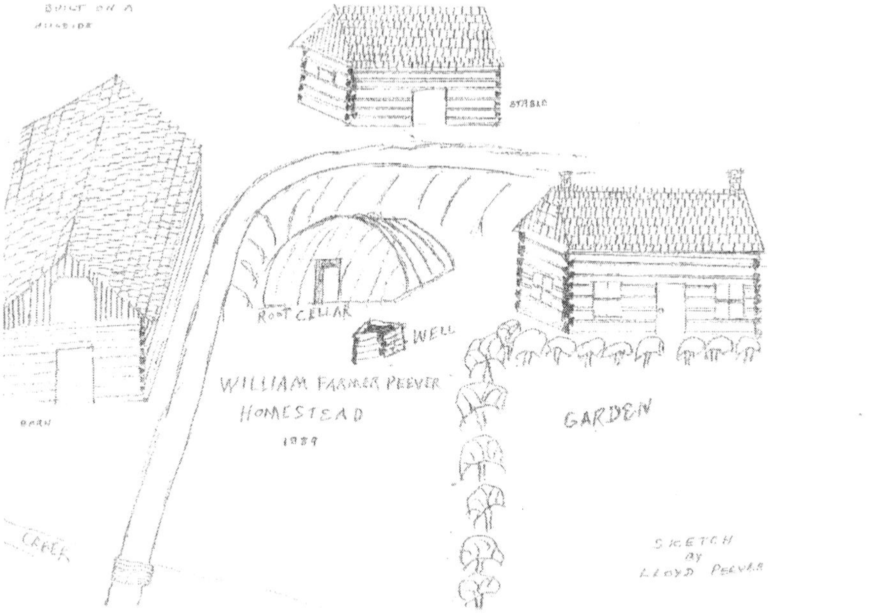


Drawing of the Peever Homestead

# ~My Mother Annie Smith's Story~

Annie scooped a tadpole from the shallow water, cupping it in her hands. The rest of the tadpoles scooted into the tufts of grass at the lake's edge. From the back door came a call, "Annie." Her mother's voice had an urgent tone.

She dropped the tadpole back into the lake and ran up to the house.

"Go quickly and find your sisters."

Annie returned from the yard leading three-year-old Iva; with Luella age seven, following sulkily.

"Children, your father is dead," said their mother.

Annie, at eleven years of age, knew that people died. Her mother had been called away many times to prepare a body for burial when someone in the village died.

But this is different, our father is dead, Annie thought to herself. What will happen to us?

Annie was tall, angular, practical and responsible beyond her years. She didn't shed tears just then; she thought about survival while Luella wailed and Iva whimpered in bewilderment. Luella wailed for she was her father's favourite and now the father she idolized was gone. One-year-old Merritt sat on the floor, his blue eyes wide with wonder at the sounds of distress.

Widowhood had come to Ellen Rea Dobbs Smith for the second time. The daughter of Irish immigrants was widowed in her twenties by her first husband, James Dobbs. She had struggled alone to care for their small son Morley in this pioneering settlement far from home and relatives in Perth, Ontario.

In the village of Golden Valley, Ellen's tall, slim form hurrying to the bedside of someone who was sick or in need of a midwife, was a familiar sight. Now after fourteen years and five more children with Alexander (Sandy) Smith, she was widowed again. Ellen sat down heavily in the rocker, pulling the two little ones into her lap. She rocked and hummed absently.

Sandy's death was expected. Pain and nausea had been his dogged companions for almost a year. In recent months he was jaundiced and bloated from the cancer that destroyed his internal organs. Like his Scotsman father Robert Robertson Smith, Sandy had been a giant of a man. He'd migrated from the Ottawa Valley north to the Parry Sound District in the 1870s. Sandy first settled in Hotham, Nippissing Township, with his first wife, Jane Miskimins. A year after she died and was buried in the new Nippissing Cemetery, Sandy married the widow Dobbs and eventually settled near the village of Golden Valley. Always the gregarious entrepreneur, he was operating a lumber camp and sawmill on Sandy Lake where they lived. He also served as Justice of the Peace for Mills Township, just as his father Robert Robertson Smith had done in Carleton County. Sandy sired eighteen children by his two wives. Sixteen survived infancy.

Alexander (Sandy) Smith was dead at the age of 60, on this warm sunny day, June 16, 1907.

"Annie, you are thirteen and a big girl. Now that school is finished, you are to go and work for the neighbour. She's just had another baby and needs somebody to help with the housework and children," said Ellen. "We need whatever you can earn. It's been two years since your father died. The sawmill is gone and there's no money coming in," she said worriedly.

School is finished! The sound of her mother's voice echoed in Annie's head.

Well that's all right. I never really fit in anyway, thought Annie. I've missed so much school in the winter because the road into Golden Valley was snowed over. By spring the other girls have paired up with somebody else and I'm left out. I'll miss the books in the library though, she said to herself as she turned from her mother.

Not only was the mill gone, due to the business inexperience of their older sons, but her eldest son Morley Dobbs had absconded with the team of horses and driven them to the railway station at Trout Creek. Morley always claimed, to anyone who would listen, that he didn't steal the horses and wagon. He insisted that he'd asked a man at the station to return them to his family. Morley left home never to return until his old age, following the death of his wife. Childless, the couple had lived somewhere in southern Ontario.

Edna, our sister, widowed and living in Port Loring in the early 1960s, took Morley in when he returned. Morley boarded with her for a few years until Edna left the area. She remembered him as an "odd duck". Morley then went to live with Bill Smith, Uncle Alex and Aunt Susie's son in Golden Valley.

Morley Dobbs is buried in Golden Valley Cemetery.

But in 1908, life held promise for Sandy's family. A letter brought exciting news! Mary, her older half-sister, was inviting Annie, now fourteen years old, to come to Eganville, near Renfrew. Mary wrote, "I have found a nice home for Annie to work in. Mrs. Mitchell will pay her ten dollars a month."

Looking up from the letter, her mother Ellen commented, "I'll make you a new dress. You'll need something suitable for Eganville."

In Eganville, Annie was happy to be near her sister Mary Ellen and brother-in-law Elisha Frances. Mrs. Mitchell, the wife of a mining magnate, treated her kindly. Annie dutifully sent money home to her penniless mother. A postcard addressed to Annie, post stamped August 2, 1911, by the Bromley Post Office, was sent by her sister Luella thanking her for a birthday gift. The postscript adds *Ma wants some money*.

Besides the postcard, saved among her few treasured things was a little brown pay packet marked ten dollars, given for her monthly wage and signed by Mrs. Mitchell. In the packet, carefully wrapped in thin tissue, nestled a nugget of rock studded with tiny raw rubies. Years later, on a visit to my home, Annie presented me with this girlhood treasure, still in its little pay packet.

"You do a bit of travelling and you need to look nice. Maybe you can have this made into a piece of jewellery," said my mother. The nugget lies in the bottom of my jewellery box, still in its packet. It means more to me in its present form as a record of my mother's early life.

When mining opened up in Cobalt, Elisha and Mary Ellen Frances moved to that boomtown. Annie went to live in Barrie with another half-sister Agnes and her husband Selby Cooke. The Cookes owned a moving and storage business in Barrie and a tourist resort on the shore of Lake Couchiching. Their son Lester (Les) later served as the mayor of Barrie for many years.

At age ten, I asked my mother how she'd learned to make beds so neatly. My mother, Annie exclaimed, "I used to work as a chambermaid in a Barrie hotel."

At age eighteen, Annie was five feet and eight inches tall, raw boned and serious in disposition. She later found work in a shoe factory but made few friends. Belonging and friendship came when Annie became a member of the Salvation Army. The jubilant music and worship was a tonic to her lonely spirit, and a Salvation Army Ensign provided kindly guidance in her young life. Financial responsibility for helping to support her mother and three younger siblings still rested on Annie's shoulders.

A postcard dated April 1914, is written in the childish hand of her ten-year-old sister Iva. The note tells of the birth of a black colt with a white star on its forehead. Added to the note is a postscript with the request to send some money to buy medicine for an ill sibling. At Annie's death, the postcard was found among her personal things.

Loneliness was soon to disappear. On a trip home to Golden Valley, the stagecoach carrying mail and passengers from the railway station at Trout Creek to the end of the road at Loring carried a charming young bachelor. Jim Peever knew Annie Smith. His younger sister Susie would soon marry Annie's older half-brother Alex. Jim invited Annie to get off the stage with him at Commanda and visit for a few days.

A vast difference in age and disposition was evident between the two. The man who was to become my father was age thirty-and my mother was just eighteen. Since age sixteen, Jim lived and worked in logging camps in winter. In the spring, he was a "river driver" in spike boots, wielding a pike pole and guiding booms of logs down swift rivers to local sawmills. It was a hazardous but free-wheeling way of life. Jim was small-boned, quick and nimble. Less agile men were often crushed to death between surging, pitching logs. Jim, like most river drivers, chewed tobacco instead of smoking. Hands were needed for balance and manoeuvring the pike pole. In his free time, Jim had an active social life, attending local dances and gatherings. He was dapper and popular with the ladies.

Annie at age 18

Old postcards stored in his steamer trunk tell the tale. Postcards were the means of communication in those days. Many were from local young ladies but a letter to Jim from his future wife advises him that she would not like a "flashy" engagement ring, preferring something modest. Devout Annie also expressed some concern about his spiritual life.

Later that year on December 2, 1914, Jim Peever and Annie Smith travelled twenty miles by democrat - a light wagon, to Powassan to be married by the Reverend C. H. Elliot at the Methodist manse.

The newlyweds returned to the home in Commanda that Jim Peever had purchased in 1913 from a Mr. Eric Campbell of Nippissing. It was perched on a western slope across the road, but facing the Peever homestead where he grew up. The two-story frame house consisted of one large common living area on the ground floor and three bedrooms on the second level at the top of a steep staircase. A tarpaper moisture barrier between the outer and inner boards was used in framing the house. It provided the only insulation. Across the road, the Peever homestead, built with foot-thick squared logs, was by comparison much sturdier and warmer in winter. Annie and Jim were to raise twelve children in that small, drafty home.

Within the year Annie bore her first son, named William after his paternal grandfather and Rea for his maternal grandmother's family name. Henceforth he was known as Rea.

"I was in the cow pasture down the road from the house intending to milk our two cows that were producing, when suddenly, I felt a crushing pain," exclaimed our mother – she often retold her harrowing story to her younger children. It's too soon! I thought. The baby isn't due for six more weeks. I turned toward home but one cow that had just calved and was heavy with milk. It followed me, mooing with her discomfort. In spite of my early labour I had to stop and milk her before she would let me go.

"Grandma Peever helped deliver Rea. He was so tiny that he could fit crosswise in the seat of the narrow rocking chair. Rea had dark curly hair and sombre brown eyes," she recalled, still smiling at the memory.

Carl was born a year later, fair of colouring and sunny of disposition. The brothers were companions and best friends as long as they lived.

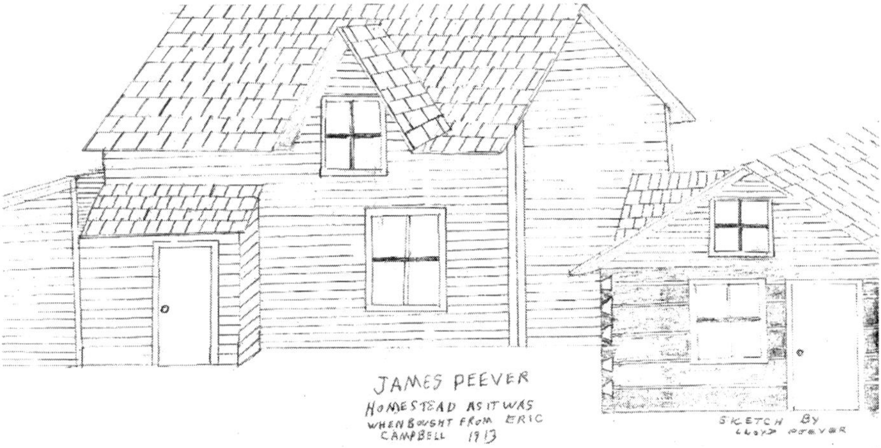


Drawing of James Peever Homestead

# ~Tending Temperamental Pigs~

With the air of an excursion, the family climbed into the wagon. The year was 1919 and the young Peever family was off to buy pigs to add to their farm stock.

"At three-years-old, I had never seen a pig," explained Carl. "Pa told me, 'The pigs are Chester White, just the breed I want. They will be long in the body so as to make lots of bacon and not too much fat.'

"Along the bumpy road toward Commanda, the wagon rumbled for a mile and then turned at the cemetery, heading northwest about four miles up the Nine Mile Bush Road (now Bennett's Road) to Yerke's farm."

The Yerkes were one the families of German, Polish and Swiss immigrants, who, in the 1860s responded to the Canadian government's drive for colonization.

In the European papers, the government advertised grants of land and four bags of seed grain per family.

Settlers hacked a clearing out of the virgin forest of the rocky Precambrian Shield where the receding Ice Age had gouged the landscape, dropping rocks and gravel in its wake. The hilly marginally productive farms yielded more rocks than crops.

This day, Jim Peever bought a pregnant sow and a yearling of good breeding stock. He loaded them into slatted wooden crates for the journey to their new home.

Well away from the farmhouse, set between the hen house and barn, a slope-roofed log pigsty awaited the pigs.

"In March, a litter of piglets was born, but the sty was too cold for their little pink bodies," recounted Carl. "Pa gathered them up in a butter firkin (a wooden tub, in English measure equal to one quarter of a barrel, in which butter was packed and sold) and set them behind the woodstove to get warm. When the piglets were warmed and lively, Pa returned them to their mother.

"As he lowered the butter firkin into the pen, the piglets cried out. With an angry snort, the protective mother pounced on the butter firkin, crushing several piglets and shattering the firkin.

"Had our mother known, she would have insisted that her butter firkin was a poor choice for a pig nursery!" laughed Carl.

Despite early mishaps, the pig-raising enterprise thrived and continued to supply the growing family with meat. Sides of bacon and hams were taken to neighbour Otto Schermer for smoking.

Otto Schermer, his wife Heddy and four-year-old daughter Lisa, his sister-in-law Louisa and her husband Wilhelm Hildebrand emigrated in 1929 from what was once known as East Berlin. They settled in the valley east of Farley's Corners.

In 1904, on a ridge commanding a sweeping view of the valley with Commanda Creek running through, the Hoffmans (previous German settlers) built a well-designed stone house and farm buildings. When Otto Schermer bought the farm he built a stone smoke house using the ample material at hand.

The Schermer smokehouse proved to be a boon for the Peever family too. Previously in summer they had to rely on salt-cured meat or meat stored for the short-term on precious ice, packed in sawdust in the icehouse. As time went on, in true neighbourly fashion, Jim Peever returned the favour by descending on the Schermer farm at harvest time with his army of sons.

"Lloyd, that sow is ready for breeding now," said Ma. "You and Howard will have to take her up to Grabouski's farm for servicing. There is nobody else here to do it!"

In winter, to maintain the family income, our father and any sons having completed the eighth grade hired themselves into the services of local logging camps: Tom Hummel's in Carr, Barney Mc Nutt's in Restoule or Empey's camp in Golden Valley. Life in a logging camp provided another kind of education for the boys. Managing and maintaining the farm fell to our mother, with the help of the younger children.

In 1938, it happened, therefore, that the task of taking the pig for breeding fell to my brothers, eleven-year-old Lloyd and ten-year-old Howard. The boys hitched the horses to the sleigh and, with the help of our mother, loaded the pig's crate onto the sleigh and drove the irritable sow up the ramp into the crate.

"You remember the Grabouski's farm?" Lloyd asked his siblings years later at a family gathering. "You turn left just past the Commanda Hall. It lies about three miles northeast, up the Alsace Road near St John's Catholic Church. For about a mile the climb is straight up. That day, at the top of the steep hill, an enormous snowdrift caused the road to disappear in a drop-off down the other side. Fearing the drop-off, the horses shied and danced. It took all my strength to hold them.

"After the breeding, the sow refused to go up the ramp to her crate. Mr. Grabouksi set the crate on the ground and we got the pig into it, but the three of us – Mr. Grabouski was a small man – couldn't lift the sow. He went into the house and brought out his buxom wife and teenage daughter Monica. They lifted that temperamental pig into the sleigh with no problem."

# ~Luella Mabel~

Luella Mabel, Annie's normally happy, bouncing two-year old is holding her belly, doubled up in pain. For two days she cries piteously. None of Annie's home remedies help. Annie gets to the nearest phone three miles away at Tom Farley's store and calls Dr. Dillaine, over 20 miles away in Powassan. He is the only doctor in the area. Dr. Delaine listens to the symptoms and instructs Annie, "There is nothing I can do for her here. Get on the train for the Sick Children's Hospital in Toronto right away! It sounds like a ruptured appendix."

With the crying infant in her arms, Jim loads Annie into the democrat and jounces for twelve miles over the stony, rough road to the railway station at Trout Creek.

The Ontario Northland train pulls to a stop at the little station. Annie, in a desperate attempt to save her baby, takes the train as far south as Gravenhurst. With a critically ill child in her arms, she has to change lines there. It seems to take forever. Annie boards the Canadian National to Toronto. Her destination is the Hospital for Sick Children.

Surgeons operate. They find that peritonitis is already destroying the ruptured bowel and the extensive surgery they must do is causing a massive loss of blood. The doctors hook up a direct transfusion line from mother to child. Their last heroic attempt fails.

Annie, just 24 years old, retraces her journey with empty arms. A little white casket rides in the baggage car.

Her headstone reads: *Luella Mabel, born 1918, died July 14th, 1921, at 2 years, 6 months and 21 days.*

The headstone, with a precious little reclining lamb on the top, and a faded photograph of a sweet-faced toddler, is all that most of us know of her. As children, we visit her grave frequently. The graveyard lies at the halfway mark between home and the one-room school two miles away in the village of Commanda.

Massive spruce trees standing guard along the fence sigh in the breeze. We speak in hushed tones as we skirt the tiny mound and caress the little lamb that is so perfectly formed that it could be alive. She is our little sister and we feel protective of her as she lies among the large gravestones of the grownups. Luella Mabel will forever be remembered as 'our little sister.'

"I remember seeing her for the first time," Rea tells us. "She looked so tiny in the bed. I asked why she didn't look like Carl and me. Ma explained that she was a girl. I was three years old."

Carl tells us his story of playing 'chase' with Luella Mabel. He says, "Rea and I and our little sister were running around the 'banking' of the house (houses, in those days, were banked with earth to insulate the cellar). She couldn't keep up with us, so Ma turned her around. She ran the opposite way and caught us. Luella Mabel laughed with delight.

"She took sick and died soon after."

In a glass display case at the Commanda Heritage Museum, we place Luella Mabel's delicate muslin baby dress and bonnet. When our mother died, we found them among her treasured things.

**Epilogue**

Carl and Rea told their stories about Luella Mabel during our last family gathering to celebrate all the spring birthdays in the family. As Carl and Rea were the only two siblings to know our little sister, I'd asked them both, "What do you remember about Luella Mabel?"

That was the last time we saw Carl. Two weeks later our smiling, happy brother was gone from us.

My mother told about her desperate journey with Luella Mabel, when, as a ten-year-old, I asked how she got the scar on her inner arm.

June and Thelma at Luella Mabel's Headstone

Registrar-General
Ontario

# Certificate of Registration of Death

(BURIAL PERMIT)

Official form prepared by the Registrar-General of Ontario, and issued by Division Registrars for Burial purposes, including transportation, as authorized by The Vital Statistics Act 1919, Section 36

I hereby certify that the particulars of the death of Luella Peever.

which occurred at the City of Toronto, in the County of York, Ontario, on the 14th day of July 1927 have been duly filed with me and registered in accordance with the provisions of The Vital Statistics Act, the Cause of Death being appendicitis

and permission for the burial of the body is hereby granted.

Given under my hand this 15 day of July 1927.

C. P. Playter
Division Registrar.

Division of Toronto, County of York.

This certificate must be obtained before the interment of any body may take place, and must be delivered at the time of burial to the superintendent or caretaker of the cemetery in which such body is interred, except as wherein otherwise provided according to The Vital Statistics Act.

OVER.

# ~Bear Among the Sheep!~

“I remember when we had sheep,” said my second oldest sister Edna. “Our mother used to send the wool from our sheep to the Bancroft Woollen Mills to be made into skeins of yarn and blankets for the family. Some of the wool she kept to card and spin. I wonder why our parents got rid of the sheep.”

Rea, the eldest, answered, “Oh, they became such a nuisance that in 1933, Pa sold the whole lot. I was nearly eighteen at the time.

“In the early days, there were so very few cars or trucks travelling on the road that the sheep grazed along the roadside and they would even lie down on the road. The traffic increased in the early 1930s when the new road was built. Pa put up fences but some sheep would always manage to find a hole in the fence to squeeze through and then they’d be killed. Bears also killed the sheep.

“Uncle Bob and Pa pastured the sheep together,” continued Rea. Their ears were marked to tell them apart. The sheep pastured on the hillside, just east of the old homestead. It was across the road from our house. The setting sun would warm that large flat rock which lies at the brow of the hill, named Cook’s rock, after an earlier settler. At the end of the day, the sheep bedded down there for the night.

“One spring day, Pa walked to our Uncle Ab’s farm at Commanda Lake five miles away in Restoule, to get some seed barley. Late that night, the sheep came tearing into the farmyard, bleating with terror. Ma woke me, saying, ‘Rea, there’s something after the sheep.’

“I got dressed, lit a lantern and took the shotgun. Up the hill I went, to see what was after the sheep. Was it renegade dogs or thieves? Everything was still. There was nothing to be seen in the field and I didn’t want to go into the bush in the dark.

“The next morning, when Pa came home, we counted the sheep.

There was one sheep missing, so Pa took the 30-30 rifle and went up a bush trail, close by the pasture. There he found a lamb and its mother. A bear had killed both and had fed off the ewe. Pa went over to Uncle Bob's, where Aunt Esther's brother Wallace McKee, a trapper, was visiting. Together they set a bear trap, using the dead sheep as bait. All day and into the evening we worked sowing the barley. Suddenly, just at dusk, the dogs began barking and the horses started rearing and snorting with fear. The bear was in the trap! But, in the thick bush where the bear was, it was already too dark. A bear would be able to crush a man before he could see it.

"There was nothing to do but wait until morning. Nobody slept that night because the dogs barked continually. At daylight, Pa and Wallace McKee went up the trail into the bush. They each carried a rifle. There in the trap was the bear, angry and dangerous. Wallace, the trapper, wanted the bear's hide, so he shot the bear in the head, taking care not to damage its skin."

"I helped Wallace McKee skin that bear! I was sixteen then," Carl declared with excitement at the memory.

Our brother Mervyn, home on a visit from British Columbia and the reason for another 'clan gathering', was excited to be included in the story. Puffing up his chest, he chimed in, "I was three when that happened. I was carried up the hill and I got to stand on the bear that killed the sheep. About the same time, I remember feeding an orphan lamb from a bottle. We got rid of the sheep shortly after."

"Yes," sighed Rea sadly, shaking his head and harking back to those difficult times, "and before Pa sold the sheep, we sheared their fleece for wool. It was no good trying to sell the sheep to the neighbours, because it was in the middle of the Depression and nobody had any money. Our father sold them to a stock dealer. That's what happened to the sheep."

# ~School Adventures~

"With every step, heavy blue clay clung to our boots," Rea recalled. "That fall, by the time we reached the sand hill our short legs could barely make the climb! When Carl and I started school in September 1922, the new road to Commanda didn't have gravel topping yet. It was just mud. I was seven and Carl was six. We started school together because Ma and Pa didn't want me making the long walk alone," said Rea, as we all sat reminiscing about our school days.

The cemetery at the top of the "Sand Hill" – at the corner of what is now called Bennett's Road – marked the halfway point in the two-mile journey to Commanda. The log schoolhouse, built in about1870, stood one mile north of the village on the old Nippissing Road and was now empty. A new frame one-room school was built in 1900 at the top of the Round Hill, one eighth of a mile north of the Commanda store. It was towards this school the boys headed. Picking up a stick from the roadside, the boys scraped the gummy mess from their boots. Their pant legs were smeared with mud. Dressed in the neat pants and matching velvet-trimmed jackets and bow ties, which Ma had so lovingly made for them to start school, Rea and Carl trudged doggedly on.

Rea remembered so many details, speaking in his slow steady drawl, "In the summer of 1922, men with teams of horses dug up the roadway with plows and cleared away rocks. Pa was hired on with his team too. A road was built, linking Port Loring to the railway station at Trout Creek. Before that, the old Rousseau Road junctioned with the Nippissing Road at Commanda and it joined up at the cemetery with the tail end of Great North Road, the 'tote road' from Golden Valley locally called the Nine Mile Bush Road. There was a stopping place on that old tote road at Benjamin Carr's that accommodated travellers and the driver of the horse-drawn covered stage. Carr's property was later bought by a German settler by the name of Bogener before the Bennett family owned it," Rea digressed. "Teams of horses levelled the ground for the new road by dragging squared timbers over it. The road ran through our farm for half a mile, coming down Peever's Hill and straight through the low ground of the 'flat', before it crossed Peever's Creek and went up the Sand Hill. Mike Magolski was the 'water boy' for the men building the road. He was about sixteen at the time," Rea recalled.

The two little boys struggled through snow up to their thighs until Christmas when Ma declared, "You boys will have to stay home until spring. I'll help you with your letters and numbers."

Ma was true to her word. She ordered a "lotto" game and children's storybooks from Eaton's Mail Order Catalogue. The game had wooden discs and cards with numbers on them, similar to today's Bingo game. Ma remembered her childhood days of being snowbound in Golden Valley.

The lotto game later served all her succeeding children when they were housebound with childhood diseases such as measles, mumps or the common cold.

"My first teacher was Miss Lehman; then there was Mrs. Graham, Miss Buchanan and then Walter Simms, who came from Loring. He taught for three years and after, his sister Agnes Simms taught us. They were great teachers," Rea stated.

"You must have been interested in nature," I, the youngest sister of the family, commented. "I remember finding a small hutch in a clearing at the edge of the balsam forest, across the road from our house. I asked Mom about it and she said, 'As a science project, Rea tried to raise pheasants. Rea earned the money to buy the pheasants by catching and skinning weasels the previous winter. The pheasants didn't survive though. Foxes got them both.'"

Rea smiled ruefully, "Yes, I was about fourteen at the time."

"School wasn't easy for me," Carl commented. "In the evening after the farm chores were done, we'd sit at the big table near the coal oil lamp to do our homework. At the time, there were eight other brothers and sisters running around so you just couldn't concentrate on homework with all the distraction."

"I loved school," Lillian chimed in.

"We always started in the morning by singing *God Save the King* and repeating the Lord's Prayer. At the end of the day we sang *Now the Day Is Over* and the teacher dismissed us with prayer.

"Preston and I were always in the same grade. Preston was smart in math, but I always needed Mom to help me with homework. I remember asking her about spelling 'enough'. Why wasn't it just spelled 'enuf'? Poor Mom! It's a good thing that with six children all in school, they all weren't in grade three. I remember that by age ten, I had to make six lunches in the mornings while Mom and the boys did the milking and the younger children fed the pigs and hens. Our dad was away working in the bush."

Lillian continued, "Often in the winter, Lisa Schermer and Alma and Walter Hoffman would come into our house to get warm on the way to school. We only had two miles to walk to school but they had to walk four miles or more."

Lillian added another incident, "Mom always said 'come straight home from school', but one spring day, on the way home, Preston and Gerald – who was the next youngest to us – were skipping stones along the road. I was walking straight ahead as Mom had instructed but one of Preston's stones hit me. I cried out in hurt, outraged that my dearly loved brother would do such a thing!

Preston claimed, 'You were walking too fast.' I answered, 'I was not! I was walking as slow as on old cow!' I had hot tears running down my face. That was the only fight we ever had," remarked Lillian, then the wife of a minister.

Lillian continued with her story, "One day in early December, Gerald, Preston and I came rushing in from school. Preston was in the lead. At the door Preston stamped snow off his feet before Mom could get the words out to take care. She gave him a swat with the tea towel, crying out in dismay, 'I just put the Christmas cakes in the oven and they've probably fallen!'

"School wasn't always fun," recalled Lillian. "One day, Helen Percy said I stole ten cents from her lunch pail. I got the strap from the teacher, Miss White. The strap didn't hurt so much but I felt terrible. I was blamed for stealing! It was another girl who took the money. When I got home, Mom took me on her knee and held me. That meant so much."

"Blaming happened to me too," chimed in younger brother Howard. "I was about seven at the time. We were playing 'Ante I Over', throwing a ball over the woodshed roof to the team on the other side. For a prank, one of the Yerke boys threw a rock instead. It hurt a child on the other side. I was blamed. The teacher, Ted Jordan, gave me the strap. Later, another child told the teacher who really did it. The teacher didn't even apologize to me for the mistake, so Pa walked down to the school. He told Mr. Jordan that if he abused the Peever children, he would have 'a man to reckon with'. After that, Pa served on the school board until the last of his children graduated."

"Mr. Jordan was a good teacher though," commented Lillian. "He taught students up to Grade Ten. When I passed my Provincial Entrance exams in 1936, I cried because I thought I couldn't go any more. Both Preston and I were allowed to stay in school through to Grade Ten."

Ted Jordan was the first teacher to institute hot lunches in schools during the Depression. He served hot cocoa one day and vegetable soup the next. Children took turns bringing ten-pound corn syrup pails of milk from home for cocoa or some root vegetables or a soup bone. At first recess older girls and boys started preparing the vegetables for soup or heating the milk for cocoa in a big pot that Mr. Jordan provided. Children brought their own enamel mug and spoon – which each washed after their meal. Hot lunches in winter continued until the Commanda School closed in 1969 when the students were bussed to Trout Creek Public School.

Lillian continued, "Our family's day began at 6:30 in the morning when Pa got up to light the fire and put the water on to heat for porridge and it ended about 9 in the evening, but Preston and I were allowed to stay up to do our homework. The house became so quiet, just the crackling of the fire and the barn owl hooting in the trees by the old log milk house, broke the silence. Soon we closed our books and headed for bed too.

"When I passed my Entrance exams in 1938, I wasn't allowed to continue in school," stated Edna. "In January, Lillian had gone to Toronto to attend Shaw's Business School that year so when next September came, I was all ready to leave for school, but our Pa said I had to stay home and help Ma with the housework and younger children. I was only twelve years old and I was so disappointed and angry. It seemed so unfair! I was too young to understand about our mother's heavy load and our dad didn't explain. In those days we were expected to do as we were told with no questions asked. It was hard to forgive them for that."

"Yes," agreed the rest. "That must have been a miserable time for you. It was wrong of them. You deserve credit for finishing your education when you became an adult."

"Howard," I said, "I remember when I was six you found a baby chipmunk and took it to school in a shoe box. When you lifted the lid to show the teacher, the chipmunk moved. Miss Kennedy, the teacher, screamed and the poor chipmunk died of shock."

"Yes, she was a funny old spinster," commented Howard. "Miss Katie Kennedy was a devout Catholic but she got in trouble with the school board for bringing Father Rouche, the priest, from Trout Creek to promote the Catholic faith in a public school. Denominational feelings ran very high in those days."

"You're right," I agreed "Just last year I met a woman at a party in Whitby. We somehow got talking about where we were from. Both of us were surprised to discover that we came from the same area. Her mother had died, explained Stella, so she lived with her uncle, a Leduka from the little settlement of Alsace. She said that she attended the Separate School in Alsace but she was taken out of school during the Depression to help her uncle cut and sell firewood. When I stated that I'd attended the Commanda School, she exclaimed, 'Oh, you were one of those Protestant pups'!" Everyone laughed.

Mervyn chimed in with his moment in the limelight at school. He said, "In the first month of school the teacher had the Grade One's standing in a row in front of her desk. She was teaching us to count. She had the students count how many fingers they had and how many toes. When she came to me, I counted ten fingers. She said, 'How many toes do you have?' I answered nine. 'Nine?' she said, 'What happened to your tenth toe?' I answered, Gerald chopped it off. In horror the teacher asked what happened. I told her that two summers ago Gerald was in the yard near the woodpile chopping firewood wood. I was four and I was standing barefoot watching him. I told her Gerald said, 'put your toe on the block and I'll chop it off.' I knew he was fooling me, so I put my foot on the block. He thought that I'd pull my foot back in time and I thought he'd stop the axe in time. I said, Ma gathered up my toe and stuck it back on while Gerald ran to the Commanda store to get someone to drive me to the doctor in Powassan. The doctor cleaned the wound and bandaged the toe in place but it didn't heal," I told the shocked teacher. My toe was the talk of the school at recess," Mervyn said, as we all laughed about the shocked faces in the schoolroom.

Howard remembered another story about school, "The winters, sometimes 25 degrees below Fahrenheit, were severely cold on the feet as we walked to school. On Sunday nights we took turns bathing in the round zinc washtub beside the big woodstove. Ma always did the washing on Monday but she told us to wash out our socks in the bath water and hang them to dry behind the stove so they'd be clean for school the next day. I was about six and always strove for Ma's approval but Lloyd, who was older by about a year-and-a-half, wouldn't wash his socks. On the way to school next morning he cried from cold feet. His socks, stiff with dirt and old sweat, didn't provide any insulation. That year, I remember Gerald, who was about twelve, crying too with cold feet for the same reason. The older ones told him, 'go back home', but he was afraid of getting in trouble for missing school. He was hopping up and down and crying, 'I don't know whether I should or not.'"

"The first winter when I started to school was terrible for me," I added. "By the time we reached the first mile by the cemetery, my feet in those black ankle rubbers would be freezing and giving such pain and there was still a mile to go! The rubbers were frozen stiff too and they chaffed my ankles. The older ones would tell me, 'Don't cry, the tears will freeze your face!' I swallowed my tears then, but by the time I got to school, I had a belly ache from swallowing my pain. To this day, I still get 'the belly ache' when stressed.

June chimed in, "Do you remember one time that winter when we were so cold on the way home from school that Lloyd and Howard made a shelter under some big spruce trees and built a fire for all five of us to get warm? We gathered around the fire under the canopy of spruce boughs and stuck sticks into our frozen leftover sandwiches and toasted them over the fire. The warmth and food revived us enough to face that long windy stretch of open flat before home."

"Yes, we had fun and adventure too. Archie missed it. He hadn't started school yet," I added.

"I remember that February, when Lloyd was about nine, he had an attack of appendicitis at school. Miss McLaughlin sent him home with me. I can still see him coming through our door, doubled up in pain," said Howard, shaking his head at the memory.

"What a terrible time," agreed Lloyd. "I lay upstairs in agony for two days with a ruptured appendix while Ma sent word for Pa to come home from Charlie Smith's logging camp. The vibration of everyone downstairs just walking across the floor was unbearable."

"It all happened in the middle of a bad snowstorm in 1937," added Howard. "Pa went and got Mr. Hubener, a German settler from up the Alsace Road. He was one of the few people in the area with a vehicle. Pa broke a trail all the way for 12 miles to the Number 11 highway through the snow with the horses by dragging a chain attached to the whiffletree. Mr. Hubener followed with Lloyd bundled up in the truck. I remember Ma standing in the doorway praying for him as they left the house. Mr. Hubener took Lloyd about 50 miles away to the hospital in North Bay," Howard concluded.

I added, "I remember the visit from Dr. R. H. Dillaine after Lloyd came home. I would have been not quite three. Mom was at the barn and there was a knock at the door. Mervyn, June and I thought it was one of the older boys fooling us. June, not yet five years old, called out, 'Come in if your nose is clean. If it's not, stay out.' We were mortified when the doctor walked in! That moment is still vivid in my memory."

"I'll surely never forget the experience!" nodded Lloyd.

"Do you remember one winter day on the way to school when we found the pail of corn syrup?" June asked. "It had fallen off a truck and the lid was open. We scooped up hands full of the sticky sweet stuff and ate it even though our bare hands got stiff from the cold. Putting our mitts over those sticky hands felt awful! We then hid our wonderful find in a snow bank and continued on to school. After school we went to where the syrup was hidden but it was gone. Someone had followed our tracks and found our buried treasure," laughed June, ruefully.

"A very serious thing happened one morning in 1943 as we rode to school with our dog team," recalled June. "Our dogs, Sport and Hunter were very fast and as we passed Pilger's Road where it joins the main road to Commanda, in the distance we saw ahead of us Dorothy Hanselman and her dog team. Dorothy was about Mervyn's age. Mervyn, who was thirteen and I age eleven, sicced the dogs to catch up with Handselman's dog-team. The dogs took off, tumbling Thelma off the sleigh. Archie still clung to the sleigh but he viewed a scary sight. Our dogs caught up to Hanselman's dogs and attacked them. What a terrible situation! Both Dorothy and Mervyn were beating at the dogs and yelling to make them stop but the dogs were mad with blood lust. They fought on, tangled in their harnesses until one of Hanselman's dogs was dead.

Our father had to pay compensation to George Hanselman for the loss of his dog. Pa forbade us to take the dog team to school anymore," said June.

"I ran to catch up and to see what was going on. I still remember the horror of that dogfight," I exclaimed, shaking my head. "Our father's punishment was well-deserved!"

"Sometimes though, on really cold days in winter when he was home, Pa would hitch up the horses and sleigh and meet us as we reached the beginning of that long cold flat. We'd huddle down in the sleigh out of the wind," remembered Archie.

"Addie Ricker had a little house in Commanda, next to the derelict Ever's hotel, just before we turned up the road to the school. I remember her inviting June and me in to get warm. We took off our boots and she had us sit with our feet on the open oven door. The frost coming out of our feet was so painful that we had to hop around. It was so kind of her though," I told the others.

"It was likely about that time in the school year when we Peever kids noticed that most of our schoolmates referred to their parents as Mom and Dad, not Ma and Pa. We wanted to be modern too so we began to refer to our parents as such even thought the older siblings continued to used the 'old fashioned' terms of Ma and Pa. Our parents didn't object.

Commanda School

"Mrs. Hannaford was our teacher when I was in second grade. She often corrected our pronunciation of words too – she likely eliminated our 'Ottawa Valley Irish' way of speaking.

"The event that stands out in my memory as the best experience of school, happened while I was doing my seat-work and listening to the grade nine and ten students on the other side of the room. Their class was reading and discussing *The Tale of Two Cities* and Sir Walter Scott's *Lady of the Lake.*

"I was drawn into that strange and tragic story of the French Revolution and entranced by the cadence and beautiful words of Scott's poetry in the *Lady of the Lake*. I fell in love with the magic of literature in that year."

Commanda Creek flowed as broad and fast as a river but still it was classified as a creek because it was shallow except in spring run-off. On the way home from school, the Commanda Creek emerged out of the forest a quarter mile west of the village and it flowed in the gorge alongside the road. There it formed rapids, spewing boiling foam over its rocky bottom. The locals referred to the area as the 'White Waters'. In winter, the White Waters steamed as spume met the frosty air. The creek descended following the curve of the road until it slowed at a tight bend, crossed the road under the bridge and slid under its prison of ice again.

In late spring, it was fun to climb down into the gorge, remove our shoes and socks and 'run the rapids,' leaping from stone to stone. Lots of times we soaked the seat of our pants as a stone tipped us into the cold water.

But the greatest test of courage and balance lay ahead at the bridge.

The framework of the white bridge was built of squared two-foot-thick beams. The first ten-foot beam slanted upward, meeting the cross-beam of the same length and joined the third beam slanting downward.

Older brothers, Lloyd, Howard and Mervyn had mastered the art of walking up the beam, across the top and down the other side, heedless of the black water swirling twenty feet below.

June, at ten, was able to manage it.

Reminding the others, I boasted, "I was eight when I first tried to 'walk the bridge'. Up the first beam, I stepped with care and trepidation.

'Don't look down!' The others warned as I placed my foot on the cross-beam.

"I looked down. The swirling water below made me dizzy. I dropped to my knees. Gripping the sides of the beam, I crawled across with my eyes fixed only on the beam, and then I stood and walked down the other side. The next year, I 'walked the bridge'."

Today, motorists speed along the straightened and paved highway 522 and they cross a utilitarian gray metal bridge over Commanda Creek, unaware of the lost mystique of the old white bridge. And townspeople will never see their old school again either.

"The school is burning!" shocked villagers in Commanda called out to each other as flames brightened the night sky one night in October of 1943.

Perched at the top of the 'Round Hill', the school's flames could be seen for miles. The wooden structure burned like dry tinder. Nothing could be saved – not school records, nor desks.

An ember falling from the big box stove was the suspected cause.

It was wartime, building materials hard to get and the community had no school. The resourceful trustees met and made arrangements to use the Commanda United Church.

In a matter of weeks, volunteers erected a partition across in front of the church's altar. Pews, organ and all church materials were stored behind the partition.

Trustees obtained desks and blackboards and school resumed.

It was all too much for the teacher Mrs. Jessie Phillips. She resigned at Christmas.

The children had an extended Christmas holiday until the end of January 1944, when one of their own Commanda residents Lisa Schermer, at eighteen, took the position.

Lisa Schermer taught grades one to ten on a letter of permission from the Ministry of Education. In summer she took studies at Toronto Normal School to obtain her teaching certification.

The little immigrant daughter of a banker from an East German city, she'd arrived in Canada at age four to settle with her parents on a farm in a rocky hollow outside the village of Commanda. Lisa was now our teacher. When she started school she'd been different from the other children. Lisa spoke no English and her mother dressed her petite only child in hair ribbons and frills. The other children made fun of her, the boys pulling at her hair ribbons and dress.

Edna, Lisa's schoolmate, and as tall as any of the boys and used to fending off three pesky older brothers, became Lisa's defender and friend.

Lisa completed her last two years of high school, boarding in Powassan. It wasn't easy for her to get a higher education. On weekends she rode her bicycle 24 miles home on Saturday and rode it back to Powassan on Sunday.

Thus, it happened that our older sister Edna's lifelong friend and schoolmate became teacher to the younger four Peever children.

Lisa maintained discipline in the school without favour, and despite her youth was held in respect.

To build a new school on the site of the old one the trustees, Otto Schermer, Frank Pilger, and Jim Peever hired Powassan builder Fred Gomoll. The trustees volunteered their labour in order to get the building completed in time for the new school year of September 1944, in spite of wartime shortages. Along one side, the new school had a bank of windows providing wonderful lighting for students. It had a teacher's office, an oil furnace and indoor chemical toilets.

While Lisa was our respected teacher during school hours, on winter weekend moonlit nights she hosted sleigh-riding parties on Schermer's Hill. At the top of the hill, she lit a bonfire to warm hands and feet. What rides we had down that mile-long winding hill by the eerie blue light of the moon! Dragging our sleighs back up to the top wasn't as much fun.

During the war years Lisa Schermer's students had a ringside seat to the discreet courtship between handsome Airman Gilbert Fry and their teacher. Lisa and Gilbert were married in Trinity Lutheran Church in April 1947. Two of her senior students, Madeline McConnell and our sister June were her bridesmaids.

"There were lots of good times at school too," remembers June, picking up the thread of conversation.

"On Valentine's Day there would be a box social. The girls brought box lunches for two and the boys would bid on them. Mom always baked something nice for our boxes and she'd help us find bits of coloured paper to decorate them. The bright boxes were arranged on the teacher's desk at the front of the room, waiting for the bidding.

"After the lunch, we went skiing and sleigh-riding down the long winding Round Hill that led to Dell Watt's farm north of the school. There was a low stone bridge at the bottom. If you didn't take care to make the curve, you could miss the bridge and land in the creek. We would go back to the classroom about 3 o'clock and hang our mitts and hats to dry on the heat shield around the big woodstove that sat in the middle of the room, until we were dismissed at 4."

"That was fun," I agreed. "It seems to me that the sun always shone brightly on Valentine's Day, but one Valentine's Day when I was about twelve, I did a bad thing.

"An older boy from my class, Gene Stenton – he had carrot-red hair – tried to kiss me on the bridge at the bottom of the Round Hill. I gave him such a push that he somersaulted right over the bridge and landed on his back in the creek. He crashed right through the ice! Fortunately, Mervyn, big, brawny and four years older than me came down the hill on his skis. He leapt down the bank and hauled Gene up out of the creek. Back at the school, Gene took off all his clothes while Mervyn hung them over the heat to dry. Gene had to stay in the cloak room for two hours while his clothes were drying. He was so mad at me!

"The next summer the Peever kids were swimming in the Commanda millpond. Gene was there too. He tried to drown me in the pond. When I was just about done for, Mervyn looked up from swimming and saw what was happening. He grabbed Gene and shook him loose from me and then gave him a bloody nose.

"I had a bad conscience though for causing all that trouble."

"It was lucky for you that Mervyn was close by," commented Archie, the youngest brother. "It seemed like the Peever lads were mostly the peacekeepers of the schoolyard. We were all about a head taller than our age-mates and that helped. I heard that Preston, although he was quiet and thoughtful, would step in to fend off bullies. He had likely grown to his full height of six-foot-four by the time he completed Grade Ten. All it took was a word from him. When I started school, Hoogie, a much older boy, was pestering me, Mervyn took after him.

"Years later, I stopped my car at the Commanda cemetery to help someone whose car was mired in the sand. I helped him free his car and I introduced myself and shook his hand. It was Hoogie. He thought that I was Mervyn. I was shocked to see that he was just a little over five feet tall. Since school days he'd never grown!"

Archie continued, "I always had to protect Jack and Donnie Bennett. They were born a year apart and were in my class but very shy, not used to mixing with people. When they got picked on, I always stepped in."

"There was no such thing as supervision on the playground in those days. The teachers went to their boarding houses or home for their noon meal. We had to look out for each other," commented Lloyd.

"Don't forget the good times those 'last day of school' picnics," exclaimed Howard. "Remember when one of the fathers loaded all the children into his farm wagon and took us up the Barrett Road to Ruth Lake?"

"Yes, I remember, and once while Lisa Schermer was our teacher, she arranged for our dad to take all of us to Rauche Lake," said June.

I added, "He put the hay rack on the wagon so the little ones wouldn't bounce out because the road was so rough. On the left, we passed the Lutheran Church, and George and Gathy Ricker's house. Further down the hill on the right we passed Andy Booth's house—now Eckensviller's—and went on across the bridge by the sawmill.

"Then there came the steep climb! The horses could hardly pull all of us up the steep Carr's Hill south of Commanda store. I was a bit scared as the wagon jounced along over loose boulders. What if the horses lose their footing and the wagon rolls backward, I worried.

"Eventually, we passed Tom Booth's farm but soon took the Rye Road to Rauche Lake where we swam and had a picnic lunch and special treats from the teacher."

"Yes," agreed all the others. "The school picnic was the highlight of the year!"

When I started to school, a boy named Weldon was in grade eight, the same as you, Lloyd. I think that Weldon liked me. He always called me 'droopy drawers'," I told them, smiling at the memory. "My purple bloomers always drooped down below my skirts. Mom ordered white fleece-lined bloomers for June and I for winter, but Eaton's Catalogue Mail Order Store always sent purple, take-or-leave-it. The elastic in all clothing was poor during the war and I was so skinny that those purple bloomers surely did droop!"

Everyone laughed while Rea declared, "That one-room school did more than give us an education; it prepared us for life!"

"Higher education after Grade Ten was another matter," exclaimed Howard. "Mom arranged for me to board with her friend in Powassan. I earned money for my board by cleaning Dr. Dillaine's office and store-room, where he kept medicines before there was a town pharmacy. I also helped him clear up his back files and sort his bills. He instructed me to dispose of one bill saying, 'Where that man went, he can't send payment.'

"The next year the Board of Education provided a bus to take students to Loring Continuation School. To meet the bus, I had to walk three miles up Peever's Hill to Farley's Corners. That meant leaving the house at 6 a.m. In the winter, I boarded at the Bain's in Loring and worked there for my board. I graduated from grade twelve that year."

"It was that way for me too," said June. "It was dark leaving the house in the morning and I returned home in the dark. That first autumn on the walk home, during hunting season, I was harassed by carloads of city hunters. Our parents agreed that it wasn't safe for me to be walking. I found a job at Berger's General Store in Arnstein. I lived with the Bergers and worked in the store after school and on weekends. I enjoyed working in the store and especially meeting kids my own age. The second year, I boarded at Len and Hilda Brooks' home in Port Loring and worked as a Mother's Helper."

I interjected, "In 1948, the Board of Education provided a bus to pick up high school kids from Restoule, Commanda and Trout Creek. They were bussed to Powassan High School. I was fortunate to be on that bus. At the school there were two portables of grade 'niners'. It was quite an adjustment to be in a crowded big-town school. June joined me at Powassan for her final year and Archie started high school at Powassan in 1950.

What a scramble it was to be ready for the bus in the morning! We had to get up at 6 a.m., dress for barn work, do the milking, then scrub and change for school. We downed our porridge and had to be at the road to catch the bus by 8 a.m. If we weren't standing at the road, the driver would roar down Peever's Hill without stopping. He wouldn't stop, even if we were running down the driveway!" I exclaimed.

Archie added, "Fitting homework in after the farm chores was always a challenge too, but we managed to get a good education in spite of all the obstacles.

# ~Building the Barn~

"We built the barn in the summer of 1935," said Mervyn.

"Thelma, you had just started to walk and talk. I remember you running after the chickens in the yard, your golden curls bobbing, calling 'chickie, chickie.' You had just returned from the Hospital for Sick Children in Toronto, where you'd been for a couple of months recovering from the mastoid operation of your ear," Mervyn, from the west on a visit, reminisced.

"Yes," chimed in Lloyd. "In about March of '35 the family all got scarlet fever. The older boys probably brought it home from the logging camp. You caught it too, Thelma. You were just ten months old. I was only eight then but I'll never forget how awful it was. You were crying in pain, and a swelling behind your ear grew into a purple abscess that covered the left side of your head," said Lloyd, with the horror of the memory mirrored in his face.

Mervyn added, "You were screaming and crying so much that Mom got Preston out of bed and sent him to Commanda, to get George Smith to come and take you to Dr. R. H. Dillaine in Powassan. Dr. Dillaine sent Mom and you to the North Bay Hospital, but they wouldn't admit you because the family at home had scarlet fever. Mom went back to Dr. Dillaine and he took money out of his pocket and instructed her, 'Get on the train and take her directly to the Hospital for Sick Children in Toronto!' I was five then but I remember it clearly."

"That was before the days of penicillin and I suffered with ear ache and chronic ear infection my entire childhood. I still have a hole behind my ear where a lot of the infected bone was removed," I commented. "Thank goodness for Dr. Dillaine. I'm lucky to be alive."

Mervyn, changing the subject, continued remembering those long-ago days, “Carl bought a 1928 Whippet, late in spring when he was nineteen. He used it to haul bags of grain to the Powassan hardware store. Carl traded the grain for nails and lime for building the barn. The lime was used in making mortar. In June, Carl also used the car to transport all the school kids to the annual school picnic.”

Lloyd added, “Carl rolled the car that summer. He was making the turn onto the road from the bottom of our steep driveway. The car skidded in the mud and rolled over, trapping Carl’s foot. Matt Peters was grading the road with a horse-drawn grader. He pulled the car upright with his team of horses. Carl had a gash on the inside of his foot. Mom washed his foot, disinfected it and stitched the gash. Emergencies were all in a day’s work for her.”

“In the spring of ’35, when I was 20, I decided to clear the flat land beyond the horse pasture,” said Rea. “Uncle Alex Smith had always said to Pa, ‘Why don’t you clear that land instead of buying hay?’ I started clearing it and Pa helped me then. We planted rye but it was planted late in the season. The frost got it before it was ready to harvest and we lost the crop but the next year we had a bumper crop.”

“Our dad wasn’t any good at building so he hired the neighbour Arnold Theil to build the barn,” continued Lloyd. “Mom was pregnant with her last child, Archie, and wasn’t well. Dad hired Mike Pearson, the old cook from the lumber camp, to help her. Old Mike always had a long pipe in his mouth, and drooled out of the corners. One day while kneading bread, Mike drooled tobacco juice into the bread pan. Mom was disgusted. She banned him from the kitchen! Mike was consigned to helping Arnold Theil with building the barn.”

“Mike slept at our house that summer,” added Mervyn. “He had the strangest habit. Instead of turning over in bed, he flipped like a fish. Everyone in the house would hear him crashing in the bed.”

Mervyn warmed to his story, “One day, as Arnold was working on building the stable with stones and mortar, I was helping him to chink the holes between with small stones. It went well, until three-year-old June appeared on the framework above. She wanted down where we were working. I held out my arms to catch her when she jumped. At five years of age, I wasn't strong enough to take her weight, and we both fell. June was hurt and crying. Arnold sent the two of us back to the house."

June interjected, "Mike Pearson comforted me as he carried me back to the house. The older kids teased me ever after, about having a boyfriend; and because I couldn't say 'Pearson'. I called him 'Mike Pearness'."

Lloyd laughed, "Poor Arnold Theil was a bachelor. Arnold was a wizened little man who lived alone in his little house; he smelled like he rarely bathed. Arnold was totally without a sense of humour. He had his patience sorely tried dealing with children running around, although he reached the limit of his patience with Preston's teenaged antics. Dad had sent Preston to help Arnold but Preston's off-the-wall hijinks drove Arnold to 'down his tools'. He demanded that Rea, who was quiet and steady, should be his helper. Rea had to leave clearing the land. Preston was assigned to work with our dad doing the clearing. Preston knew better than to raise our dad's quick temper!"

Rea interjected, "When the stable was built, the neighbours came for the barn-raising. Many of them said 'this barn is so big, you'll never fill it' but the next year the barn was so full that we had to build a haystack outside."

"The roof had to wait until everyone's harvest was in," said Mervyn. "In November, our neighbours Otto Schermer and his brother-law Bill Hildebrand helped Dad, Carl and Preston to put the galvanized tin roof on. The next day, they all went deer hunting together."

# ~Wind and Fire and Other Disasters~

## Fire on the Roof!

"It was the summer of 1930," related Lloyd to his younger siblings during another family occasion, as he told them of incidents that had happened when he was little. "We were eating our noon meal when we noticed cinders falling past the window. We all rushed outside to see what was happening. Cinders from the chimney fire had set the cedar shingles around it ablaze!

"Edna, who was five, stood with her mouth full of biscuit, looking up and bawling in terror, as sparks and flames shot from the chimney, licking at the shingles on the roof of the house. That image seared into my memory when I was three and remains vivid to this day," Lloyd declared.

"Mom directed operations like a field marshal. Although she was very pregnant, Mom and Rea, then age fifteen, hoisted a ladder against the roof and fourteen-year-old Carl hurried up it with a pail of water, wetting down the shingles. Mom raced into the house, calling to Gerald, age six, to follow her. She lifted him into the attic, handed him a pail of water and a dipper with instructions to douse any sparks or cinders that fell through the roof from the from the flaming chimney. In short order the crisis was over - except for repairing the roof.

"Our dad would have to see to the roof when he came home from working at the sawmill in Commanda.

"Mom had thrown some kindling into the stove to quickly heat the oven. She was baking biscuits for the noon meal and the high heat ignited the residue in the chimney. The biscuits were sure good though. There is nothing so good as fresh biscuits and maple syrup!" Lloyd laughed.

"It was only a few months later on August 21 that Carl took all the younger kids, including Gerald, Edna, myself and even two-year-old Howard, to the 'Sand Hill' near the Commanda cemetery to pick blueberries. When we returned, there was a silver-haired baby boy. Aunt Fanny was there again to help with Mervyn's birth," concluded Lloyd.

## The Minnow Spring

"We were splashing icy water from the minnow spring onto a rock just to hear it sizzle, one hot day in the summer of 1931," related Lloyd. "Edna, who was six by then, leaned far over the edge of the spring to get a good scoop and she slipped head first right into the three-foot-deep water. I grabbed her by the belt of her dress and tugged, but I was only four years old and not as heavy as she. I kept on tugging and finally, I built up enough momentum that she came up out of the water with a WHOOSH. Edna coughed and sputtered, wiping the water out of her face. We didn't play at the minnow spring after that experience," Lloyd smiled.

## Snowshoes

"Billy Barton was the best snowshoe maker in the area," stated Lloyd as he continued his memories of the 1930s. "Billy had been married to our dad's younger sister Isabelle, who died in 1923 after the terrible Spanish flu pandemic went through the whole world, carried by troops returning home after World War I."

Although the flu epidemic was officially deemed over by 1920, it was still moving through some isolated villages in Northern Ontario. The flu reached Hotham in 1923, a little hamlet situated between Powassan and Nippissing – now incorporated into Nippissing. Aunt Belle died of it that year, and so did others in the area.

Dr. Harcourt, a brusque physician served Powassan and the whole rural area, just as did Dr. Dilliane, who followed him. Dr. Harcourt was called to her deathbed on March 23, 1923. Aunt Belle's Certificate of Death from pneumonia, secondary to influenza was co-signed by Angus Floyd of Nippissing and registered on April 3, 1923.

Miraculously, none of her five children died of it. The eldest boy Seymour was in the Hospital for Sick Children in Toronto, due to a ruptured appendix. He returned on the day of his mother's funeral and was taken to a neighbour's house. He asked for his mother and was told that she was dead. Seymour was ten years old.

Seymour had four younger siblings; the youngest was two when she died. What a tragedy!

"Later," said Lloyd, "Billy Barton married our cousin Irene, Ed Peever's daughter from Powassan, and they had five more children.

"It was in the winter of 1932 that Carl took snowshoe frames and a raw cowhide to Billy in Hotham –about ten miles from Commanda. As everyone used the barter system in those days, Billy got to keep the cowhide for his work of webbing the snowshoes.

"Carl drove our dog team when he went back to pick up the finished snowshoes but as he pulled into the yard, the Barton's pit bull attacked Hunter, our lead dog."

Lloyd continued the story, shaking his head sadly. "Carl brought the dog home on the sleigh. Hunter's head, front leg joint and paw were lacerated. I was heart-broken to see Hunter in such a state. Hunter was born on the day of my birth, you see. We were both five years old that spring," stated Lloyd.

"Mom bathed and dressed Hunter's wounds and nursed the dog in the house, until his recovery. It was very special to have Hunter in the house, as farm dogs were always kept outdoors in their own doghouse," concluded Lloyd.

## Winter Winds

"I awoke to hear our mother calling, Gerald! Lloyd! The house is blowing down! Come quick and help me prop it up."

"While sixteen-year-old Gerald and I, age twelve, hurried out into the howling wind, Edna, fourteen, bundled the younger children in blankets and herded them outside.

"Mom was out there in the wind, grappling with cedar poles that had been piled behind the house to make rail fencing for the garden, come spring. Gerald and I grabbed hold of a long pole and, with Mom steadying it we rammed the small end against the wall, just under the eaves. We then jammed the butt end of the pole into the partly frozen earth, piling rocks around the end to anchor the pole firmly. Our mother directed two more poles to be erected against the house for good measure."

"As usual, the men-folk were away in the logging camps. Jim, our dad, and brothers Rea and Carl were at Tom Hummel's camp in Carr. Preston was 'chore boy' at Barnie McNutt's camp in Restoule that fateful winter of 1938."

## The Gong

The gong was attached to the corner of the 'summer kitchen.' It rang to announce meal times for the family working in the fields. The gong also announced emergencies.

It was maple syrup time in the early spring of 1939. Granular snow still lay on the ground. At mid-morning Rea, Gerald, Lloyd and Eric Howes were in the sugar bush gathering sap. Dad had taken the team of horses and gone to the Trout Creek General Store for spring seeding supplies.

Suddenly, a cry from June, age seven, "Mom Look! Uncle Bob's house is on fire!"

Smoke billowed from the roof of Uncle Bob and Aunt Esther's Peever's house across the road, built next to the Peever homestead. Our mother rushed out to the summer kitchen with June and me trailing at her heels. Mom banged on the gong with all her might.

My five- year-old body was filled with a sense of horror at the scene, and then from the bush, emerged Eric and our older brothers, running toward the burning house. From a distance, they looked like tiny bugs crawling across the field. It seemed to take forever to cover the quarter mile to the house engulfed in flames.

Years later, reminiscing Rea told his story of what happened next, "Ignoring the flames, I removed as much of the dishes and furniture as I could from downstairs. Eric dashed upstairs and threw bedding and whatever else he could see, out the window to Gerald and Lloyd. I didn't think of the portrait of our grandparents, William and Maria on the wall. It burned up along with Bob and Esther's little house."

"Well, I was the first to spot the fire," chimed in visiting neighbour, Lisa (Schermer) Fry. "It was a Saturday and Alma Hoffman and I had stopped in at Bob and Esther Peever's on our four-mile trek home from picking up the mail at the post office in Commanda Store. As we were leaving their house we stopped to admire the big beaver pelt that Bob had nailed, stretched and drying on the back door. It was then that we noticed the flames shoot from the roof.

"Esther was boiling down maple syrup in the kitchen. She left the kitchen to chat with us and that's when the syrup boiled over and caught fire. We alerted Esther and she ran to the kitchen but it was too late. The kitchen was all in flames.

"Young Florence began howling in terror and calling out, 'my dolly, my dolly', while pointing up the stairs. Esther started up the stairs to get the doll but Florence howled for her to come back. Together they fled the house.

"There was nothing Alma and I could do to help, so we went on home," declared Lisa.

Lloyd picked up the story, "In the evening Gerald and I walked over to the burned-out house. There we found Uncle Bob boiling a pail of eggs over the coals for his supper. As usual, he was humming a tune to himself.

"Uncle Bob had been away tending his beaver traps when the fire occurred. When he returned to their burned out house, he sent Esther and ten-year-old Florence and her older brother Ronnie, to stay the night with Esther's father Tom McKee, in Restoule."

Rea sadly concluded the story, "And it wasn't only their loss, it was mine too. I had already bought the farm from Bob. After the fire, Bob and Esther moved into the vacant log homestead, and later, left Commanda for a trap line further north.

"War was declared in September 1939. I joined the army and, along the way, got married. My wife Margaret didn't want to farm. My dreams of farming were burned up in that fire," said Rea, with regret.

We have no visual record of our grandparents. The gong signaled the loss of dreams and of memories.

# ~The Baptism~

In winter all the side-roads leading to the little United Church in Commanda were snowed over. Nobody would be attending church. The circuit minister who served Nippissing, Carr and Commanda, reached our home on a Friday night. The Peever household on the main Trout Creek -Port Loring Road held the greatest number of his Commanda congregants. He, therefore, held the service in our home.

Rev. John Wetzel was the minister in 1937. When he discovered that the Peever children had not been baptised, he set about to rectify the matter. To our Salvation Army mother, adult immersion was the norm, but the sacrament of child baptism wouldn't hurt. Her children would be baptised.

That winter, our dad was the teamster in at Charlie Smith's logging camp, beyond Commanda. It was up the old Nippissing Road past the Booth's farm. Carl and Rea were in camp behind Loring, and Preston was chore boy at Empy's camp at Restoule. My mind's eye at three years still sees all remaining eight of us, Gerald, Edna, Lloyd, Howard, Mervyn, June and myself, with Archie, 20 months younger, held in arms; all lined up across the floor.

The Reverend Wetzel, with a cereal bowl in his hand, said a prayer then walked along the line of children, saying our names and sprinkling each of us.

Did it make a difference in our lives? Who is to know? Each of us kept the faith, serving God and others in the human family.

# ~The Milk House~

"You're not supposed to play here in the milk house. This place has to be kept clean and cool for the milk and cream," Mom scolds five- year-old Archie and me, age seven. We've crept into this cool dark place to get out of the hot sun. As there are no windows in here, we left the door slightly ajar for light. Archie and I are just playing house but Mom spots the open door. It should be kept closed against the heat. She herds us out.

The milk house was built by digging down into the earth about four feet. It was built with hand-squared and chinked pine logs to a total height of only about eight feet. The milk house has an attic. A thick layer of sawdust used for insulation, lies on the floor of the attic.

Behind our house grows a tall row of five Balm of Gilead trees. The sixth Balm of Gilead tree stands opposite the last tree in the row. Those two trees standing like sentinels, shade the milk house. The trees are not native to the Parry Sound District. They had been planted by Eric Campbell, the original owner. True to their name, in spring they produce a balm or salve from their buds.

To produce the salve, our older brothers climb a ladder and pick the buds. Mom gently steams them to loosen the outer covering and then she presses the buds in a sieve. The buds yield a thick yellow antiseptic-smelling salve that she stores in sterile jars for use on cuts and scrapes. A separate jar is reserved for treating cows' udders and teats when they become chapped or cracked. The Balm of Gilead salve is a very effective healing agent.

In summer, our milk, cream and butter are stored on the earthen floor of the milk house. Five-gallon cream cans are placed on the floor. They are filled with chilled cream. When full, the cans of cream are picked up at the roadside by Oliver Moore's stage and transported to the railway station in Trout Creek. They are shipped by train to the creamery in Toronto.

Oliver Moore's big green lumbering stage starts out from Loring on its four-day, round-trip to the railway station at Trout Creek. Oliver Moore picks up cans of cream, parcels, mail and passengers stopping at every home along the way.

During the summer, Mom ships about three cans of cream per week. The monthly "cream cheques" provide cash for basic groceries and for new school shoes for us each September.

A hand-cranked churn, along with a butter dish carved from the bole of an enormous maple tree is stored in the milk house too. When we churn sour cream into butter, the buttermilk is drained off and stored in two-quart sealers. The buttermilk makes a cool refreshing drink for our dad and our brothers who are working in the fields.

Using a large hand-curved maple paddle, Mom mixes the freshly churned butter with salt and presses out any remaining buttermilk.

Mom uses a wooden butter-printer to make one-pound butter prints. She stores the prints of butter in a large covered crock.

When we girls reach about twelve years one of our chores in summer is churning butter. The girls in the family are entrusted to mix and print it. A certain amount of wrist strength is required to manipulate the paddle and the butter-printer. Maturity is required to understand that care and cleanliness must be maintained.

Six-quart baskets of early Ida Red apples are stored in the milk house too. Later, peaches will be stored for eating or for preserving for winter. Our mother buys them from Mr. Friedman.

Mr. Friedman lives in Toronto. He sells fruit from his truck to the housewives along the Trout Creek-Loring road. On his return journey, Mr. Friedman's truck will be filled with livestock that he buys from farmers along the way. He makes money, both in selling fruit to housewives, and by selling livestock to slaughterhouses in Toronto.

Mr. Friedman is Jewish. He wears a skullcap or yarmulke. He is the first Jewish man we children have ever seen. If it is mealtime when he calls on our family, Mr. Friedman declines to eat with us. After our meal he asks to use our stove to prepare his own food using his own utensils. Sometimes Mr. Friedman's teenaged son Manny accompanies him. Manny is the first fat boy we have ever seen. Farm boys don't become fat because they burn all their calories doing manual labour.

In return for our mother's hospitality, Mr. Friedman offers her bruised fruit that he's culled from his baskets. These are gratefully accepted and will be immediately salvaged; the good parts cut up and stewed for dessert.

One day, I spy a ladder propped against the loft above the milk house and I climb up. I've never been up here before. I put my head through the open door.

How curious! Old bed frames are propped against the wall. Nobody is in the loft except a family of "chimney swifts," small brown birds, cousins of barn swallows, whose feet seem to stick to the walls. Their nests of mud are also stuck like wall sconces to the aged grey pine beams. In the nests are scrawny looking babies, their naked heads and necks peeking over the edge.

Finding my older brother Lloyd, I ask him, "Why are there bed frames in the milk house loft? Who slept there?"

"Well," he answers me, launching into a story of times past, "During the 'Great Depression' in the 1930s, the government created employment by commissioning road building. Up to that time there was only a narrow winding road between Trout Creek and Loring. The Ontario government wanted the road to be widened to the status of a County road.

"Road-building gave work to local men but, in addition, Government welfare provided transportation for unemployed men from Toronto to these work sites. There was a tent camp set up for men who were working on the road. The camp was in Jack Schwartz's field, on the right side of where Schermer's Road joins the main road. A cook prepared food to all the workers.

"We supplied the camp with five gallons of milk each day from our farm. We also supplied cream, eggs, beef and pork; sometimes mutton too. I remember when I was about four or five years old Carl took me with him to deliver supplies. That day, our dog team hauled the supplies up the long Peever's Hill. For about a mile, the dogs had to haul their load uphill all the way to the camp.

"When we got there, cook gave us each a big slice of blueberry pie. That stands out in my memory!" Lloyd exclaimed.

"Three or four of the road-builders slept on straw ticks in our milk house loft. It was more comfortable than sleeping on the cold ground in the tent-camp. Those poor men from Toronto arrived here without warm clothing. They had no idea how cold it gets up here.

"After the men got off the train, they had to walk ten miles from Trout Creek to Commanda and another three more to the tent camp," explained Lloyd.

I interrupt his story, "So that's why Dad still goes down to the road when he sees a stranger walking! He always invites them to come up to the house for something to eat. Dad remembers when those were poor, hungry men walked the roads. He still expects that anyone on foot might be hungry too."

Lloyd nods, going back to his story, "The road was built with picks and shovels. It was very hard work.

"Dad got work on the road too, using our team of horses. Our horses dragged a broad scraper. It was a big scoop steered by wooden handles. The scraper scooped up earth, loosened by the men wielding picks and shovels. Dad had to be strong to steer that big scraper loaded with earth.

"Local men had to do 'Statute Labour' in lieu of land tax and a team of horses was equal to the work of one man. When Dad completed his Statute Labour, he continued working, but then he was paid for it. Money earned building the road and by supplying food and shelter to the workers, really helped us through the Depression," explained Lloyd, finishing his story and going back to hoeing the garden while my eight year old mind continues to think about the milk house and the special place it holds in our family life.

An ice house is built against the side of the milk house. The ice house is not as sturdy. It is built from pine boards. The ice house is filled with blocks of ice, packed in sawdust.

In winter, when the ice is deemed thick enough, our father drives the team of horses to Mud Lake. Armed with an axe, a special crosscut saw, with every other tooth broken off, and huge ice tongs, our dad chops and saws two-foot blocks of ice. He heaves the blocks onto the sleigh until there is about twenty blocks piled about seven feet high. He places chains around the sleigh's box to support the weight.

If ice-cutting happens on a Saturday, our biggest brothers will help. Smaller children are not allowed in that venture because of the danger of slipping into the icy water. Dad will have to cut and haul ice for about a week to get the ice house filled.

To keep our meat fresh in summer our mother cuts it up and packs it in large crocks set on the ice blocks. The meat, usually venison, will keep there for about a month. Mom also slices some meat and packs it in two-quart sealers. This meat will keep for three or four days, set in the minnow spring that bubbles ice-cold water out of the hillside below the well.

Mom cooks meat stored in the minnow spring first; one portion for adults and a half-portion for children.

In summer, our meat is usually salt-cured pork or fresh venison, although our summer diet is primarily fresh vegetables with mounds of new potatoes topped with butter because fresh meat can't be stored for long in the heat of summer. In1939, just before our brother Carl enlists in the army; he buys domestic rabbits, one male and two female ducks, all for breeding purposes. Carl wants to ensure that the family will have a ready source of fresh meat. He reasons that smaller animals could be consumed the same day that they were slaughtered, eliminating the problem of storage.

The ducks weren't a success. Foxes got two of them and the third was found dead, having choked on a June bug.

The rabbits, however, reproduce rapidly, as rabbits do. Around the rabbit hutch, Mom and the older boys build a roomy pen made from chicken wire. The furry rabbits make pets for us children as well as providing satisfying rabbit stew.

Some of the rabbits do escape by digging under the wire fencing. Having cross-bred with wild rabbits, in winter, we see patchy white and brown rabbits hopping around the entrance to the Balsams. It isn't long before they are wiped out by wild animals because their brown fur makes them more visible in winter.

The best thing about having ice though, is – ice cream! In summer, we usually make ice cream in the evening, after the chores are done.

In the afternoon, Mom cooks a custardy filling of eggs, cream, sugar and flavouring then sets it to cool in the milk house. After the milking is done and calves are fed, one of our older brothers goes to the ice house and chips enough ice for the ice cream maker.

Mom fits the filled two-quart container into its wooden tub. One of the boys pours ice in the tub and pours in some salt on the ice encircling the container, to speed up the freezing process.

We children will take turns cranking the handle that turns the container round and round and moves the paddles inside it in a beating motion. It takes about twenty minutes until the handle feels too stiff to turn. That's a signal that the ice cream is ready. What a cool delicious treat on a warm evening!

Mom spoons ice cream out into dessert dishes.

I have my own special pink fluted ice cream dish. I bought it at Mr. Charlie Hoffman's General Store in Commanda in 1940.

I remember that I was given ten cents for my sixth birthday. It just happened that on this very day in May, the IODE ladies – Imperial Order Daughters of the Empire – resplendent in elegant dresses and hats - came to school to talk to the students about helping the soldiers in the war by buying War Saving Stamps.

I thought of my brothers Rea, Carl and Preston in the army. I was so impressed by their talk that I gave my birthday money to the war effort. Somehow one of those elegant ladies heard that I'd given my birthday money.

The woman presented me with a gift of ten cents. After school that day I marched right down to the Commanda Store with my new birthday money. There on a shelf, I saw the most beautiful ice cream dish! It cost just ten cents.

Mom kept my dish on the top shelf of her prized china cabinet. She kept it safe just for me. Seventy six years later the pink fluted dish sits on my dresser filled with potpourri.

## Postscript

In about 1949, hydroelectric power lines were strung all through Northern Ontario. Our father didn't have to cut and haul heavy loads of ice for the ice house anymore.

After the war, Edna's husband Les Bain became an electrician. He worked long hours wiring the homes of everyone in the Loring - Trout Creek area. Les wired our new house that Howard designed and built in 1949, with Lloyd assisting. Lloyd bought and laid hardwood floors in the living and dining room. Together, they finished the kitchen. Our mother had a modern home and, for first time, a refrigerator.

The milk house still served the family though, as long as there was a herd of milk cows.

# ~The Peever Fortune~

The Peevers have inherited a fortune!

In the last year of The Great Depression of the 1930s, the news spread by word-of-mouth all the way from the Ottawa Valley to Northern Ontario. It was like a fairy tale. It sounded like a Cinderella story.

How did it happen?

How big was the fortune? Nobody seemed to know.

Such was the excitement that Jim Peever's, brother-in-law Bill Hodgins, (Aunt Fanny's husband) walked three miles through mud and mushy snow from his home on Schermer's Road in Commanda, to the logging camp on Commanda Lake in Restoule to tell Jim that the Peevers had come into a fortune. Bill Hodgins was outfitted with a new set of clothing and boots - all bought on account. He advised Jim that he wouldn't need to work again; that Jim should just quit his job.

Jim answered pragmatically, "I'll spend the money when I see it."

A few months later, in 1939, an official-looking envelope arrived at the Commanda Post Office addressed to James T. W. Peever. Enclosed was a letter from a New York City law firm, acting on behalf of the Carr Estate. The lawyer requested proof of the lineage of the said James T. W. Peever. The letter instructed that the sum of $1.00 should be enclosed as a token of good faith.

Annie, who handled all correspondence, completed the forms and gave all the requested information. Jim signed the forms and enclosed a $1.00 bill. He took the important-looking letter to the post office which was located in the Commanda General Store.

The lawyers were searching out the nearest relatives of a Carr couple who had died in Manhattan, New York. The Carrs were Irish immigrants who'd settled on a tract of land in New York State. New York City had grown up around their land. In those years of expansion, the City purchased Carr's land for a considerable sum.

Today, Rockefeller Centre stands on a part of the property formerly owned by the Carrs. Jim Peever's uncle Albert, the tenth child of John and Ellen Peever, the first Peever settlers in Fitzroy Township, was married to Elizabeth Carr.

Elizabeth Carr Peever, a direct relative of the New York Carrs, had inherited the money. Elizabeth died childless in 1929. Her husband Albert Peever died in the early spring of 1939, leaving the legacy to his late siblings' descendents.

Lawyers for Albert's estate were, therefore, searching for remaining descendents of Albert's siblings. That was tall order because Albert's ten siblings had all produced large families.

In mid-summer that year, two lawyers and their wives arrived south of North Bay, at the farm of Jim Peever's older sister Ellen (Nellie) Peever Anderson and her husband William, just outside the town of Powassan.

The lawyers and their wives were having a wonderful holiday touring Ontario in a luxury car visiting Peever descendants all at the expense of the "Carr Estate". They'd likely gone to see the Dionne quintuplets in nearby Calendar who were a great novelty and tourist attraction in North America during the Depression years. The senior lawyer was pleased to pose in his city suit, complete with gold watch fob, for a photograph with Nellie and farmer Anderson, in his overalls.

Jim Peever of Commanda didn't rate a visit, but soon after a cheque arrived, made out to James T. W. Peever for the magnificent sum of $22.00.

In 1939, $22.00 had four times the buying power compared to the present day. Jim Peever took his "fortune" and bought a second-hand two-seater democrat - a horse-drawn buggy. The shiny padded leather bench-seats had springs. What comfort!

We children felt very stylish when our father drove us to school in our new democrat. We felt as rich as Rockefeller.

Peever Fortune Lawyers with William and Nellie (Peever) Anderson

# ~Christmas in Commanda~

## The Christmas Concert

Snowflakes, giant white snowflakes are drifting down. Caught on outstretched tongues, they feel cool and wet. Snowflakes settle on coat collars and sleeves, their intricate patterns are clear against the dark wool clothing insulating the small children. Looking up into the dove-grey sky, the downward path of each snowflake can be tracked before it lands. Suddenly, individual flakes become a deluge and we are enshrouded in a soft white cocoon. Footsteps are muffled as we trudge the second remaining mile to school.

In my belly there is a delicious knot of excitement and anticipation. This is the morning of my first Christmas concert. We have been practising our recitations, plays and intricate drills for a month. Today we will rehearse on the big stage at the Commanda Community Hall.

Each of us will be dressed in our best. Instead of black rubber ankle boots, I will wear a stylish pair of white leather snow boots with real fur at the tops. The white boots arrived last week in a parcel of clothing that city cousins have outgrown – thank goodness for city cousins and their thoughtful parents. My sister and I will have ringlets. Her dark hair, tied with a red ribbon, is a contrast to my blonde with blue ribbon. I think about how our mother heats the curling iron on the coals in the woodstove, wipes the soot off on a cloth and applies it to a hank of hair. The hair gives off a hot smell. I always sit very still through this process to avoid an accidental brand on my neck or ear.

The draughty Commanda Community Hall smells slightly of stale cigarette smoke and the tang of fresh floor wax and cedar boughs. Students stretch red and green paper garlands across the ceiling, fastening a red paper bell in the centre. They set up chairs are for tonight's audience. A Christmas tree is dragged onto a corner of the stage and decorated.

Parents and older siblings arrive. Folks from neighbouring villages come too – for the entertainment and for the food, and the dance that will follow. The era of television hasn't arrived to jade appreciation of home-grown talent, or the pleasure of meeting neighbours and participating in lively dancing.

The concert is over. Santa hands out a gift to each child, paid for from proceeds of last year's concert. The year is 1940, and for most children of large families and small incomes, store-bought toys are treasured. After the gifts, sandwiches brought in six-quart baskets by parents are passed through the rows to everyone.

The local dance band tunes its instruments while chairs are dragged to the walls. Chairs piled with coats become makeshift beds for sleepy little ones. Soon, the caller announces the first square dance, which is followed by shottises and interspersed with 'round dances.'

Blowing steam from their nostrils, the horses are led from the open shed. Our father hitches them to a low sleigh for the trip home. My sister and brothers and I are all bundled into a bed of straw in the sleigh. We huddle under the heavy buffalo robe for the journey home. The midnight-blue night is filled with magic as I lie on my back under a canopy of stars, listening to sleigh runners squeak over frosty snow. Silvery tinkling sleigh bells echo against dark walls made by trees flanking the road. I fall asleep.

### Christmas Eve

In the afternoon, armed with a saw and a length of rope, Dad sets out for the forest to cut the Christmas tree. The snow is thigh-high as we younger children, June age eight, Archie age four and me at age six wade excitedly behind him. Our father is in a rare good mood. He is as happy as we are to be free in the forest, away from farm chores. With our help, he chooses a fat spruce which is both straight and tall. The tree leaves a trail of snow as we drag it across the floor but Mom doesn't protest. Tall and majestic, the tree touches the ceiling, filling the entire corner of the room.

Mom bustles in orderly preparation while an air of controlled excitement overtakes our household as Christmas day approaches. The goose is plucked and hung in the woodshed, ready for stuffing. An enormous plum pudding hangs there too in its cheesecloth shroud, while pies sit cooling out of harm's way. The house has been cleaned; fresh straw ticks are laid out on the floor upstairs for the youngest children. We younger children must all give up our beds to our older brothers who are home on leave from the army. They'll be accompanied by a buddy or two who can't make it to their own homes for Christmas. The small house embraces everyone. How handsome and grown up Rea and Carl look in their uniforms! Preston isn't here. At nineteen, he is already in England, soon to be shipped to Holland. As she works, Ma worries, "Why did the youngest of the three have to be the first to go overseas?"

In the evening, when the farm animals are fed and the chores are done, the family sings Christmas carols while everyone takes a hand in decorating the tree. Dad sits in his rocker with four-year-old Archie and me in his lap and sings "...now tell me dear old Santa Claus what you'll bring to me?" It is my favourite Christmas song because it gives voice to all the wonder and anticipation that I'm feeling. At six years, I still believe in Santa and his "brownies" that peep in windows and report to Santa if children are being good. I feel a shiver up my back at the thought of "the little people" watching me. Finally, we are bundled off to bed.

"You boys take these warm quilts. You'll have to make beds for yourselves in the stable. There won't be room for you to sleep in the house for the next few days," says Mom, handing them the lantern. The boys pull on coats and boots, pick up a coal oil lantern and head for their beds in the stable.

The 'feed alley' in the stable where the hay is dropped from the barn above, through the trap door, is bordered by mangers on both sides. It makes an ideal place to spread their beds. In the steamy warmth of the stable, Lloyd, Howard and Mervyn, ages twelve, eleven and ten respectively, make cosy beds in the soft hay and then carefully put out the lantern. On one side of the feed alley the horses stamp a welcome and reach out and nuzzle the boys and then they resume feeding from their mangers. The cows on the other side of their makeshift bedroom continue their rhythmic chewing. It didn't occur to the boys that Jesus spent his first Christmas Eve in a stable. They were in good company.

Downstairs, I hear nuts being rattled into bowls and amid low laughter the crackle of paper as presents are wrapped. The grownups feel the special wonder of Christmas too.

**Christmas Day!**

Eight-year-old June rattles the straw tick, waking Archie and me as she reaches for her stocking at the bottom of our bed. Santa did come! These are the stockings we'd left for Santa, now filled with nuts, candy, a rosy apple and the biggest orange I've ever seen! Oranges are such a rare treat that I don't want to eat mine right away. I smell it and examine the little bump on one end and anticipate biting into a juicy section. We eat some bell-shaped cream candies while we get dressed.

A breakfast of oatmeal is bubbling on the woodstove and the kettle sends up steam to help warm the house and dispatch the winter chill. The space around the Christmas tree is piled with so many colourful presents! Dad reminds us sternly that we won't be opening presents until all the farm chores are done.

Stamping the snow off on the porch, Lloyd, Howard and Mervyn burst into the house. They have fed the stock and are ready for a good meal of porridge and hot tea with slabs of fresh bread and honey. We all sit down together and give thanks for our food. I feel too excited to eat and it seems to take so long for the rest of the chores to be completed. The goose is stuffed and roasting in the oven.

Carl makes jokes as he calls out names and hands each one a present. The pile of presents dwindles quickly. The boys get warm pants and the very latest in headgear – helmets with attached goggles. The leather hats, with tie-down earflaps, lined with a wool fabric, look like real aviator helmets.

Thanks to Carl, June and I get our very first snowsuits. They are two-piece, made of Melton cloth, scratchy and smelling of wool. No more, as we tramp through the snow to school, will the wind and snow whip up our skirts and wet those black ribbed stockings, causing our knees to be chafed and red. The older brothers share a crokinole board. Our parents receive their first radio. Since hydroelectric power will not be strung through the area for another ten years, two wet-cell batteries the size of a car battery, are attached to the radio. Later, a pole will be hoisted outside with an attached wire, acting as an aerial, connecting us to the outside world and bringing in the disturbing news of the war.

Santa has been generous this year too. Due to wartime demand, the beaver pelts our father sold brought a good price.

Archie gets a sleigh of golden shellacked wood, trimmed in red. He'll no longer have to suffer being pushed off the bobsled by his bigger brothers. I can't express the wonder as I receive my first pair of store-bought red skies and poles. There is a pair of snowshoes under the tree for June - just the right size for an eight-year-old. How thrilled we are as we bundle into our snowsuits for the first time and rush outside to try out our new presents.

We children are starving by the time Christmas dinner is on the table. Steaming bowls of fluffy 'riced' potatoes adorn the table - made by placing potatoes in a gadget that looks like an oversized garlic press makes riced potatoes. The cooked potato is forced through holes in the bowl of the gadget. It is a tedious process and therefore reserved for special occasions. My father's favourite fowl, dark and pungent roast goose is passed around the table, followed by bowls of stuffing and gravy.

Sauce for the plum pudding keeps warm on the side of the large cook-stove, which shines from its fresh coat of 'stove blacking.' Spicy steam wafts from the pot where the pudding is heating. The rich dark pudding, filled with fruit and shiny from the ground suet, is ready for serving.

"Please Ma, don't put sauce on my pudding," I say. The golden caramel sauce smells so tempting, but I know from experience that it is too rich for my tender tummy. Earlier I'd watched, fascinated as sugar was browned with gobs of butter in the smoking iron pan, then it sizzled as

Mom stirred in boiling water, finally beating in fresh cream and essence of vanilla. Wonderful but deadly rich! I'm thinking that after dinner I want to be able to sample the nuts and hard candy, especially the hot red and white striped cinnamon sticks.

It is evening and the house is still, the soldier boys have gone to the Commanda Hall to enjoy the annual Christmas dance. In the morning they'll be gone back to their army camps to await embarkation to the war raging far away in Europe. Already I miss my big brothers and the excitement and laughter they bring. Christmas is gone for a whole year. As I say my prayers and crawl into the scratchy straw tick, I feel sad. "Do others feel the same let down?"

I am alone with my thoughts.

# ~Memories of Preston~

"I wish that I remembered more of our home life when I first entered the family at age three and a half. I don't know why I don't. There would be more Preston stories to tell," said Lillian.

We were all sitting together at a family reunion, remembering those who weren't with us. Lillian continued, "I remember when we were six and were walking home from school – the teacher let the Grade Ones out at 2:30. A man from the village picked us up in his car. He asked how old we were. I said I was six and Preston said he was six."

"'So you are twins?' the man said.

"'No, we aren't twins,' I said.

"The driver said, 'How come you are both six?' Puzzled, we said, we don't know.

"Preston was smarter in mathematics and always saw through problems sooner but I was better in grammar than he. We were in the same grade all the way through school. Preston and I stayed in school at Commanda through grade ten. Ted Jordan was our teacher," Lillian said.

Lloyd added, "Preston was always quiet and studious in school but when Roger, a skinny and hateful boy who lived up the hill toward the Booth farm bullied me and other younger kids, Preston would always defend us. He was lean but tall for his age."

Lillian said, "I remember that always in the late fall when butchering day came, Preston didn't want to be around the farm. He couldn't stand seeing the pigs being butchered. After the pigs were butchered and their bristles scraped off, they would be hung by the heels from the big elm tree beyond the creek to chill before being cured in salt brine, or else sent to Schermer's smoke house. Mom would send Preston to the store at Commanda for kitchen supplies on those days.

"Preston didn't like to eat fish either," commented Lillian, as an afterthought.

She continued, "I remember also that Preston liked to get into the cupboard when Mom was away. One day he found raisins and decided to make candy. I knew that he shouldn't do it without permission but he decided to do it anyway. I guess I liked the idea of a treat too," she said, with a guilty laugh.

"Oh," exclaimed Lloyd, "He made the best fudge! And he loved to cook too. Mom finally gave him his own cookbook. In it he wrote silly rhymes and comments. For example, a recipe directed to put ingredients in a bowl. Preston scribbled in the margin: or pot, pan, kettle or pail."

Edna added, laughing, "I remember one day when we planned a picnic on the high rock that we called Commanda Mountain, but we didn't know what to take to eat. Preston solved the problem. He threw a stone at the rooster and broke its leg. Then he told Mom that the rooster had a broken leg, so he killed it. He plucked and cleaned the rooster. We cooked that bird over a fire up on the mountain and had a delicious picnic from our ill-gotten rooster. "

"He was inventive all right," said Lloyd. "Remember when he built 'the Pine Shack' as a workshop? He built himself a forge to heat metal so he could repair the farm machinery. He even bought a hacksaw and drills. Like his brothers, he made his pocket money by snaring weasels and other small fur-bearing animals and selling their skins. The 'Pine Shack' stood for many years after Preston grew up and left the farm."

Lloyd added, "When Preston was about fifteen, in the spring of 1938, despite having a cough, he went fishing on Commanda Lake with Rea, Carl and Uncle Willie's sons Harvey and Fred. He got very sick while out on the ice, complaining of pain behind his shoulder blade."

Archie added, "His cousins hauled him on their sled across Commanda Lake and got Allan Grawbarger to drive him to the doctor in Powassan and from there to the North Bay hospital. They figure that they saved his life. Harvey and Fred both told me that story since I moved to Iroquois Falls where they now live. The Grawbargers were married to Uncle Ab Peever's daughters and lived on adjoining farms in Bear Valley."

Lloyd continued, "He had pneumonia and pleurisy. Those were the days before penicillin. Preston had to have surgery to drain the fluid from around his lungs. He was in hospital for a long time. I can still picture

Preston sitting in the sun on the bench outside the 'cook house' (summer kitchen) after he came home from hospital. He looked so weak and thin.

"Preston used to always carry Archie around his shoulders. He took Archie with him to the barn and everywhere. I guess that's how come Archie caught pneumonia too. Archie, who was two, came down with pneumonia and pleurisy a few days after Preston and he had surgery too. They were in the North Bay hospital at the same time. They both carried identical scars under their left shoulder blades."

"The first time that Preston and I were separated was in the winter of 1938, when I left home at sixteen to attend Shaw's Business School in Toronto," sighed Lillian.

Lloyd chimed in, "That was the winter Preston worked as 'chore boy' for Barnie McNutt in the bush at Restoule. One day, he brought home a dog team. One dog was a black collie and the other was an enormous Great Dane. The Dane had a shiny blue-black coat. Preston used the dog team for transport back and forth from the logging camp. He also bought a guitar and taught himself to play it. The following summer, he worked in Commanda at the saw mill."

June added, "I remember him playing the guitar and singing the song, *Red River Valley*. He also sang *Little Red Wing*, the song about the Indian maiden.

"Preston bought each of us a big sucker for Christmas the winter that he worked at Barney McNutt's. He hung all the suckers on the tree, each with our names on them. Preston sure had a lot of little ones to buy for!"

Lillian continued the story, "During the summer when we were seventeen, I worked at mom's sister Aunt Agnes and Uncle Silby Cooke's store at Big Bay Point on Lake Simcoe. Preston and I were together again.

"He worked with Aunt Agnes' son Lester (Les) delivering ice to the cottagers at Big Bay Point. Les and Preston became inseparable. They were the same age and both had dark, swarthy colouring. They were both tall but Preston, at six-feet and four inches, was taller while Les was sturdier. They looked like brothers and loved each other like brothers. Preston and Les forged a close friendship. When the war was declared in 1939, Preston joined the army but unfortunately for them, his cousin Les was declared medically unfit and couldn't follow him."

"War was declared in September 1939. I remember lying across my bed in the girl's sleeping cabin, crying because my brothers would have to go to war. Sure enough, as soon as Preston turned eighteen he joined the army. He was transferred to the Provost Corps. Rea and Carl joined up a few months later. Edna enlisted in the Air Force too, when she was eighteen."

I broke in, "Before Preston went overseas he came home for a visit. That was the time when he brought June and Archie and me each a present. I don't remember what he gave June but I clearly remember that he gave me a 'Wettums Doll'. It was a rubber doll and it came with a small celluloid bottle with a removable red nipple and tiny flannel diapers. The doll's mouth was shaped like an 'O'. It was just the size to fit the nipple. I was entranced with this magical doll that could drink from a bottle and wet its diapers. Archie's gift was a foot-long, red 'Sandy Andy' dump truck. A removable tin driver sat in the cab of the truck. The best thing about the truck was that it had a trip-lever that tipped up the truck bed, opened the tailgate and could dump its load of sand! Archie played with that truck for years."

"I do remember the little red truck!" Archie exclaimed. "I used to pretend that I was Preston, hauling ice with it, because that was one of the jobs he did when he worked for the Cookes."

"Preston was sent home to recuperate from an appendectomy not long after he enlisted. He was already wearing the uniform of the Military Police. He showed us younger children how he had to train and to march. He looked so tall and impressive in his uniform with its white lanyard at the shoulder," I interjected.

Archie continued, "When Preston came home on embarkation leave, he had a lot of people to visit in a short time but he took time for me. He put on the boxing gloves, sat on a little red chair and boxed with me. He then took out his guitar and played and sang some songs. One of my favourites was *The Wreck of the Old '97*. I always used to cry when he sang it and I cried that time too. That is the last time I heard him sing it. When he came home from the war, I don't think he had his guitar with him.

"Carl had an ex-girlfriend 'Gertie'. We used to refer to her as 'Gertie Goose Grease'. Gertie made a play for Preston when Carl started dating

Ella Gorham (whom he later married.) It didn't last but she managed 'to get in the way' while we, especially Mom, were trying to say our last good-byes. Everyone was having a hard time emotionally as Preston was so young. Mercifully, at five, I was too young to understand. For some time after, I used to think that our brothers were in training when in fact they were in combat. I guess that Mom didn't bother to set me straight, so eventually someone else did."

Lillian broke in, "Preston went overseas when he was barely nineteen. He was stationed in Surrey, England for a time. That is where he met Audrey Robinson. Later Preston was posted to Belgium and Holland. He kept in touch with his sweetheart in England, spending his leaves with Audrey and her family. Mrs. Robinson opened their home to Carl also when he arrived in England. In May of 1943, Preston and Audrey were married. Preston was twenty-one and Audrey was eighteen. Carl was there to be his best man."

I added, "Mom made a three-tier wedding cake and shipped it, along with staples like sugar, because of the severe rationing in England. Due to all the problems with wartime shipping, the cake didn't arrive in time. The Robinsons had to use their rationing stamps to buy a cake from a bake shop, but they wrote that they enjoyed Mom's cake when it did arrive."

Archie interjected, "Life in England must have been really hard considering the restricted rations. I heard later that Preston didn't eat while visiting Audrey's home because he didn't want to use their precious rations. If Preston's metabolism was like mine, he probably needed to eat for two men!"

"Mom had a hand-operated canning machine. She canned beefsteak and butter and shipped it to Mrs. Robinson throughout the war," I said. "Mom also sent away to Eaton's mail-order store for dress material and a pattern. She made Audrey a dress with a sweetheart neckline. That was a popular neckline during the war. If only she'd known that Audrey had studied dressmaking and design at school, it would have been more practical to have sent the material and let Audrey make the dress for herself. Audrey always had a wonderful sense of style," I commented.

Archie recalled, "I remember that Preston sent home a parcel from England and in it was a little yellow duck calendar dated 1944. The pages of the calendar were glued to the duck. It appealed to me, as I was just a little kid."

Lillian added, "Sandra was born on December 13, 1944. I have snapshots of Preston holding her. Wartime was particularly difficult for young mothers with babies. Little Sandra was terrified of the noise from the bombs."

"Preston was the first of the brothers to return home when the war ended. He arrived in the winter of 1945. He said that soldiers were crowded in hammocks below decks of their troopship, crossing the Atlantic. Preston was sick with pneumonia when he got home. He coughed and coughed. I remember him lying in the big bed at the top of the stairs. Mom kept mustard plasters on his chest," I stated.

"Oh," said Archie, "I remember when he arrived home and ducked through the door, I thought that he looked like the pictures we were seeing of starving prisoners. His eyes seemed sunken and dark. He was still in uniform and didn't stay long but he promised to come back next summer and bring Audrey. He promised to take me back with them. I had all winter to look forward to the trip."

"Ironically, Preston had sold his guitar to an army buddy before he went overseas. When he arrived in barracks, he was surprised to find his old buddy was there with the guitar. Preston bought back the guitar and kept it during the war but somehow, he didn't have it with him when he arrived home," I recalled.

Lillian interjected, "Preston returned to Barrie as soon as he was discharged. That first Sunday night Uncle Silby and Aunt Agnes Cooke took Preston and me to the Peoples Church in Toronto to hear a special speaker. There, Preston surrendered his life to God. It changed his whole perspective. When Audrey arrived as a war bride, they went to live in Orillia," added Lillian.

With a nod, Lloyd confirmed Lillian's account of Preston's activities, "Preston set up a cartage and storage business in Orillia and called it Arrow Movers. It was a franchise of Cooke Cartage and Storage in Barrie. He also bought a large house. Preston and Audrey lived in the front part of the house and stored furniture in the back rooms. They rented the upstairs of the house to Rea and Margaret until Rea was able to buy his own house on Moffat Street. Rea lived there on Moffat Street for the rest of his life."

Archie broke in with his piece of the story, "When Preston arrived back from overseas in the winter of 1945 he promised that he would return in the next summer with his wife Audrey. He said that he'd take me back to Orillia with them, and he did."

"They came in June of 1946 for Carl and Ella's wedding," I reminded him. "Preston and Audrey stayed at the hotel in Port Loring. Ella's home was in Loring and the wedding was in the United Church there. I remember that I was twelve when I first met Audrey on the day of Carl's wedding. I thought she was the most beautiful woman I had ever seen. Audrey admired my 'frock' that Mom had made from a silky blue material with tiny pink and yellow embossed flowers. We four children were walking along the road in Port Loring near Boutz's store singing an old folk song when Preston and Audrey walked up to us. Audrey began singing with us. We were surprised that she knew the song."

"I was eleven when I visited them in Orillia in the summer of 1947," said Archie, "I could see how Preston adored his little girl Sandra. He would pick her up and carry her around with him as he did me when I was little. Then he'd set her down and she'd run a few steps and hop and run again. Preston would laugh with delight and tell her to do it again. Sandra would have been about two-and-a-half-years old then.

"Every day while he was at work, I would take Sandra for a walk. We often went to the park, which was quite a long walk for her. Lots of old ladies would remark about the 'nice boy' taking his sister for a walk. I would explain that she was my little niece.

"I thought that Sandra was the cutest little girl I had ever seen and I hoped that I would have one of my own someday. And of course I did, but Becky had blue eyes instead of soft brown eyes. Sandra had long lashes and soft brown curls that framed her little face."

Archie continued, "The city of Orillia sponsored a picnic in the park with free ice cream and cotton candy for the children. Sandra and I were there and we were having a wonderful time, until I discovered that I had lost my wallet. This was very serious because I had money in it to buy my train ticket back home. I began looking for it and told some people suggested that I ask at the booth 'over there.' Fortunately, whoever found it had been honest and turned in the wallet with the money still in it. I was so shaken that I took Sandra's hand and headed for home.

"Sometimes I would ride with Preston on his bus run around the end of Lake Couchiching to the Rama Indian Reserve. When he wasn't driving the bus, he took a jeep and delivered bundles of newspapers to small stores and tourist outfits around the lake. It was lots of fun for me. On one of those trips, I remember seeing mannequins in store windows for the first time and wondered how people could stand so still.

"Soon it was time to take the train north to Trout Creek. I had to wait at Trout Creek train station for the stage. At the station I met and played with a couple of boys my age who helped themselves to handfuls of blueberries from baskets sitting on the station platform. I got a taste myself before someone told us that we shouldn't be doing that.

"I don't remember the rest of the trip home. It seemed like a non-event. I think Mom was the only one who noticed that I had been away on such an earth-shaking, eye-opening and life-changing trip. About the time that I was settling back into the home routine, we got the news that Preston was sick with polio. Sandra was sick too with whooping cough. Mom went to Orillia to look after Sandra so that Audrey, who was three or four months pregnant with Valerie, could visit Preston in the hospital."

Lloyd explained, "The previous year when the moving business was slow, Preston took a job driving a bus route through the Rama reserve to help with the cash flow. In August he helped a sick man off the bus. The man was diagnosed with polio and within days Preston was ill with it too."

Archie added, "When Preston got sick and started 'acting funny' – delirious with a high fever – Audrey called the Cookes and Uncle Silby came from Barrie and drove Preston to the Hospital. He was diagnosed and transferred to Riverdale Hospital in Toronto."

Lloyd continued, "In those days, Riverdale Hospital had become the 'isolation hospital' for southern Ontario, that's why Preston was taken there. He was diagnosed with bulbar polio, the most lethal strain of the virus and placed in an iron lung that mechanically forced his lungs to breathe. Within a week of contracting the disease, Preston was dead."

Archie broke in, "I remember that it was a Sunday morning when we got the news. The morning chores were done and Mervyn and I, Thelma and June were in the yard. A taxi driver pulled into the yard. The driver gave Mervyn the message verbally and then asked for his taxi fare. Howard came from the house and paid the driver. The message had come by telegram to the Trout Creek station and because of the urgency the stationmaster telephoned Farley's Store with the message. Nobody else had telephone service in those days. Tom Farley dispatched a taxi with the message.

Archie continued, "I don't know who in the family went to the funeral but I know that Mervyn, June, Thelma and I didn't go. We did go to church at Commanda that afternoon. That was the day when heaven became a real place for me. At night I would lie in bed and picture reuniting with Preston there."

"When I heard the news," I told them, "I ran to the outhouse and cried. It was the one place of privacy. Someone told me later that our dad went to the barn and cried. Unfortunately in our family, we had not learned to share our grief, or to look to one another for support or comfort. Each of us grieved alone."

Lillian said, "Preston's body was taken directly from Riverdale Hospital in a sealed casket and buried in Mount Pleasant Cemetery, Toronto, with only a graveside service. Mom and Audrey weren't allowed to go to the funeral. They were quarantined in the house. What a sad time for Audrey. She was a widow at twenty-one."

Archie continued, "Mr. And Mrs. Claredge, Rea's wife's grandparents were visiting at the time. Mrs. Claredge took over the role of 'Mom'. When Gerald arrived home from Winnipeg to attend the funeral it was dark and he gave her a hug and kiss. He thought she was our mother."

I clarified, "Mrs. Claredge oversaw the cooking but I took over making the bread and churning the butter she was a 'city woman' and didn't know how to do those things. I was thirteen at the time.

"Mrs. Claredge must have gotten tired of eating the fried salt pork that was our summer staple, due to the lack of electricity to keep fresh meat. One day Mr. Claredge walked the two miles to Commanda store, where he bought fat farmer's sausages. For supper that night Mrs. Claredge made 'toad in the hole.' She wrapped pieces of sausage in dough and baked them. They tasted so good that I would have liked more but there was only enough for one piece each.

"While Mom was still away in quarantine with Audrey, a new gas-driven washing machine arrived from Eaton's department store in Toronto. Lloyd had saved money from his new job in Toronto and he ordered it to lighten Mom's workload. Mervyn, just sixteen, assembled it and got the gas motor running. He set it up in the woodshed which also served as the summer kitchen. It was an exciting occasion to have a modern washing machine even though hydro-electric power didn't come to Commanda for another two years.

"It's funny the things that stand out in one's memory at a time like that," I concluded.

"Audrey was quite young to be a wife and mother and her parenting and culinary skills weren't developed yet. I noticed earlier that summer when I visited, Preston was doing quite a bit of the cooking and he handled any of Sandra's disciplinary problems with gentleness and understanding. To have the whole responsibility thrust upon Audrey while she was so young, and also pregnant with Valerie, must have been really hard," commented Archie.

"When Audrey came to visit us in Commanda a year later the change in her was dramatic; the blush of youth so quickly gone. She asked our dad, whom she considered to be the head of the family, for his advice as to whether or not she should remarry. I still remember his words," continued Archie. 'If you can find someone you could love as much as you loved Preston then by all means marry him,' he said.

Archie recalled, "Then Audrey's face crumpled and her lips trembled. She turned away to get control and answered over her shoulder, 'I could never find anyone that I could love like I loved Preston! There is a man, however, who wants to marry me and I don't know what to do.'"

Audrey did remarry. She had two more children, Terry and Danny. When her second husband died she re-established her ties to the Peever family. She attended the 1996 Commanda Peever reunion, where Preston's brothers and sisters were delighted to greet their beloved sister-in-law.

Audrey died April 4, 2001 at age seventy-five.

# ~Mrs. Sullivan~

Beneath the massive spruce tree in the graveyard, a living soul resided. The spreading branches that touched the ground formed a roomy tent. Nearby, her uncle, the late Langton Carr, first Member of Parliament for the East Parry Sound District, rested in grander style under a large granite headstone. Her meagre stores of bread, tins of sardines and jar of peanut butter sat on an old blanket inside an opening in the branches.

Annie Sullivan was not home. In a rumpled cotton dress, her shapeless body bitten by sand flies and mosquitoes, she haunted the farm that was once her home. About a mile up the Nine-Mile Bush Road (now named Bennett's Road) stood the homestead, legally occupied by Tom Bennett and his sons, Tom Jr. and George. In her disorganised mind the farm had been stolen from her and nobody would help.

Occasionally, Mrs Sullivan turned up at our home.

Our mother, who would root through her stores to find a warm winter coat for one of our schoolmates, who made room among her own dozen children for an alienated teen friend of her son, also welcomed Mrs. Sullivan. They often sat in the shade of the Balm of Gilead trees shelling peas or snapping beans.

Our mother would gently steer the conversation away from Mrs. Sullivan's delusions. For a time Mrs. Sullivan would respond companionably, her dishevelled greying, blonde head bent over the basket of beans.

We children didn't fear her although we were aware that she was different. As three-year-old Archie and I played at their feet, my five-year-old ears picked up her tale. She was being terrorised in the night by men "yipping and yowling like a W-O-L-F," trying to drive her away. Her attempt to spare our childish understanding failed because I had already learned to read and spell, thanks to my older siblings.

Annie Sullivan was as intelligent as she was delusional. She confided to our mother how she had convinced the doctors at the mental hospital that she was well by agreeing with their statements. When summer came, Annie wanted to be at her old home in Commanda.

Thus, fortified by a hearty meal, contact with reality, a bath and shampoo and wood ticks removed from her scalp, Mrs. Sullivan shuffled off to her retreat in the cemetery.

When the weather turned cold, or if her mental state deteriorated, Mrs. Sullivan's son would arrive to take her back to Toronto. Most likely Charlie Hoffman, the kindly proprietor of the Commanda General Store notified him.

June encountered Mrs. Sullivan one day when she was about fourteen. It was after the Second World War when June was visiting Carl and Ella who, at the time, were living on Balliol Street in Toronto. June was playing on the street with some other kids. They dared her to knock on the door of a nearby house. Naively June knocked. Who should open the door but Mrs. Sullivan! She recognized June. Mrs. Sullivan was delighted to see Annie's Peever's daughter from Commanda. She invited June in for tea and cookies. The children who dared her were astounded!

June told her story to the family when she returned home from her visit to Toronto. June related how Mrs Sullivan had all kinds of barriers by her front door, and an axe. She told June that people frequently harassed her. June described Mrs. Sullivan as living alone and still a little "strange."

Nobody saw Mrs. Sullivan in Commanda after that day.

On reflection, it would seem that the plight of the mentally ill has not changed much since 1939. Although we could not have realized it at the time, Mrs. Sullivan was the first "bag lady" and the first paranoid schizophrenic whom we were to encounter in our lifetime.

In Commanda there were two places where Mrs. Sullivan seemed to connect with reality, at our home and at the Commanda Store.

The Commanda Store was built in about 1885 by James Arthurs. It was purchased in 1906 by a German immigrant August Schwartz, father of Alvina Schwartz Peever, wife of our uncle William Alexander Peever. August Schwartz died in 1920 and left the store to his two sons Anthony and Ben. In 1928 the store was sold to Florence Smith. She ran it with the help of her son George. In 1945 Charlie Hoffman purchased the store. The store was then bought in 1957 by George Hanselman. He died in 1977.

In 1979 the store became the Commanda Museum providing an enduring record of the lives of hardy folk who settled there and harvested the white pine forest.

Commanda Store

# ~Sundays! Sundays!~ Summer Escapades

### The Balsams

We'd all grown up and scattered, but, like homing pigeons, on a 24th of May weekend we'd gathered for another "bush picnic" at Mud Lake.

It was there that Lloyd launched into the story of building his first log cabin. He related, "Across the road from our farm we built our first log cabin at the edge of the clearing above Cook's Rock – it was named after settlers who'd build a cabin above that rock but then moved on. We built our cabin walls of saplings in just the fashion of log cabin building. Then for a roof, we salvaged a piece of corrugated tin from the roof of the old barn that blew down in about 1930.

"It was six years later that Preston, Gerald and I built our first cabin," Lloyd stated. "An oil drum became a stove. We cut a door in one end of the drum so wood could be put in. A piece of downspout from the old barn was fashioned into a stovepipe. On cool days a fire made the cabin cozy. We made seats for the cabin from tree stumps. Next we built a fire pit outside the door where we buried potatoes and carrots in ashes and cooked them in their skins.

"The cabin was our refuge from the steady routine of farm chores. We were age fourteen, twelve and nine respectively when we built it but as the years went by the cabin fell into disuse."

Lloyd continued his story, "A dense copse of balsam trees directly across from our house that we call The Balsams was the site of the next cabin that came to life in the early 1940s. Halfway up the hillside Gerald and I, Howard and Mervyn cleared a spot in the bush for the new cabin. Again we scavenged parts from the ruins of the first cabin.

"The forest floor was sandy, a thick padding of balsam needles afforded a deep silence and the air held a sharp tang of balsam. In the stillness one day we looked up from our work to see a deer watching us from not more than ten feet away. I'm sure the deer wondered who were these interlopers disturbing the peace of the forest! We stood stalk still until the deer wandered away. Gerald was around just long enough that summer to help erect the cabin and hoist the slanted tin roof over the beams, before leaving for Toronto to find a man's job.

"I set up the old stove and stovepipe, salvaged from our first cabin. We knocked together boards to make a door and hinged it with pieces of leather straps. You younger kids, June, Thelma and Archie were age ten, eight and six. We recruited you three to chink the cracks between the walls of saplings with moss, to keep out the drafts. An old green bench and sawed off logs provided furniture. We had a few tin plates and spoons, and a small pail sufficed as a 'tea pail' or kettle."

June interjected, "Before Gerald left he undertook to teach us younger ones how to find our way home from The Balsams alone. He set us in the right direction and disappeared. We nervously picked our way through the dense trees toward home; looking for blazes on trees to mark the way. The forest floor was too springy from the padding of needles to show a trodden path. When we emerged through the trees into bright sunlight we found ourselves in a swampy area, about a hundred yards off the proper entrance to The Balsams.

"Gerald suddenly reappeared. He had been shadowing us all the way to be sure that we reached safety."

I laughed and added, "The next thing you boys did was to build an outhouse a short distance away, to the side of the cabin. You dug a trench and erected a frame made from saplings over it. Poles were secured across the framework, spaced wide enough to support the buttocks. The open-air outhouse afforded comfort but no privacy." I smiled ruefully at the others gathered for our Mud Lake picnic.

"I also remember you boys building a fire pit. We younger ones had to search the forest nearby for rocks, just the right size, to surround the pit. There were always lots of vegetables from our garden to roast in the coals or to be cooked, buried in a pail full of damp sand. The roasted potatoes and carrots had a very sweet, smoky flavour and were delicious – if one could ignore the gritty sand still clinging to them.

"Before leaving for home the older boys were always careful to douse the fire with water and then they kicked sand over the site as well. They took great care to prevent a forest fire."

Archie added, "On a Saturday for a special treat, sometimes Mom would make hot dog rolls. She'd dispatch one of the children to the Commanda store to buy wieners for a Sunday picnic up on the hill at Cook's Rock. Store-bought wieners were a treat as we raised all of our meat but never made wieners.

"The original fire pit still existed there and sitting perched on the rock or on the steep hillside above the giant rock we devoured our wonderful picnic, while enjoying a sweeping view. As far as the eye could see the valley and flat land beyond was our Peever farm."

Archie emphasized, "But even though it was Sunday all of us had to be home by 4 p.m. to begin the evening chores of herding the cows to the milking ground, feeding the hens and gathering the eggs before supper."

I concluded, "On Sundays I recall that we ate more lightly. In summer meal preparation meant several of us picking and husking a large pot of corn. June or I had the task of finessing a bucket of new potatoes out of potato hills without disturbing the growth of smaller potatoes on the stem. The potatoes had to be scrubbed clean and the muddy water carefully poured on plants in the garden. Remember that water was carried by hand and it was never wasted.

"The meal often featured a platter of fried eggs accompanied by corn on the cob and new potatoes, slathered with home-churned butter. After supper we had to milk the cows and return them to pasture and to feed the calves and pigs but it still felt like a day of rest and adventure. The day ended as we gathered around the big table. Mom read a Bible passage by lamplight and Dad led all of us in singing hymns."

"Sundays were great fun!" We all agreed.

## Epilogue

In later years, Archie, reminiscing about our cabin in the Balsams said to me, "Just before Lloyd sold the farm, Kathy and I and our three little children came south from Nakina for a visit. We stayed in Mom and Dad's empty cottage. One morning I arose early and leaving the family sleeping, I 'walked the farm' for the last time saying goodbye to the land.

"I strolled through the Balsams and came upon our cabin. A tree had fallen on the roof but that sturdy cabin still stood as we'd left it when we left our childhood behind."

## Going Down For the Last Time

Sunday! The morning farm chores are done and we are free for the rest of the day.

The five of us head up the trail through the forest. The woods are cool in dappled sunlight filtering though the leaves. Barefoot, we tread softly, careful not to break twigs underfoot or kick loose stones. We speak in muted tones and only when necessary. Our father has taught us to respect the sanctity of nature.

A red fox raises his head to observe the silent procession. His pungent scent is still wet at the base of a tree. We touch each other and point. The fox watches for a moment before ambling deeper into the bush.

Winding through a marshy area, wet marsh grasses crowd in against my bare legs. I carefully scan the path ahead for snakes. I don't like snakes. I don't like their silent, sudden appearance under my feet; or the way they curl up on the path ahead, flicking their slender pink tongues while I stand transfixed with fear. As the smallest of the troupe, I don't want to bring shame upon myself by crying out.

My brothers, Lloyd, Howard and Mervyn and my sister June and me proceed up the trail toward the clearing. We are in age respectively fifteen, fourteen, twelve, ten, and eight. We pass the ruins of our Uncle Willie's old farm, abandoned to the shallow, rocky soil and wild berry bushes. An old torn shoe and a few rusted pans lie in the hollow that was once a cellar, make the place look forlorn.

We take the stony, overgrown path to the secluded lake nestling like an oval sapphire set in a giant granite ring.

Our wooden rowboat is pulled up at the marshy waters' edge. We leave our clothes on the shore to keep dry, scramble in into the leaky boat and sit in the bottom while the eldest pushes off from shore. Our brothers row across the lake that is a half-mile across and only a mile in length from its spring-fed inlet to its marshy outlet. The far shore of the lake is open and rocky.

Leaping out onto the rocks, they pull the boat up after us. Our brothers take off up the rocky hillside in search of adventure and of wild fruits or berries to assuage their constant appetites.

My sister June and I sit on a smooth rock in the warm sun. In a test of nerve and timing we dangle our toes in the water, enticing the shiny black leeches to crawl out of the mud. Just as the leeches reach our toes, we pull back our feet. The leeches sink back into the mud to await more unwary prey.

Our brothers return, hot from running and foraging over the rocks. We all clamber into the boat to go swimming, heading for the centre of the lake that is free from mud and leeches.

Cool water slides smoothly over sun-parched skin. The boat rocks gently with our splashes.

I feel tired suddenly and give a kick to reach the boat. A puff of wind takes it beyond my grasp. I'm sinking but I use the last of my strength to swim after it. The boat still drifts forward. I feel myself slide beneath the water, and in one desperate effort, I claw my way to the surface.

Nobody is near.

Exhausted, I am aware that I'm drowning; my long blonde hair drifts upward past my face.

Suddenly a hand grasps my hair and with a shout, June pulls me to the surface.

I don't recall anything beyond that moment.

The incident is never mentioned to our parents for as children, we are expected to be responsible for ourselves and for each other.

Fifty years later my sister June and I make a return visit to our home area. On our semi-annual visit to Edna at her home in Powassan, we reminisce around Edna's dining table.

June says, "Remember when you nearly drowned in Mud Lake? You were going down for the last time when I caught sight of your hair drifting down, just beneath me."

With an intake of breath, the memory and the drowning sensation come flooding back.

## Charging Bull

Hurray! It's Sunday again!

Mom has the breakfast table nicely laid. Breakfast is a special treat on Sunday now – store- bought cereal and glasses of juice grace the table. It is a welcome change from our weekly diet of rib-sticking oatmeal porridge.

Thanks to Prime Minister Mackenzie King and the Marsh Report of 1943, we receive the Family Allowance, as do all families because of the Second World War. *The Family Allowance Act of 1944* was instituted to alleviate financial hardship of families while the men folk diverted their wage-earning power to fight in the war, instead of providing for their families.

To our family it means that our mother has purchasing power. What is more powerful than Purchasing Power! Unwittingly, Mackenzie King raised the status of Canadian women for all time by putting money directly the hands of Canadian mothers.

To our family, the Family Allowance means that the National Grocers' truck stops at our home to unload food in bulk. Twenty-pound bags of cereal, fifty-pound sacks of flour, five-pound blocks of cheese, large cans of orange and tomato juice, all paid for with the Family Allowance cheque.

It means a nice breakfast on Sunday morning.

It also means dreaded cod liver oil!

I gag on it, but Mom holds my nose and spoons it down my throat.

Annie is determined that her children will be healthy.

This Sunday, farm chores done, we head out for a day of freedom, our trusty dog Sport at our heels.

Sport is our lead sled dog in winter, herd-dog in summer, and always our companion in fun and adventure. Sport is the son of fox-colored Maggie, a Red Bone Hound bred for speed and "giving tongue." Her loud *AARRUUH* can be heard for miles, guiding hunters to their quarry.

Sport's sire is Preston's powerful, sleek, black Great Dane. Sport is both fast and powerful. His hide is the color of denim. Sport's hound's nose can pick up the scent of a marauding bear in the bush. He keeps us safe.

Mervyn is leading the way, June and Thelma with the youngest, daydreamy Archie, trailing behind. We are, respectively, age fourteen, twelve, ten and eight. Barefoot, with the warm June sun or our backs, we climb the hill behind our grandparents' old homestead and head into the bush.

It is only lately that Archie is allowed to come along too. Mom kept her last baby close to her side for as long as she could. He still has the large, angry scar under his left shoulder blade; a souvenir of life-saving surgery for pleurisy and pneumonia at age two.

We are headed to The Chute in the gorge on Commanda Creek. The creek separates our land from Frank Pilger's farm and Ephraim McConnell's household on the other side. The chute was built in earlier years for driving logs through the gorge during the powerful surge of spring runoff. River-drivers created the chute by lining the sides of the gorge with logs to form a V shape, to channel logs over the rocky gorge bottom. The logs roared down the narrow gorge and shot across the rapids to deep water. Below the rapids, river-drivers guided them to the local mill.

Today, small mills are gone. Truck drivers haul logs to larger, central mills.

Hanging over the boiling fury of the chute sits an enormous black granite rock. The receding Ice Age formed it in the shape of a giant high-backed chair.

The roar of the chute is deafening. We have to shout to hear each other.

Sunshine warms the chair as spray from roiling water drenches us. We finally climb down from our perch and hug the bank as we tread over tree roots clinging to it. Soon we reach the calm shallows below the rapids.

Warm pools walled off by rock ridges are a great place to bathe - clothes and all and to search for crayfish and clams. Clams lie with their shells open just enough to catch food that drifts downstream. They "clam up" as soon as they're touched.

Crayfish make a tasty snack for Sport. He stands close as we overturn small rocks. When the crayfish shoot out, with teeth bared, Sport nabs them and crunches them down. Sport knows enough to bare his teeth to protect his lips from the crayfish's pincers.

On we go following the creek downstream.

Commanda Creek soon leads us beside our neighbour Schermer's field. Finding a dip in the terrain, we crawl under the page-wire fence into his field. The other three kids amble on but I find a patch of wild strawberries – the first of the season.

The strawberries are juicy and warm from the sun. Warm wild strawberries give off such an irresistible aroma that I'm entranced. Pure bliss! I stuff handfuls of juicy berries into my mouth.

A bellow! I look up to see a red bull, head down, horns glistening in the sun; bearing down on me. The bull has me trapped against the fence. There is no escape!

My piercing scream rends the air and brings Sport, fast and powerful, to the scene. Sport grabs the maddened bull by the heels. The bull turns on him. Sport slashes the bull's lowered muzzle with his teeth.

Mervyn hears the racket and runs back to boost me over the fence. Mervyn hoists himself over too, as Sport drives off the bull. Our siblings aren't taking any chances. They find a low spot and crawl back under the fence. We head back head home the way we came.

# ~Winter Adventures~

## Pants on Fire

When the morning chores of feeding livestock and milking the cows are completed, the animals are driven outdoors for a day of fresh air and exercise. We are free again until late afternoon.

Strapping on skis, our trusty dog Sport bounding along, all six of us: Lloyd, Howard, Mervyn, June, me, and the youngest, eight-year-old Archie, take off up the logging road behind the farm. We are heading toward Mud Lake looking for adventure. In the forest, protected from the wind, we are comfortable and can travel easily on skis over the deep snow.

While dining with siblings during one of his rare visits to family in Ontario, Mervyn reminisces, "Do you remember when Howard set his pants on fire?" The table erupts with knowing laughter.

Mervyn launches into his story, "As we came upon a grove of tall hemlock trees, at the base of one tree Sport began barking excitedly. Looking up, we spotted a porcupine near the top. We knew that porcupines are a scourge to hemlock trees. They feed on the bark and they'll eventually kill the tree, so Howard, sixteen, elected to climb the tree and knock the animal down.

"Climbing a hemlock is a challenge. Those trees grow very tall. Their lowest branches could be ten feet or more above the ground," Mervyn explains. "Howard shinnied up 'til he reached its branches and then climbed up to where the porcupine clung. Howard dislodged the animal with his boot and the animal tumbled to the ground. We had to hold the dog back or he would have been 'quilled' by the frightened porcupine."

Mervyn's siblings all begin to laugh at the picture of happened next.

Mervyn continued, "As Howard began to slide down the last ten feet of the tree, friction lit matches in his pocket and as the fire burned his leg, Howard had to let go. He dropped the rest of the way. Howard sure shed his burning pants in a hurry!" exclaimed Mervyn, amid laughter.

"That wasn't the only incident to happen that day," Archie confessed, "As usual, my chore was to feed the hens and gather the eggs. That morning there were two eggs in their nests already. Hurriedly I just put them in my pocket. I was afraid you older ones would leave me behind so I ran directly from the henhouse and strapped on my skis. In the bush I tripped, as my ski caught on a branch. As I went down, I felt the eggs crush against my thigh. 'Oh no,' I groaned inwardly, as the slimy raw eggs soaked into my thigh.

"I never told you older ones because I didn't want to get laughed at," said Archie embarrassed still.

"Aaw," the others sympathize, acknowledging the pain of being the youngest.

**Lost In a Whiteout**

Suddenly a deluge of snow enshrouds me, muffling all sound, obliterating my footsteps into the swamp. I call out to my brother, "Archie! Help! I'm lost!"

Silence.

On a mid-February Sunday afternoon, three of us, June age sixteen, Archie twelve, and myself age fourteen, trek half a mile up the bush trail behind our farm to go skating at a spot we called 'the wet hole'. A recent thaw flooded this low-lying area making an ideal skating rink. Before changing into our skates, we build a small fire to ward off the cold.

Surrounded by swamp, the air is still and the weak sun behind a leaden sky gives the place an eerie jaundiced aura. We skate for an hour or so and decide to head home. Farm chores have to be done before supper.

June is withdrawn and morose because her boyfriend fails to call this weekend. She pulls off her skates and, without a word, starts down the trail. Wanting to comfort her in her sadness, I hurry into my boots. Leaving Archie to douse our fire I attempt to cut through the swamp and intercept my sister on the trail. Minutes into the swamp I'm enveloped in a dense cloudburst of snow falling over me like a ruptured feather bed.

I can see nothing but ghostly outlines of trees crowding in around me. I have no idea which way to turn. Hoping to get my bearings I call out to my brother. He hears me close by but thinks I'm fooling. He doesn't answer. I stand listening but there is no sound in the forest but my own breathing.

I feel panic rising but I quash it resolutely. I must keep my head to survive. Instead, I pray, "Dear God, help me to find the way out of here." Home is to the south. Moss grows on the north side of the trees, I tell myself as I try to get my bearings.

Taking a firm grip on the skates slung over my shoulder, I tramp my way out of the swamp through knee-high snow.

The forest opens up but fear rises in my chest so I stop and pray again, check the moss on the trees and walk on. Soon I come to the Bennett's fence line, our nearest neighbour a mile to the east of our home. Here I make a near-fatal mistake. I turn away from the fence line, determined to go south.

The light is fading, I'm tired and I feel a pain in my side from a recent appendectomy. I trudge on for more miles. I must get home before dark!

Finally, I reach the edge of a small frozen lake. Now I know where I am! I recognize Cadge Lake from summer hikes with my older brothers and realize that I've ended up two miles north of the skating rink instead of south. If I hadn't stumbled on Cadge Lake...in the direction I'm walking, fifty miles of wilderness lies ahead of me!

The realization takes my breath away. Taking a deep breath, I turn south.

I know that another small lake lies between me and the trail home.

Thankfully, the snow has stopped falling as I carefully skirt the end of Cadge Lake, find Mud Lake and skirt it too. What joy and relief when I find blazes marking the trail crossing "Bill's Field" and turn toward home!

Night is falling as I meet my young brother coming up the trail. Archie, who has always been afraid in the bush at night, has come to look for me. I run, crashing into him in wild elation. Laughing, we both go sprawling on the icy hill above the farm.

"Always stay together when you are out in the bush," our father sternly admonishes all three of us at supper.

I learn that nobody knew that I was missing. Archie thought that I was with June. June was unaware that I'd tried to catch up with her. Only Mom, as she started supper, asked, "Where's Thelma?"

Nothing more is said about the incident.

The wind picks up, the temperature drops and a winter storm descends in earnest.

I say my prayers and crawl into bed. Lying in a warm bed as the howling wind rattles my windowpane; I know that I could not have survived this night in the wilderness. Again I thank God for bringing me home safely.

**Epilogue:**

In adulthood we haven't changed much.

Archie would become a minister, seeking lost souls in Ontario's northland.

I became a social worker, reaching out to heal those in emotional pain.

June became a full-time homemaker.

# ~Seasons on the Farm~

## Ice-fishing

*Swish, swish, swish* sing our skis as we glide across granular snow on our five-mile trip in early March, to Restoule and a day of fishing.

Sun! Glorious sun, glancing off the ice of wind-blown Commanda Lake, heralds the opening of ice-fishing season. Mervyn leads the way with powerful strokes of skis and poles, followed close behind by June and me. Our backs carry fishing gear and an auger for boring fishing holes, and most important, our lunch. We are age fourteen, twelve and ten, looking forward to a day in the sun, relief from Saturday chores, and the excitement of catching some fat pickerel.

Mervyn bores and chisels out two fishing holes, not far off-shore. June and I gather dry driftwood sticks for a fire to warm our hands and to boil tea. We drag a small, dry log out onto the ice to make a seat near the fire. June gets the fire going while Mervyn baits our hooks with minnows that we've brought along. June dips some water into a pail that will hold our catch, and we're all set.

June is the first to land her fish. What excitement! A pickerel, its spiny dorsal fin erect as it protests at being yanked out of the water. She carefully removes the hook from the fish's mouth and places it in the pail, but June is so excited that she steps backward into Mervyn's fish-hole, getting a boot-full of water. Wet feet are a hazard in cold weather. Steam rises from the wet sock-clad foot she extends to the fire while Mervyn props her wet rubber boot upside-down on a stick near the fire, her fishing put on hold.

Mervyn is the next to catch a fish, a large pike that gives him a fight to tests his skills, but he finally lands it flopping, onto the ice. The sun is high in a sparkling blue sky. We feel it's warmth through our heavy woollen coats. Our stomachs tell us that it is noontime. As our tea pail boils over the fire, I notice that 50 feet away; toward the shore, the ice has opened up and a current seems to be flowing in the strip of water. Soon a duck lands in the open water. It is not a reassuring sight! We can hear a low rumbling under the ice.

Mervyn deems that we are far enough out from shore to be safe. The fish-hole shows that the ice we're sitting on is two feet thick. We catch a few more fish. Soon the wood in the fire burns down and shifts, dropping June's boot into the coals. She leaps to snatch it out. Too late - the side of her boot is melted. It's a signal that it is time to go.

The afternoon sun is still warm as we pack up our gear. June slips on her wounded boot. Mervyn puts the fish on a stringer over his shoulder as we strap on our skis, grab our poles and set off across a corner of the lake toward home, our faces sun and wind-burned.

With each stroke of the skis we hear the ice under us crack and groan, sending shivers of fear through us. Nobody comments. We know that skiing is safer than walking because our weight is well distributed and we are moving very fast.

What a relief to reach solid ground! We turn toward home.

Proudly we present Mom with her favourite food, the first fresh-caught fish of the season!

Lloyd and Howard Ice Fishing 1937

## Home from the Logging Camps

Heavy packsacks hit the floor with a thump. Our dad, Preston, Rea, Carl and their friend Eric are home from the logging camps. We are excited to see them. The house is suddenly full to capacity again and bursting with sound, all telling their stories.

The men have spent the winter living in close quarters of various bunkhouses. Their packs contain soiled clothing AND bedbugs. Under their skin, the men's bodies carry a parasite that causes the "itch." At the nape of their necks, where heavy collars rub, carbuncles form angry red pustules.

Annie goes into action. To kill parasites, she doses the men with sulphur, mixed with honey - to make it marginally palatable. After bathing, hot salt water compresses are applied to carbuncles to draw out the infection. Mom excises these and paints neck areas with iodine, covering them with a dressing. When the infection has drained, she applies antiseptic Balm of Gilead salve for healing.

The men should have left their packs outside overnight to freeze the vermin they carried. Unwittingly, in short order, their packs cause the household to be infested with bedbugs. The children wake up with welts. We search our beds and find the pesky critters lurking under bed covers, fat with our blood. We can hear the scratching of their feet under the wallpaper as they hide out during daylight.

"Mom we've got bedbugs!" we call out. When we've gone off to school mom goes through the bedrooms with Flytox spray, even ungluing wallpaper to spray their hiding places. It takes a few repeats of Flytox to eradicate the bedbugs for another season.

For the men it's time to get out on the land again, fertilizing the fields. They fill the sleigh-box with loads of manure from the pile behind the barn. The horses pull load after load while the men fork manure out across the fields. As the snow melts the nutrients from the manure will be carried into the earth for another growing season.

Our brothers and their friend Eric will be looking for work at sawmills in the area as soon as the ice breaks up on lakes and rivers, leaving Dad with most of the tilling and seeding.

**Maple Syrup Time**

Drip, drip, and plink, plonk. Clear beads of sap form on spiles and roll off into sap-pails, creating an early April symphony resounding through the maple bush. Crystallized snow still lies on the ground. Sunny days and cold nights are just the right combination for a good run of sap to be boiled down into maple syrup.

Spring is an exciting season - the earthy smell of spring, the feel of spring sunshine is in the air. Days are longer. Winter is losing its grip on the land and snow is less deep to wade through. The sun is warmer. There's a promise of freedom and new energy! Everyone feels it.

The woods are full of the songs of over-wintering birds: jays, chickadees and whisky jacks. Male partridges are already drumming to attract mates and early crows add their raspy caw-caws. In the barnyard, cows are gambolling about like silly yearlings and the horses roll on the ground, rubbing off their heavy growth of winter hair. Hens are freed from the henhouse to scratch away the snow, searching for bits of grain and grit, while the rooster prances around them, crowing for attention.

Saturday! And the swarm of Peever kids are in the sugar bush carrying pails of sap and emptying them into the big sap-pan. They're crunching through shin-high snow, calling to each other and laughing. It feels like an excursion, almost like the excitement of hunting Easter eggs.

During the week when our dad is alone with the task of gathering sap, he hitches the team of horses to the low stone-boat, sets five-gallon cream cans on it and empties sap-pails into the cans as he visits each tree. The horses haul the cans to the sap-pan.

The pan is about four feet wide by eight feet long and three feet deep. It sits on a four-foot high stone frame. Over the stone fireplace boiling sap is reduced to maple syrup. It takes all day to boil down a pan of sap.

Steam rises above the sap-pan. The smell of fresh maple syrup is in the air, mixed with the tang of wood-smoke.

At the end of the day, Dad and the older siblings carefully carry pails of syrup to the house. Mom fills large cooking pots. She brings the syrup back to the boil and then pours the hot syrup into sterilized two-quart sealers. This is our annual supply of maple syrup. Sometimes she helps us make maple sugar candy, reducing a smaller pot of syrup until a spoonful, dropped in cold water, forms a ball. We beat in some fresh cream and pour the candy into a buttered cake pan to cool – a wonderful treat on a Saturday night!

Maple syrup time lasts for two or three weeks, depending on the weather. The season makes for long days of carry pails of sap and longer days for our mother, who works into the evening preserving the syrup. The season is usually in full swing in time for Pancake Tuesday. This day we're treated to platters full of pancakes, running with butter and fresh maple syrup, celebrating the day and nature's wonderful bounty.

Lent doesn't affect the Peever family's diet directly but further up the road beyond Schermer's turn, the family of Frank Hummel observes the season of Lent by abstaining from meat. Peevers supply the large Hummel family with a wooden crate of twelve dozen eggs. When the crate is empty it is returned for refilling. With the cash received, the Peevers buy one of the huge frozen salmon that lies in crushed ice at Charlie Hoffman's Commanda Store. Salmon, stocked only in Lent, is a rare and delectable treat.

### Alder Whistles

Every year when the pussy willows bloom, we know that it's time to make new alder whistles. Alders grow along the creek that runs in front of the balsam forest. Older brothers show the next younger ones how to make them. "This is how you make a whistle," said Lloyd to June and I, and Archie the youngest.

Taking his jackknife from his pocket, Lloyd instructs: "Choose a straight alder limb about as thick as my middle finger and cut it. Now cut off a piece about four inches long," He says as he beats the stick gently against a rock. "Now you can slide the skin off."

Grasping the slippery, naked, white stick Lloyd cuts notches along it and flattens and shapes the mouthpiece, finally he slides the skin back on and makes openings in the skin for the sound to emerge. He hands his jackknife to June. "Now you make one," Lloyd says. Ten-year- old June struggles to cut a piece the right size. June, a tomboy, handles the knife with confidence. She manages to produce her first alder whistle.

"Look at that!" June crows as she tootles on her whistle.

"Now it's your turn Thelma," Lloyd hands me the knife. My hands, barley strong enough to handle the knife at eight- years-old, I choose a slightly smaller stick to cut. Grunting with the effort, I manage to cut off a length from the alder limb.

"Don't forget to beat your stick to loosen the skin," reminds Lloyd, holding out a flat stone. Lloyd tests the stick to check if the skin is loose enough. He hands it back to me. "Now slide the skin off carefully," he instructs.

Lloyd puts his hands over Archie's small ones. Together they cut a piece for a whistle. "Now, Archie, you beat your whistle until the skin is loose, but don't beat it too hard!" Lloyd cautions.

Soon Archie's alder whistle is notched and shaped. He dances around delighted with his creation, unaware that when he is grown, he will play a real trumpet.

Lloyd couldn't see then, that in years to come, the farm would be his and he would be teaching his own children how to make alder whistles.

## Soap Making

Chunks of frozen pork fat, stripped in the fall from the bellies of butchered pigs, stink as they're rendered over the outdoor fire. To keep the unpleasant smell out of the house, Mom builds a fire-pit in the yard near the woodpile. Over the fire she sets an old preserving kettle filled with pork fat. The pot sizzles and sputters and gives off a smell of over-heated fat. She stirs the pot with a long wooden stick, making sure that the pieces of solid fat are exposed to the heat, until all the white chunks are reduced to brown twists and rendered fat. Removing the pot from the fire she fishes out and discards the brown rendered remains.

The next step is tricky. Mom carefully removes flakes from a tin labelled Gillett's Lye. Standing as far back as she can from the acrid fumes she stirs lye into the pot of rendered fat. The pot bubbles up like a witch's cauldron. A surprising thing happens. As she stirs, the light brown rendered fat turns white. It is time now to pour the mixture into two 9 x 13 metal cake pans to cool. When cooled and solid, she'll cut it into bars of laundry soap.

On wash day Mom shaves a bar of soap into a large oblong zinc boiler of water containing soiled white clothes. The boiler sits for an hour to simmer on the back of the woodstove. Stirred from time-to-time, the clothes come out amazingly white and clean, ready for a rub on the scrub-board in the big wash tub and final rinsing and wringing.

Hand washing for the large family lasts all day and fills three long clotheslines. In winter, a line full of our brothers' white combination underwear frozen stiff on the clothesline, dances like a child's strip of paper cut-out men.

In 1939, Mom gets a washing machine, though she still shaves soap into the old boiler on the stove soaking the white clothes. Broad wooden legs of the washing machine support a barrel-shaped wooden tub, its staves held together by three broad iron bands. On the sturdy lid is a wooden handle, which is attached to a circular iron cogged wheel. Six wooden six-inch long smoothed wooden pegs are attached to the underside of the lid. The handle is pulled and pushed. The wheel gyrates to a half-turn with each stroke of the handle. Clothes in the washer swish back and forth like a modern top-loading machine. A hand-turned wringer is mounted on the washer. The wooden washer considerably lightens Mom's workload.

In summer the washer is toted out into the yard. When the children are home from school they take turns pulling and pushing the handle, activating the gyrating mechanism. They lug pails of water from the well for rinsing while the older children rinse the clothes in a galvanized tub and feed clean clothes through the hand-cranked wringer.

## Calving Time

Springtime on the farm truly brings the renewal of life. It is the season when cows are giving birth. At 6 a.m. Mervyn, age sixteen, comes running from the stable where he's gone to fork morning hay into the mangers. He calls out, "Dad, one of the cows is in trouble trying to deliver."

While Dad is getting his boots on, Mervyn, ever hungry, grabs up a slice of bread and honey and heads to the stable with him. Dad, down on his knees focused on assisting the poor cow, stands up from his bloody task. And what does he see but Mervyn standing back gnawing away on his piece of bread! The sight is more that Dad can stomach. He gags and, with a roar, knocks the bread flying and gives Mervyn a clout.

Our mother keeps a book for recording when each cow is bred and her time of expected calving. Usually the calving is routine but sometimes drama accompanies the event.

The cows are in uproar one spring morning; mooing and stamping when, at fourteen, I go to do the milking. A cow tied in her stall is birthing early. The bull smells blood. He's tugged himself loose from his tether and somehow has made his way to the cow stalls. The bull is trying to mount the panicked cow while the cow is sidestepping, all the while trying to protect her calf lying at her feet, still in its birthing sac.

Seeing this, I back out the door and run to the house. Only Mom is at home. She comes running with me. Opening the stable door Mom views the mayhem. She grabs a pitchfork.

"Thelma!" she yells. "Open the stable door and stand well clear." She goes after the bull, jabbing him in the hind quarters.

The bull turns on my mother. I'm scared for her but Mom stands her ground, thrusting at him with the fork. The maddened bull is the first to back down. He turns tail and heads out the open door. I slam it shut behind him while Mom unties the frightened cow and leads her to a clean stall, reserved for calving cows. We clean the calf and carry the newborn to his mother. I clean up the birthing mess in the other stall while Mom goes on to the granary and scoops up a pail of oats.

Our mother always revives cows that have just given birth with a nice meal of hot oats. She has a three-legged iron stew pot that, when she lifts a stove lid, can be set directly over the coals. The pot filled with oats and some water stews until the grains are fat and soft. I carry the pail of hot oats to a very deserving cow.

A few weeks later, before catching the bus to high school, I again go to the stable to do the morning milking. Another cow is in distress! I quickly assess the situation, shove up my sleeves and assist the cow in delivering twins. I scrub up, change clothes and still make it to the bus in time.

After the first few days calves are separated from their mothers and placed together in a penned area. Calves are fed skim milk, fortified with special calf meal. The calves have to be taught to drink from a pail by inserting one's fingers into the calf's mouth and guiding its nose into the pail of milk. The calves soon discover how to suck up milk from a pail.

The family needs the cow's whole milk for making butter and cream.

**Easter**

Conspiracy and excitement on Saturday evening after the smallest children are tucked into bed. Now older sister and brothers can colour the Easter eggs. Edna, Lloyd and Howard boil eggs together with some vinegar and onion skins, for colouring. When the eggs are cooled, with crayon, they draw colourful patterns on eggs dyed yellow by onion skins or on red eggs, dyed with pickled beet juice.

Packing the eggs carefully into baskets the boys make a trip to the barn in the early morning. They feed the animals and then hide the eggs in nests on the barn floor around the bottom edges of hay mows.

After breakfast excited children dress warmly and troop out to the barn in search of what the Easter Bunny has left.

At Easter time the boys get new store-bought shirts but Mom always makes new colourful cotton dresses for the girls. She looks in the Eaton's catalogue to see the latest styles. Mom sketches a pattern onto brown wrapping paper, making a pattern, and then fits it on our body, getting the fit just right and cuts out the material. The dresses are usually pretty pastel prints with full skirts, tied in bows at the back. The sizing in the material even makes them smell new!

On Easter Sunday afternoon Mom treks off on the 2-mile walk to church with all her children in tow. The organ resounds with a familiar hymn: *Christ the Lord is Risen Today*. We feel as if we've all been reborn.

## The Stone Boat

April showers have washed the last snow from fields and forest. The world smells fresh and clean. Again it's the time for tilling the land.

The horses plod along dragging the heavy stone boat, its runners made of 2 x 4 timbers, tapered at the front ends. Heavy planks form a platform over the runners making it look more like a sled for giants than a boat. Our horses pull the stone boat over furrows that were ploughed the previous autumn.

Stones make a dull thump as they land on the thick planks. The children pick more stones from the earth – big ones and small ones. Stones seem to grow in the fields during the winter, working their way to the surface, aided by the heaving and receding of winter frost.

Lift and heave. Lift and heave.

Picking rocks is tedious, back-breaking work. Rough stones scuff the hands of children and adults alike but the work must be done. Stones will break the disking machine that the horses will pull over the field. The sharp disk blades break up sod furrows and prepare the land for the broad multi-tooth harrow to rake the earth smooth; preparing the field for the seeder that plants oats, rye, barley or turnips, all grown to feed livestock.

The stone boat takes its load of stones to a hedge-row of rocks, separating the field. Unloading begins: *Wham. Wham.* We fling the rocks, making the pile taller. All four of us, Mervyn, June, Archie and I, jump on the stone boat for a ride back to the field. Our dad guides the horses to the unpicked furrows. It's the only fun we'll have this day.

## Spring Flowers

Mother's Day and the May sun is shining! Mom is smiling. She does feel special today.

The three youngest go to the woods searching for flowers to bring her. Clusters of yellow, patches of blue and blankets of white flowers flourish at the base of trees in the sugar bush where we've gathered sap just a month before. We have to pull away the covering of last fall's leaves to find the shy, pink, sweet-scented Mayflowers.

Tiny rills of clear water trickle their way to join larger streams that we hop over, or teeter across on fallen logs. The ground is wet and spongy under rubber-clad feet and wet knees as we kneel to pick the flowers. Breathtaking swaths of white trilliums flourish close to the forest edge but we don't pick them. Their bulbs will die if we pick the foliage. Their red-petalled cousins go unpicked too. They smell bad. We call them skunk lilies.

Home again! We present Mom with fistfuls of wild flowers. Bouquets of yellow adder tongues, with their splotchy green foliage – sometimes called dog-toothed violets, blue violets and white Dutchman's britches – wild orchids make colourful bouquets. Delicate little pink Mayflowers form a separate bouquet. Back home, each of us scurries around the house looking for jars to hold our Mother's Day tributes.

In a few weeks the lilacs will be blooming in the yard across the road at the old homestead. Grandma Peever's abandoned garden will be encircled by blossoming plum and hawthorn trees.

Mr. Brunne "the honey man" from Arnstein owns an apiary. The Brunne family were German immigrants who settled in Arnstein in the mid 1800s. Mr. Brunne is a quiet devout man. Our parents have great respect for him.

In spring year after year, Mr. Brunne places his beehives around the periphery of our fields. In return for allowing his bees on our property, every fall he provides us with a square, seventy- pound stainless steel container of creamed honey. The honey lasts the Peever family for a full year. Our breakfast always consists of a bowl of oatmeal, cream of wheat or corn meal porridge, sweetened with brown sugar; followed by a thick slice of home-baked bread and honey. Mr. Brunne's honey is a vital source of energy in our diet.

## Potato Planting

May 24th is Queen Victoria's birthday. Britain and her former colonies still celebrate the day.

It is just the ideal time for potato planting - the peak time of black fly infestation too!

It's a school holiday and all the Peever children are in the field planting potato-sets into furrows. Two fields of potatoes are needed to feed the family for the year. We bend our backs, carefully placing the potato-sets, with sprout side upward, so they will produce a whole hill of potatoes at harvest time.

Black flies torture us, biting any exposed surface and crawling behind, and into ears, noses and hair. Flies rise up from the wet soil in swarms, lighting on our faces and hands and crawling up sleeves. We have to keep lips tightly closed to prevent inhaling the pests! They leave blotches of blood where they bite. They leave our hair matted with blood and incredible itching and burning welts where the flies have bitten.

On Saturday we'll have to plant the second field and feed our blood to these insatiable black flies, I muse. I stand, drawing myself up to my six-year-old height and swear to the sky above, "When I'm of age, I'll leave this miserable land!"

## Ball Game

In early June, the days grow longer. After the chores are done, there is still enough daylight to have a ballgame in the front yard. The pitcher safely stands with his back to an open field. The woodshed can take the brunt of a wild pitch if need be. Windows in the house will be spared.

What fun! We all get a turn at bat and run the bases. Dad comes out to join the fun and calls Mom away from her work to join in too. It is a rare occasion when our parents take time to play.

**Potato Dusting**

The alarm clock jangles, *brring, brring, brring.* Five a.m. and it's still dark. We groan as we roll out of bed. All the children know what is ahead of us – dusting the potato rows with potato-bug killer. If we don't kill the bugs as they hatch, we'll have to pick those squishy orange bugs off the plants before they form hard shells and lay more eggs. We have to save our potato crop or we'll be hungry next winter. Dusting has to be done while the dew is wet on the plants and the wind is calm.

Donning warm coats against the morning chill we stumble out the door, our stomachs empty. There will be time to eat when the job is done.

Each of us picks up a tin can, its bottom punched with holes like a large salt shaker. When we get to the potato field our dad fills each of our cans with pale green arsenic insecticide powder.

Each person takes a potato row and carefully dusts every plant in the row by gently shaking the container over and around the plant. We don't talk and we try to turn our heads away from the can as we shake out the insecticide. Even so, insecticide dust still irritates our nostrils and gets on our bare hands and under our nails.

Home again, scrubbing our hands and faces thoroughly, we change into our school clothes and after a hurried breakfast, head off to school.

Nobody is aware that the inhaled arsenic will stay in the bones of the children for a lifetime.

## First Fruits of the Season

Aaah, rhubarb pie, fresh and tart, still warm from the oven! What a welcome change from winter desserts of preserved fruit, raisin-filled, rib-sticking rice pudding or maple syrup poured over warm Johnny-cake. The only unwelcome dessert is tapioca pudding. We call it fish-eye pudding because the clear gummy tapioca's white centres make them resemble slimy fish eyes. But the first rhubarb of spring brings the promise of summer's bounty. Stewed or in pies, rhubarb that still grows in abundance in Grandma Peever's garden, almost a hundred years since planted, makes a welcome treat.

Between the rows of newly sown lettuce, peas and onion sets, grows wild lamb's quarters. How these early spring sprigs got their name in a mystery. The tender green plants taste somewhat like spinach and are rich in iron. Steamed and topped with butter, they are a nutritious change from root vegetables – until shoots of asparagus poke their heads out of the soft earth too.

Soon wild morels will spring up under a sandy carpet of pine needles covering the forest floor. Sautéed, these beige coloured earthy-tasting fungi are delicious, however, their bounty is doubled- edged. The cattle love them too but when the cows eat morels, their milk takes on an unpleasant flavour. The creamery devalues our cream because it tastes "off".

## June Sunshine

The sun beats down mercilessly on three-year-old Archie and me – just turned five. Aunt Esther, who lives across the road on the original Peever homestead, leads the two of us by the hand. It is unusual that Aunt Esther, not our mother is walking with us. We've climbed to the top of the Sand Hill on the way to Commanda School. We children have walked a mile.

Tired and thirsty, we've got another mile to walk. The weather is very hot for June and the sand gives off waves of heat.

The school is noisy and crowded. Dr. R.H. Delaine is at the school inoculating children against smallpox. Children of all ages are standing in line with their sleeves rolled all the way up to the shoulder. Our older siblings are there too. Parents accompany preschool children. June, in grade one, sees our neighbour Mrs. Leola Pilger nursing her baby as she waits with the Pilger children. June has never seen a nursing baby before.

This is the first time that children in our area are immunized. The vaccination feels like we're being punched half-a-dozen times in the upper arm. The children will feel feverish and a round brown scab will form over the spot for about 10 days.

The doctor is inoculating families alphabetically and as he vaccinates the last of the Yerke children he exclaims, "Well, that's the last of the Mohicans!" Everyone thought he was very droll and repeated the phrase throughout the community.

Finally it's summer! How wonderful for the girls to run bare-legged. Free of the sturdy cotton camisoles with attached garters. In winter, garters hold up itchy black ribbed woollen stockings. The girls are also happy to run free of heavy rubbers- except for rainy days. On rainy days June and I go to school in style.

From her Air Force Station – as it was closing down at war's end – Edna purchased and sent home a yellow rubber dingy cover. Leaving the snaps intact Mom fashioned two rain capes for the girls. The ponchos are attractive and highly effective. At school, the girls are the envy of other kids. Their schoolmates often ask, "Are your new clothes *maden* or *boughten*?" They ask because our mother turns items from boxes of used clothing, sent by city cousins, into stylish outfits. Overcoats are often transformed into warm coats and pants for the boys too.

But today the sun is shining and it's time to take our first swim of the season in Commanda Creek! On our way home from school, as soon as the 24th of May passes, it's traditional for us to celebrate by taking our first swim in Commanda Creek.

Around the bend beyond the white bridge the boys pick a spot to swim. The girls walk around the next bend, remove their clothing and jump into the icy water for a quick and vigorous swim. Tingling, we strip the water off our limbs and pull on our clothes. We feel clean and alive and warmed by the sun.

Saturday morning, the risk of frost has passed and it's time to help our mother plant the garden. Mom started the tomato seeds indoors in late February. At the same time she gave each of the younger children, June, Archie and me, a flower pot of our own and balsam flower seeds to plant in the pots. We each had a window sill for our own pot, to water and watch our flowers grow and bloom.

Now in early June, tomato plants are ready to be set out in rows. Carefully we stake up their spindly stems and mound the warm soft earth around them, enjoying the feel of warm earth squishing up between our bare toes.

Mom stakes out straight rows for several varieties of beans. We walk along the lines making hills while Mom walks behind us scooping out shallow beds for the children to drop in beans and sweet corn and peas. The seeds are gently covered and the hills patted in place. Mom has started cucumber, cabbages, cauliflower, celery, and cantaloupe plants in a cold frame on the sunny side of the house. We plant these next.

When they are grown we trade surplus fresh vegetables, like large white cauliflowers, at Commanda Store for staples like sugar or plugs of chewing tobacco for our dad. Nobody wants to be near Jim Peever when he runs out of his Big Ben chewing tobacco!

The sun feels hot, beating down on winter-whitened skin. A tall white pine at the bottom of the garden looks like an inviting place to find shade but we know not to stand near that tree. The tree is infested with wood ticks. We've all experienced a stinging sensation and found ticks with their heads burrowed beneath our scalp or shoulders. The horrible pests must be able to smell blood, for they will drop unnoticed onto unsuspecting humans or animals. Daubing the protruding body with wet salt or burning it with a lighted match, is the only safe way to extract the ticks. We shudder with revulsion at the memory and avoid the tree.

The first wild strawberries appear on sunny hillsides about a week before the end of school. They thrive in untilled hayfields, nestled among green sprouts of timothy hay. Something else is nestling deep in the grass.

Little brown sparrows –'grass-birds' we call them – are nesting on the ground. The parents set up a chirping noise and hop away from the nest, hoping to lure away predators. Some nests hold little speckled eggs and others, the tiniest of baby birds. We children hope the fat snakes that inhabit the nearby marshy ground don't find them.

Green oats rustle as out steps a little spotted fawn. It came to the fence and stuck its head through the wire to gaze at the strange sight of a boy on his way to school. Archie stands transfixed, gazing back into innocent big eyes, seeing long ears erect and almost opaque, the morning sun filtering through them. Time stands still for a moment before the boy and the fawn go their separate ways.

# ~Summer Adventures~

## Mrs. Stanfield

"We're going fishing on Jack's Lake today," announces Mrs. Stanfield.

It is the summer of 1940 and four-year-old Archie, I at six-years-old, and eight-year-old June are being cared for in Golden Valley by our mother's friend Mrs. Stanfield. The reason for our stay is not explained – we just find ourselves there in her roomy, well-appointed house.

Mrs. Stanfield looks old to our young eyes. She looks like a Victorian cameo with her luxuriant white hair piled on top of her head. Her small, plump, well-corseted frame is clothed in a high-necked, full-skirted dress that falls just above her ankles. Mrs. Stanfield's head shakes when she speaks. And she speaks authoritatively to everyone – to us, to her bird-like companion Bella Rayment and to her ancient, arthritic husband Archie.

"Isn't that right, Archie?" she demands from her silent husband.

"Yes, Saphronia," he mutters resignedly.

Even her name sounds exotic. It is clear that the Stanfields are not native-born to Golden Valley. They hail from somewhere in southern Ontario.

We are off to Jack Lake; Mrs. Stanfield, Bella and we three children, laden with fishing rods, a pail for caught fish and a picnic lunch. Arthritic Old Archie is not with us. Even Mrs. Stanfield is smiling and seems to be enjoying our excitement. The lake is about a half-hour walk from behind the Stanfield property. Pulled up on shore is a rowboat. We stow our gear and clamber aboard while the adults push the boat into the water. Mrs.

Stanfield is at the oars, Bella in the bow and the three children sit very still in the stern.

Out at the fishing spot Archie moves from the stern up to sit beside Mrs. Stanfield. She baits our hooks and we toss lines into the water. Noon arrives in no time and we enjoy their tasty lunch. The fish are biting and we all catch a few.

Mid-afternoon, Bella takes the oars and rows toward home. The children are silently impressed that two women can handle a boat so well. There will be several excursions to Jack Lake during our stay.

After the evening meal in their roomy kitchen, Mrs. Stanfield reads from the Bible and says a prayer. This is curious for us children who experience Bible reading and devotions only on Sunday nights.

Old Archie is in a rare talkative mood. He tells us how beautiful his Saphronia was as a young woman, while she smiles benignly. We ask questions, "Why has Bella a different last name?" Bella smiles, she is pleased to be the centre of attention, while Mrs. Stanfield tells us Bella's story.

"You see, we didn't have any children of our own," relates Mrs. Stanfield. "Dr. Bernardo in England sent orphan children to Canada and we chose Bella."

"Why is she so small?" We ask with childish candour. "Will she grow any bigger?"

Bella is just a little more than four-and-a-half feet tall. The adults laugh at our questions. Whether it was due to genetics or early malnutrition, they didn't give an answer. We notice that Bella clearly does not have the status of a daughter of the family. She is differential in doing their bidding but a fondness between all of them is evident.

We notice another curious thing. Mr. Stanfield sleeps in a room off the kitchen, while Bella shares a room upstairs with Mrs. Stanfield – likely because we three are sleeping in Bella's bed. We also notice that Old Archie moans when he moves and he swears under his breath. Mrs. Stanfield doesn't appear to hear him.

We have never seen a parlour as spacious or as beautiful. It stretches across the entire front of the house. The stuffed furniture all matches, mahogany cabinets and china figurines abound and in one corner is a grand piano. We are not allowed beyond the door.

Another day and another outing! Mrs. Stanfield and Bella walk us a mile down the road to Cameron's General Store in Golden Valley. The three of us are fitted with red canvas shoes.

How pretty they are and light on the feet! Our new shoes are so different from our scuffed, sturdy leather shoes. We're thrilled to have new shoes and they feel so light! We feel as we could run like the wind. Little did we know that our treasured canvas shoes will not stand up to dew-dampened grass or the farm's rough terrain. The toes will wear through before summer's end. There are so many new experiences that we don't even feel homesick, but the Stanfield's and their grey clapboard house return to us in dreams even in adulthood. Their kindness remembered.

## School's Out

School's out! The Peever kids feel both liberated and isolated. Free from classes and homework but isolated from the company of other children. There is a shift – a different morning routine for everyone. The extra pairs of hands change our parent's routines too.

After the morning milking is done, the older brothers head to the fields with their dad. The younger boys are left to feed the calves and drive the cattle to pasture. Lloyd, although still in his early teens, sets about to repair the farm machinery. Jim Peever has no aptitude or patience for repairing machinery, broken by the rocky ground. Jim is happy to leave this task to his young son.

Mom is relieved to get out of the house, leaving the endless pile of dishes to the younger girls; she goes out to hoe the garden. The girls are instructed to sweep the floor after the dishes are put away. It seems that no sooner than the dishes are away, the girls must start preparing the noon meal. New potatoes to dig out of the kitchen garden, enough for dinner and supper – boiled for dinner and home-fried for supper; lettuce to be picked for a salad. She comes back to the kitchen in time to fry the meat. Farm families need two large meals each day to provide energy for the heavy work they perform.

The men return, stamping clods of earth from their feet before entering the house. They wash up while bowls of steaming food are placed on the table. The big teapot sits brewing atop the reservoir of hot water that is attached to the woodstove. Mom says a hurried and breathless grace before everyone digs in.

By mid-afternoon the children have a few hours of free time to play. Older brother Carl's abandoned 1928 Whippet car sits in the yard behind the woodpile. Carl is far away with the Canadian Army, manning giant anti-aircraft guns, fighting his way through Sicily and Italy. He will return with his hearing gone from the constant blasts. His laughing blue eyes will hide the trauma of surviving his unit having been being blasted off an Italian mountainside by landmines; mines that were laid by the retreating enemy. Carl will not speak of it until a year before his death, when he tells of the nightmares that have persisted for a lifetime, waking him soaked in sweat. Nor would Carl speak of out-rolling the tank that was bouncing down the mountain behind him, nor of finding his buddy with the back of his head blasted away, or of reliving the carnage that wiped out his unit. In his letter home, he only writes of breaking an arm in a road accident.

The elegant, vintage, chrome-laden Whippet has leather seats and beige-coloured roller blinds on all the windows. It is of no consequence to us that the engine needs an overhaul and doesn't run. Mervyn, the eldest of the four of us, is the driver for our imaginary journey. Like the Bronte children of yore, isolation is no barrier to our combined imaginations. Building on each other's narrative we are transported away from the confines of the farm to magical towns, having adventures and conversations with people we meet on our journey.

Mom's voice calling brings us back to reality. It feels like waking up from a dream. The mind is reluctant. It wants to stay in fantasy land but it's time for chores again. Each of us has assigned routine chores before supper. Archie, the youngest, must feed the hens and gather the eggs. June and Mervyn carry in wood to fill the wood box and they carry the evening supply of water from the well. My task is to fill the coal oil lamps, clean the lamp glasses and to assist in preparation of the evening meal. These tasks don't vary with the season.

## Haying Season

July is haying season. The old adage "Make hay while the sun shines," is a true imperative. Dad labours, mowing the hay in a distant field. Over the rattle of the mower he is unable to hear the gong announcing the noon meal.

Years before, when the three youngest were little, June, Archie and I ran barefoot to the field to summon our dad. There was a treat in store for us. He'd unhook the horses from the mower and lift us onto the broad backs of his team of black Percherons. June sat astride Duke's back while Archie sat up toward Doc's neck, grasping a fistful of mane for security. I would sit behind Archie, my legs barely reaching across the broader span of Doc's back. Dad walked along beside, with a hand steadying the two youngest, as the horses plodded into the farmyard and down to the creek for a well-deserved drink of water. The children were lifted down and scampered to the house to get washed up, while Dad led the horses into the barn.

Fragrant new-mown hay lies drying in the sun. As soon as the hay is dry enough, all hands will turn out to coil the hay into mounds. The next day, the wagon is fitted with the broad wings of the hay-rack. The older boys hoist tidy coils of hay into the wagon, while Jim levels the hay and drives the horses from coil to coil. There is an urgency to get the hay into the barn before rain-showers come.

Dad backs the wagon through the open barn doors. The boys ride the wagon to help with the unloading. Lloyd pulls down the gigantic hay-fork that runs on a track along the inside peak of the barn. He positions the fork's open maw over the hay-load while Dad hitches the horses to a pulley. As the horses go forward, the pulley snaps the hay-fork closed and lifts its load of hay up and along the track. Lloyd swings the load over the haymow and trips the mechanism to open the fork. It opens with a clang, dropping its load into the haymow. Howard levels the hay in the mow. The procedure is repeated until the wagon is empty. Dad hitches the horses up to the wagon again and drives them back to the field until the field is cleared of hay.

As afternoon wears on, Howard, next younger than Lloyd, is dispatched from the fields to round up the cattle and herd them home to the milking ground. Howard saddles fleet-footed Prince and off they go up bush trails towards the marshes around Mud Lake. There the grass grows tall and succulent. Both Howard and the horse enjoy the freedom of a good ride.

After supper, all hands, except our dad, turn out to do the milking – Dad claims that he never got the knack of milking cows. He carries pails of mash to feed the pigs. The boys run pails of milk through the cream separator and feed the calves. The girls tackle the dishes while Mom dismantles the cream separator and washes the parts. Dad drives the cattle to pasture again. By 8 p.m. the chores are done. We get to listen, on the battery radio, to an episode of The Lone Ranger.

On the rare occasion that our parents are out for the evening, teen brothers, Lloyd and Howard tune in the radio to The Green Hornet or Inner Sanctum. The sound effects of the doomsday-voiced narrators, spooky music and creaking doors terrify seven- year-old Archie. He covers his ears and shouts from his bed, "Turn...That...Thing...Off!"

What a terrible thing to be the youngest of a large family!

Edna is now seventeen and one persistent fellow skis six miles from Bear Valley every Sunday to visit her and every Sunday Edna during that winter, desperate to avoid him, climbs out her bedroom window onto the woodshed roof. She shinnies down the drainpipe and escapes over the fields to spend the day at the neighbouring Bennett farm, a mile away.

Edna is very strong due to having to take on heavy work in the barn while the men are away in the bush. She is injured one summer, however. Duke, one of our huge Percheron horses, has fallen down in the horse pasture and is unable to get up. Our dad calls for Edna to come and help him and boys to get the horse on his feet. As they heave on Duke's hind quarters, Edna pulls on the lead at his head. With a mighty lurch, the horse comes forward onto his feet, throwing Edna backward onto a rock. Even the youngest in the family feel afraid for her, sensing the severity of her pain. Edna will suffer back pain for the rest of her life.

The year is now 1943; Edna is eighteen and is gone from the farm. She is no longer available in her unhappy role as mother's helper and guardian of the younger children. The younger ones suffer some bullying as a result but Lloyd soon steps in as mentor and guardian.

### Berry Picking

Early July is the season for picking strawberries. Dad happily leaves farm chores to Lloyd and Howard and takes the four youngest on berry-picking expeditions to Bill's Field. The untilled farm is home to masses of wild berries. Nothing is left of Uncle Willie's (Bill's) abandoned homestead except the cellar framed by a low wall of stones, rusted bits of a stove and the leather sole of a boot. Desolation and sadness hangs in the air. We quickly skirt around it and move on to the berry patch.

A few weeks later, Lloyd and Howard are the leaders of a raspberry picking expedition. We head about two miles up Peever's Hill to the old site of Tom Hummel's sawmill. Raspberry canes taller than our heads grow out of the fertile spongy piles of rotting sawdust. The berries are enormous.

Suddenly, bear alert! A lumbering mother bear appears. She bawls for her cubs.

Danger! We are between the mother and her cubs.

Lloyd and Howard herd Mervyn, June, Archie and me away to safety. We look back to see the cubs scurry up a tall beech tree. There are no lower limbs but the cubs are light and their sharp claws penetrate the smooth black bark of the beech as they scramble high up to safety. Mother bear continues to snort and smash around in the under-brush threateningly, to drive us away. We circle around the near-sighted bear until we're downwind of her and then go back to our picking.

What excitement! Our dad is taking us on a trip to Golden Valley. He'll combine a visit to his youngest sister Susan with a berry picking excursion. June and I and Archie grab our berry pails and straw hats. Dad takes extra baskets for the raspberries and we all troop down to the road at about 10 a.m. to await Moore's stage.

Oliver Moore will have picked up cream cans from the Trout Creek railway station and dropped off cans to all the farms on his route between Trout Creek and Loring. He picks up passengers like us and delivers them to their destinations.

The heavy dark green, rectangular stage has two rows of padded brown leather bench-seats that accommodate about eight people. Behind the passengers, bags of mail for village post offices, boxes and packages from Toronto Simpsons' or Eaton's mail-order stores, and rows of cream cans returning from the creamery for delivery to farms along the way.

We three children can barely contain our excitement but we sit, with decorum, taking in everything we see. The stage stops at Tom Farley's store to leave off mail for Carr residents, then rumbles down the steep perilous Tricky Hill with its sharp ess-bend at the bottom, onward to Bear Valley. At stops grizzled farmers are happy to exchange a few words and hear the latest news.

Finally, in early afternoon, we arrive in Golden Valley at Aunt Susie and Uncle Alex Smith's cosy home. Aunt Susie is our dad's sister and her husband Alex is our mother's older brother. Aunt Susie is small and dark haired, with a dimple in her chin like our dad's. Uncle Alex is tall and blonde, raw-boned like our mother.

We are happy to see our cousin Joan too. Joan is one year younger than June and one year older than me. We don't get to see each other very often. Joan's older brothers Melville and Bill are away in the army. Her older sisters Audrey and Velma are married.

After a bite to eat, the children run off to play while the adults chat.

The next morning, Aunt Susie, with a large cooking pot in hand, leads Jim and the children down an old logging road to her favourite raspberry patch. The picking is good and we soon fill all our containers. The rest of the day is for play and visiting. Moore's stage won't be coming by on its return trip to Commanda until the next morning.

That evening, Uncle Alex entertains the children by taking out his false teeth and chomping them at us, acting like a boogie man. We scream, run and hide. We are not used to adults acting silly. Joan leads us to her room where we play quietly until bedtime.

In the morning Moore's stage stops while our dad takes his leave of

Susie and Alex while we clamber on board with our baskets of raspberries and wave goodbye to Joan.

August is the month for picking blackberries and blueberries. Bill's Field bordering on Mud Lake is the prime place for picking blackberries.

Before the war Lillian came home for her holidays. She loved picking berries, a love that persisted all her life long. Lillian always sang quietly to herself as she worked. Years later, in a conversation about those early days, youngest brother Archie recalled, "It was a treat to go berry-picking picking with Lillian. We had our big sister to ourselves for the whole day. I used to be so scared of bees, wasps and hornets that, I'm afraid, I didn't get much picking done. But Lillian was so gentle and kind. She didn't scold when my berry can was nearly empty."

Berry Picking

I add, "I remember one time Edna and Lillian were both home for a holiday and we four girls, Lillian, Edna, June and I went blackberry picking for the whole day. We packed a picnic lunch and a large thermos of tea. At noon we sat on our favourite rock overlooking Mud Lake and enjoyed our lunch. We returned home with two eleven quart baskets, two six quart baskets and our berry cans all full. Mom would sure be busy preserving all those blackberries berries!"

During blackberry season people from Commanda, Carr, Restoule and Bear Valley would drive into our yard and take the trail through our field, trekking up the logging road to Bill's Field to pick berries. Our dad always made them welcome.

Archie recounts this memory of blackberry season, "As I grew older, I was often asked to go along as a guide for folks wanting to pick berries. One day I accompanied Carol Schwartz, Ben and Gladys' teenage daughter to Bill's Field. She was quietly singing a tune. I asked her what she was singing and she said, 'Oh, you'd be offended.' I said, no, I wouldn't. She then sang *Ave Maria*, in her beautiful contralto voice. Carol explained that she was taking voice lessons and was practising her piece."

Ben Schwartz and Gladys (Watt) Schwartz were both born in Commanda and spent summers there but as Ben was Commissioner of Roads for the Parry Sound District, his family lived the rest of the year in Parry Sound.

Archie continued his berry picking stories, "I remember the time that Dad took us younger kids picking gooseberries up on the rocks that bordered our farm and Bennett's. June got stung on the mouth by a big black hornet. Her mouth swelled grotesquely and she was crying. Dad shooed all of us back from the big hanging nest. He took a long stick and knocked the nest down and lit it on fire. It didn't make June's mouth feel any better but all of us felt that 'justice had been done'."

I add to Archie's gooseberry story. "The older boys, Gerald, Lloyd and Howard would often take potato sacks and go up to that same spot picking gooseberries. When they returned home, June and I had the job of removing the prickles and stems. We'd sit on an old quilt under the Balm of Gilead trees, rolling the sacks of gooseberries on the sun-baked ground to break off the prickles. Then we'd have to pinch the stems off. When they were cleaned, Mom would make a big batch of gooseberry pies. The tart, sweet, gooseberry pies made all the work worth the effort!"

Blueberry picking is always an adventure because we have to travel away from home to access good blueberry picking. The storekeeper Charlie Hoffman and his wife invited Archie and me, when we were young teens, along on a blueberry picking excursion near the village of Hotham. When leaving his car by the side of the road, Mr. Hoffman said to Archie, "Now remember the position of the sun so we can find our way back to the car."

All four wandered over the rocks, finding pockets of blueberries thriving in mossy hollows. When noon came, Mr. Hoffman turned in the direction of the sun to return to the car for our food and drink.

"No," argued Archie. "Remember the sun has moved in the past 3 hours. We have to head east to find the car."

Mr. Hoffman took some persuading but he reluctantly followed Archie's lead to the car.

In 1951, Lloyd takes his summer holidays, returning home from his job in Toronto. He has brought along his fiancée, Eunice Hutcheson. The two of them, along with fourteen-year-old Archie and me, age sixteen, load the farm pickup truck with the canoe, lunches and berry baskets. We drive to the town dock in Port Loring and launch the canoe in the Pickerel River.

With Archie in the bow and Lloyd in the stern, we swiftly paddle downriver. Steep granite encases the river for several miles. Finally a break in the rocks provides a landing spot. We step ashore onto low rocks, dragging the canoe well clear of the river.

Plump blueberries grow in abundance. We easily fill our baskets. Mid-afternoon clouds gather with a spattering of rain, signalling that it's time to leave. The water is a little choppy as Lloyd and Archie launch the canoe. Eunice and I sit mid-ship surrounded with full berry baskets. The heavily loaded canoe now sits low in the water.

Lloyd and Archie are paddling upstream. The wind and waves pick up, forcing the paddlers to keep manoeuvring the loaded canoe's nose into the waves. A line squall slops water over the gunwales. Eunice and I bail steadily. We're not making much headway. The sky is darkening and the waves are threatening.

Behind us we hear the thrum of a large engine. Lloyd Rogerson's big tour boat pulls ahead of us. He is returning a boatload of tourists to his resort. He calls out, "Do you want a lift?"

"Yes!" we yell with relief.

Rogerson's passengers give us a hand in boarding and assist Lloyd and Archie in lifting the canoe and placing it across the end of the tour boat. We sit wet and bedraggled at the rear of the boat, silently thanking God for being saved from a risky situation.

Lloyd Rogerson, native son, a WWII Air Force pilot and now local business man and resort owner, sets us down safely at Port Loring town dock. We give him our heartfelt thanks.

The best chokecherries grow along the brow of the steep hill above our late grandparent's homestead. When crushed, strained, boiled with sugar and preserved, the syrup makes a tasty cherry topping for pancakes or hot biscuits.

Older brother Carl liked to relate this story of teenaged rebellion in a teetotal household. "I decided to try to make cherry wine. I mashed the cherries and strained them into a two-quart sealer and put some sugar in too. Aunt Luella was home from Toronto on a visit. She'd become rather prim and religious and she scolded me for making wine. As she walked away, I picked up a handful of the mash and threw it. The mash hit her on the ass. She was wearing a yellow chiffon dress. The stain never came out," Carl said with chagrin, but with a devilish smile that carried satisfaction, too.

Carl continued, "I tightened the lid on the jar and put it in the cellar to ferment. Tightening the lid was a mistake. Two weeks later, there was such a big bang in the cellar! I went running down and found that my jar of cherry wine had exploded. There was sticky cherry juice and shards of glass all over the cellar. What a mess to clean up!" Carl laughed.

## Harvest Time

The end of World War II marks the beginning of more prosperous times, of no more rationing or gasoline restrictions. The grim shadow of war, the dreaded news of losing a son is lifted. Young men are home on the farm again.

In late July and August long hot hours of "haying" are celebrated by community harvest dances in villages like Golden Valley, Restoule and Commanda. On a Saturday night everyone washes off sweat from toiling in hot dusty fields. Young bucks with hair slicked down, muscles rippling under white shirts; sleeves rolled to the elbow, are driving the family pick-up trucks. They're looking for fun, female company and a little excitement.

Girls in cotton eyelet blouses and dirndl skirts are at the community hall. Their parents are at the dance too, to dance a little, chat with neighbours and to keep an eye on their daughters.

The music strikes up and a caller takes the stage for a square dance. Young men lolling against the walls, eyeing their prospects, make their move and invite girls to the floor. Squares form along age lines. Older couples form their own, leaving the young people to themselves.

Slower, more intimate round dance music scares off less confident males. The girls simply solve the problem by dancing with each other, while their faint-hearted counterparts lean against the walls together eying the girls again or they slip outside to get their courage from bottle.

The last dance is announced. It's now or never for a young man looking for romance. He asks the girl of his choice if he can drive her home. The offer entails more than a drive home. A wise girl will thank him for the offer but, if interested, invites him to Sunday dinner instead. She'll go home with her parents or an older brother.

The grain in the fields, oats, barley and rye are golden and ready to be mowed. The binder cuts and binds the grain stalks into sheaves with twine. Family members follow along lifting the sheaves upright and standing them in clusters of three to dry, heads tilted inwards to form conical stooks. If rain falls, less water will soak into the stooks. It is a dusty, scratchy chore because nature protects grain heads with barbs that scratch and cut tender hands as the sheaves are handled.

A day in the sun dries the sheaves. Jim drives the horses to the field where his sons hook a fork prong into the twine and heave the sheaves into the wagon. Load after load goes into the barn waiting threshing time.

This is the season for making sauerkraut. Our mother, with help from her daughters, shreds cabbage, fresh from the garden, into two ten-gallon crocks. She layers the cabbage with liberally sprinkled sea salt and over top of filled crocks. Mom sends the younger boys to cut tender branches of cherries leaves. For flavour, she places cherry leaves over the shredded cabbage, sets a large plate weighted down by a flat stone on top of the mixture and covers it all with the lid. She leaves it in the cool Milk House to ferment.

## Threshers

"The threshers are due here tomorrow," Mom reminds our dad and Mervyn after morning milking. "I'd like to go out to Powassan and get supplies for making a nice dinner for the threshing gang. I'm planning to make lemon meringue pies."

Housewives take pride in providing a good meal for the threshing gang.

An hour after Mervyn and our parents leave in the pickup truck, Wilma Pilger, just sixteen, pulls into the yard with the family car. She is here to announce that the threshers are running ahead of schedule and will be at our farm within hours.

"The granary isn't ready. The men planned to do that today!" I, one year older than Wilma, exclaim. Both of us grab brooms and run to the granary. We dismantle bins, quickly sweeping out dust and mouse droppings, replace the boards into their slots and clear the area of clutter. Wilma goes on her way.

Frank Pilger is Wilma's dad. Frank owns the threshing machine and the huge tractor that pulls it. He lives opposite our farm, on the other side of Commanda Creek.

At threshing time, neighbouring men in the area form a co-op team, travelling with the threshing machine from farm to farm. As each farmer's grain is threshed, he joins the team until everyone's grain is threshed.

I dash to the Ice House to retrieve the large hip of beef that Mom's been saving for threshing day. I rinse, pat it dry, season and pop the roast in the oven, stoking the woodstove.

*What can I put in pies?* I mutter to myself as I look through the cupboards. Ah, raisins!

I wash the entire bag of raisins and put them to simmer while I make pastry for three large pies. The pies are baking in the oven as the noisy old fashioned tractor, pulling the threshing machine, chugs into the farmyard. Men walking and men driving, follow the machine.

Within minutes the threshing machine, now attached to a wide belt powered by the tractor motor, starts up. Threshing is in full swing when Mervyn, driving our Studebaker pickup truck, rolls into the yard.

Mom is aghast. Just one hour until the men will want their noon meal! She rushes into the house to find meal preparation well in hand. With amazed relief she turns in to help.

Water, soap and towels sit on a bench outside for the men to wash dust off hands and faces.

At noon, men sit down to roast beef, mashed potatoes and gravy with plenty of salad, accompanied by homemade horseradish and pickles; followed by plump raisin pies, still warm from the oven and gallons of tea.

In the midst of my busyness, I look up and meet Weldon's eyes. He sits at the table with the rest of the men. We haven't seen each other since public school. Weldon's eyes note that the curvaceous young woman is no longer his little "Droopy Drawers."

A secret smile passes between us. We've both grown up.

Before the first frost of September the tender plants, beans, corn and tomatoes have to be picked. Mom packs yellow beans into two-quart sealers, pours in boiling hot mustard sauce and seals the sterilized jars. The beans are preserved in their vinegar and pickling spices. They'll be a treat in winter.

All the children join in husking bags of corn and slicing the nibblets from cobs. The nibblets are spooned into 32-ounce cans, some salt and boiling water added. Our mother's new canning machine seals the lids tight. The cans are stacked into a large preserving kettle to boil. The canning machine was another gift from Carl before he left for war. Some of the cans of vegetables, meat and butter are shipped to England for Preston's new wife and in-laws, to ease their British stringent rationing.

Many of the tomatoes are still green. They are stored in the cool Milk House to prolong their ripening. The ripe ones are turned into jars of delicious chilli sauce.

In late October, cabbages, cauliflower, turnips, onions, carrots and celery must all be harvested and stored in bins in the cellar. The whole family works tirelessly, because all of it is our winter food supply.

**Fishing**

Between harvest and fall ploughing there is time for the men-folk to take a break and go fishing. Dad sticks his hook and line in his back pocket. No fancy fishing rod of him! He will cut a forked sapling the length of a fishing rod from the alders growing along the banks of Peever's Creek that separates his land from Bennett's. He cuts the ends of the sapling's forks back until they are about three inches in length. Next he unwinds the fishing line from the small forked stick in his pocket and attaches it at the base of the sapling's fork. He weaves the remaining line in a figure eight formation back and forth around the two forks a few times to anchor the line. Dad digs out a worm from the creek bank and baits the hook. He walks along the bank to his favourite spot and drops in the line.

Our dad loves the silence and solitude, the smell of cool, damp earth and the chirping of birds in the bushes. He'll return home after a couple of hours with two or three iridescent brook trout on another slim forked alder twig, his fishing line and hook in his back pocket. Mom receives his gift of fresh brook trout with joy and love like a city wife receives a bouquet of flowers.

On a Sunday afternoon our parents leave the younger children in the care of older siblings. They are going to "The Chute" on a rare outing together. Up the hill behind the old Peever homestead, into the bush and down into the gorge of Commanda Creek. Big vigorous trout lurk, waiting for nutrients at the base of the chute's water fall.

Jim and Annie attach lines to their newly made rods, bait their hooks and make their way in companionable silence along the shore, over tippy rocks, slick with spray from the chute. The thundering chute makes conversation impossible.

Jim tosses in a line and retrieves it after it is swept downstream in the current. He tosses it in again. A couple of tosses and a trout 'strikes' the bait. He gives the rod a slight jerk to set the hook, swings the trout clear of the rocks and lands it, flapping onto the shore behind him. Jim catches a few more and slips their gills over a forked sapling for safekeeping.

Annie isn't so lucky and she's frustrated. As her line is washed downstream one more time, she steps further out onto rocks in the stream. Annie slips off the wet rock and throws up her arms as she loses her balance. The line swings back and the fish hook 'imbeds' itself in her hand between her thumb and index finger. Jim helps her back to shore.

At the house they examine the hand. There is no way to remove the hook without doing damage. Jim walks to the Commanda store and asks the then-proprietor George Smith to drive them to see Dr. Delaine in Powassan.

The hook was firmly imbedded; it required a doctor to safely remove the fish hook.

The older Peever brothers, those who have city jobs, take their holidays to join the brothers still on the farm. With canoe, a tent, fishing gear and food staples, the brothers take off for two weeks of canoeing and portaging through the lakes and rivers back of Loring, living off the land and their few staples. From the days of working in the lumber camps in winter, older brothers know the water systems well.

Archie remembers clearly his first fishing expedition with his big brothers. Years later he tells this story to me: "I was twelve years old in

1948 when I got to go for the first time with our older brothers Rea and Lloyd. Usually Mervyn, six years older than me, was invited and I had to stay home and do the farm chores but that year they asked me.

"We started out at Wilson Lake in Port Loring and portaged from there to Bass Lake. Rea led us to an abandoned logger's bunk house to sleep for the night. The bunk house was infested with porcupines. Rea cleared them out and we settled down to sleep, but during the night, one of them came back. In the melee of getting rid of the porcupine, Rea knocked down some boards that fell with a crash, right beside me. I was so worn out from our trek that I was 'dead to the world'. The racket didn't even rouse me.

"We found that we were out of minnows, so Rea and I canoed across Bass Lake to another smaller lake to catch minnows in our minnow trap. While we were trolling across the lake, Rea caught a big pike. He laid it in the bottom of the canoe instead of putting it on a stringer, but soon it started flapping around. When Rea reached down to grab it, the pike fastened his teeth onto Rea's thumb. Rea had to pry the pike's mouth open to free his thumb. Rea wound his handkerchief around the deep cut in his thumb to staunch the bleeding while we paddled back across Bass Lake to our campsite. When we arrived, Lloyd was frying fish for supper.

"The next day we portaged across to Fox Lake. There we watched in wonder a beautiful deer feeding in the shallows. The fishing trip was 'a coming of age' event in my life."

As the years pass, the brothers' tradition of getting together in summer for two weeks of bonding and fishing persists. The venue changes when Carl buys a farm near New Liskeard and Archie settles in Iroquois Falls. They soon establish a fishing/hunting camp site on Chin Lake just south of Cochrane. The brothers, from eldest to youngest: Rea, Carl, Lloyd, Howard - flying in from California on occasion, or Mervyn – making the trip from British Columbia when he could, and Archie, all gather to make two weeks together a unique occasion. They are joined by Carl's son Bryan from Timmins. The group drive to the end of the road and portage their boat, motor and gear a mile or so through the bush to the lake. Their food supplies always include six dozen varieties of cookies and squares supplied by Lloyd's wife Eunice. They set up their camp across on the far side of Chin Lake.

Carl has commissioned a large custom-made tent for their camping needs. There is plenty of room to stow their gear. There is a sleeping area and space to set up their cook-stove, near the tents' opening. Their tent is cosy even when the temperatures drop below zero.

**Hunting Season**

In late October, available brothers trek north again for moose season, hoping for early cold and snow to preserve the moose meat, until they can transport it to town for cutting up and freezing.

After more than fifty years of camping together, Archie makes a series of errors. Archie is delayed and doesn't make the crossing with his brothers to their camp for the moose hunt.

At the end of a busy day, Archie makes the forty mile drive from his home in Iroquois Falls to the portage site alone. Archie, in a rush, portages to the lake with his canoe, motor, paddles, his 22 rifle and his 30-30 moose-rifle. He forgets two crucial items, the gas can and his life jacket.

Archie launches the canoe but without the weight of the can of gas in the bow for balance, the stern rides too low and the propeller catches in floating deadwood near the shore. Archie moves forward in the canoe, to balance it, and paddles out into the lake until sufficiently clear of the deadwood. In the clear from deadwood, he makes a move back toward the stern, and the canoe flips upside-down. The 22 rifle sinks. Thrown into the water, Archie turns the canoe upright and swims, pushing the canoe in front of him, back to shore.

*I must light a fire to warm myself*, Archie says to himself. He is soaking wet and shivering as he strikes a match - strikes a second match. His matches are wet and won't light. Archie shouts across the lake to the camp. No answer! Frantically, he tries to start the motor. The wet motor doesn't start.

Night is falling.

Archie fires his 30-30 rifle. In the stillness, the report echoes off the trees all around the lake. The campers hear but can't determine the direction. Hypothermia has set in and Archie is finding it difficult to think. He is getting weaker but he climbs into the canoe and paddles toward the camp.

As he nears shore, Archie feebly calls out. Bryan, the youngest of the group, hears the call. The campers grab up a light and run to the shore, waving him in. Archie is nearing collapse. His brothers, half drag, half carry him into the camp. They strip off Archie's wet clothes, rub him down, put him in his warm sleeping bag and get some hot tea into him. Archie isn't able to eat the hot food awaiting him until the hypothermia has passed.

Recalling the event ten years later, Archie comments, "It was a life and death experience."

Fishing or moose hunting is never the brothers' primary purpose. Being together in the wilderness, sharing the happenings in each others' lives is the real reason.

At eighty-seven, Rea is aware, deep inside, that he wouldn't make the trip again. Before they leave camp, Rea hands his trusty .22 rifle to his youngest brother Archie for safe keeping.

Archie, afterwards commented to me, "I had a hard time not to cry. I was so touched by his gift and its significance."

Rea passed away before another summer rolled around. Rea, Carl, Howard and Mervyn are all gone now. The two remaining brothers and their nephew Bryan still meet for fishing in summer, and "moose watching," in the fall – if they don't have a tag for shooting a moose.

Lloyd likes to sit in a notch in a tree and "call" moose. He is able to replicate the sound they make. In fall, a female will come to check out a prospective mate. A male will come ready to challenge a rival in his territory. Lloyd is getting to know in his joints that his time of tramping through wilderness terrain is nearing an end. The brothers' special time of bonding under the stars will soon be just a fond memory.

## Potato Harvest

It is a Saturday morning in autumn. The sun rises in a clear sky. The dry autumn day is ideal for harvesting potatoes, because potatoes have to dry before bagging or they will rot.

"Hurry up with your chores!" calls our dad. "We need to get out and dig the potatoes."

Dad hitches the team to the plough, throws the lines over his right shoulder, grasping the plough handles firmly. He steers the tip of the plough along beside the hills of potato stocks. His neat furrow unearths the potatoes. The children follow along behind, lifting potatoes clear of the furrow and placing them in clusters where they'll dry.

By noon the field of potatoes are dug and left drying. After their noon meal, they'll all go out to the field, emptying buckets of collected potatoes into jute bags.

At the end of the day, Dad hitches the horses up to the wagon. Out in the potato field, bags of potatoes are loaded into it. Back at the house, our father and the bigger boys swing fifty-pound bags of potatoes on their backs and tote them from the wagon into the cellar. They empty bags into waiting potato bins.

The following Saturday, we dig a second field of potatoes. It is back-breaking work but our winter supply of potatoes is safely stored in the cellar.

Thanksgiving is a very real time for farmers who live on the land, who live from the land and depend on the elements for a good crop. We give heartfelt thanks to God for our daily bread.

The Peever's Thanksgiving dinner in never turkey. On the day before Thanksgiving our brothers usually return from hunting, with a brace of wild ducks and partridges. They pluck and clean the birds.

Thanksgiving Day, Mom stuffs the ducks, lays them crosswise like cordwood in two-tiers in the giant roaster. The aroma of rich dark meat blending with stuffing spices fills the house. As we sit down to a festive Thanksgiving meal, the table is laden with vegetables that the family has grown and harvested. Pumpkins from the garden become spicy pumpkin pie, served with our own whipped cream. There is tart cranberry pie too. Older brothers have made a trip to the marsh to gather a sack of cranberries. There are still enough cranberries, stored in the cellar, to last until Christmas.

**Winter**

The smell of snow is in the air. A thrill of excitement shoots through the children. It is mid-November and the first dusting of snow peppers the brittle blades of frozen grass. We run to haul our sleighs and toboggan out of the woodshed.

Mom laughs at our excitement. "You'll be sick of it before the snow is gone again," she warns.

What we're tired of is the drizzly dark days of early November. We're tired of the dampness that chills the bones, and of the farmyard turned to glutinous ooze that sucks at our boots.

Mervyn and June rough-house in the barn on those dull November Saturdays or they swing from the hay-fork chain in the peak of the barn. With a three-story drop to the barn floor, it's a risky pastime.

I, two years younger than my sister, would rather stay indoors and go exploring through boxes in the attic. The attic is stuffed with interesting things like Mom's boxes of buttons.

There are buttons of every size and colour. Crystal buttons that look like jewels, ivory, carved into tiny roses and lilies and tarnished silver buttons. There is an ivory-handled gadget with a hook on the end.

"What is this?" I ask my mother, taking it downstairs where she's working.

"It's a button hook," Mom answers. "Years ago it was very fashionable for ladies to have long rows of little buttons on their dresses. They used the button hook to pull buttons through button loops."

Another box is full of dress patterns. On each package are illustrations of ladies in long dresses. The dresses are narrowed at the ankles.

"How could anyone walk in such a dress?" I ask.

"Those were called hobble skirts. They were the fashion in the twenties," Mom answers. She doesn't say why she still keeps the patterns.

They all look like beautiful things from another world.

Eight-year-old Archie plays downstairs with a pinball game that Lloyd made for him.

Lloyd, now fifteen, remembers playing with a pin ball game, seven years ago when he was recovering from a ruptured appendix in the North Bay hospital. He fashions a 12 x 12 inch sloping board, and for a barrier, edges it with a half-inch curved strip of pliable pine. Lloyd carves a grooved runway with numbered holes along the route, inserting old gramophone needles for pins at the holes. He attaches another short strip of pliable wood to provide propulsion for the ball – a marble.

Archie loves to play with his treasured game.

By the time Lloyd reaches retirement age he will have become a noted carver and artisan.

## Butchering

Early winter is the time for butchering livestock to provide the winter supply of meat for the family. Saturdays are chosen because the older boys are available to help their dad.

I, like my older brother Preston, hate butchering day. June, older by two years, tortures me by giving a running report of the proceedings. If possible, Mom will send me away on an errand to the Commanda Store.

On a cold dry day, a cow fattened for beef, is lead out to the big elm tree. A well-placed shot to the head quickly ends its life. The men attach a rope and pulley to a sturdy branch, hoisting the animal up by the heels.

My father quickly slits its throat to drain out the blood. He and my brothers remove the entrails and skin the animal. One of the boys carries a pan containing the heart, liver and tongue to the house.

The smell of warm blood revolts me but Mom washes the meat until the water runs clear.

She'll fry fresh liver for the noon meal. The heart and tongue will be simmered with spices and sliced to make school lunches.

The beef is quartered and hung in the woodshed where it will remain frozen, to be used throughout the winter. While the beef hangs to firm up, Dad puts its hide to soak in the woodshed in an old boiler with water and tan bark. After weeks of the tanning process he'll remove the hair with a drawknife, then "work" the hide, kneading and rubbing to make it supple. The leather will be used to repair horse harness, make webbing in snowshoes and to make laces for leather work boots.

Deer hides are cured the same way. Mom makes double soled "shoe pacs" (heavy knee-length moccasins) for our dad to wear in the bush, or moccasins for the children. The deer skin shoe pacs are warmer on the feet than rubber boots in the cold weather when Dad is working as a teamster, standing atop a load of logs.

Two pigs will be slaughtered also. Dad takes hams and bacon over to Schermer's smoke house.

No part of the animal is wasted. Pork hocks will be simmered with sauerkraut for a hearty meal. The remaining pork will hang frozen in the shed, with the beef, or be cured in salt brine.

Mom takes a pair of side ribs, makes a savoury stuffing, fills the cavity with dressing and binds the two sides together. Placed in the family's enormous roast pan and baked, the aroma of fresh pork and spices is mouth watering. Along with baked potatoes and cabbage salad, it makes a tasty fall meal for the large family.

Mom removes the fatty skin and simmers the pigs' heads, grinds the glutinous meat, adding spices. She packs the head cheese mixture into bread pans to shape and set. These blocks of head cheese will be sliced and spread with homemade mustard for her children's lunches.

Winter provides its own natural freezer for preserving meat for the family.

## Firewood

Snow is clean. It makes the hills our playground!

We celebrate the coming of winter but our father is aware of the need to keep the family warm. Dad takes the axe and saw and tramps up into the maple bush. He is looking for deadwood or trees blown down by the high winds of November. He'll cut them for next winter's supply of firewood.

Although Dad wouldn't know the meaning of the word, he is a conservationist. He treats the forest like his garden. To him, "clear cutting" is a sacrilege. He cuts only the trees he needs for firewood or lumber. He hitches up the team of horses, and with the cant hook, rolls the logs onto the sleigh, hauling the load into the yard.

He'll hire his nephew Hughie Peever, son of his late brother Ab to bring his wood cutter. Hughie lives on Ab (John Albert) Peever's homestead on the shores of Commanda Lake. His large gas-driven machine predates the chain saw. It will cut logs into two-foot rounds.

Dad with his sharp axe splits these blocks into sticks of firewood. We work along beside him, stacking the firewood in neat rows to form woodpiles. There is a technique to piling wood. Rows of sticks are each fitted snugly into crevices in the row of sticks below, always with the bark side outward. A compactly built woodpile will repel snow or rain, preventing the wood from becoming wet and useless for burning. The woodpile will stand for a year while the wood dries and "seasons." We'll burn last year's cut wood in the stove this winter.

Tragically, Hughie Peever's woodcutting machine malfunctioned one day while cutting up logs for a family in the area. The rotating chain of teeth broke, sending a loose end flying upward. Hughie was decapitated. In this rural area where everyone knows and cares about each other, people were shocked. They rallied to provide comfort and support to his wife and children. Hughie lies in the Commanda cemetery beside his father John Albert Peever and his mother Emily.

**Winter Travel**

By mid-December, the snow already lies deep. Winter sets in with earnest.

Reminiscing recently, older brother Lloyd tells me a story about the winter of 1930, before I was born.

Lloyd recounts: "In the winter of 1930, travel was still on single-lane wagon roads. Bill Gael and his family lived on the shores of Commanda Lake, near to Grimm's place. Every Sunday Bill and his wife, devout Catholics, bundled the children, Paddy, Bernard, Frank, Lloyd, a girl whose name I can't recall, but she became a nun – and the youngest, Kathleen, into the sleigh. He'd put a lighted coal oil lantern under the covers in the sleigh to keep the family from freezing while they made the trip to St. John's Catholic Church in Alsace. In those days Catholics had to fast before mass. It was a fourteen mile trip each way. On the way, the Gaels always stopped at our house to get warm.

Bill Gael was on the horns of a dilemma. In the fall he had sold his fatted livestock and he was afraid to leave his money unattended in his house while he went to church. The nearest bank was 60 miles away in North Bay. But he didn't want to carry his money into church. Bill solved the problem by entrusting his leather bag of money to our dad, a Protestant – an Orangeman at that!" laughed Lloyd because; in those days mutual religious prejudice was the norm.

"On the return trip, Gaels arrived back at our house about 2 p.m. Mom fed the starving- hungry family a meal of fried eggs, hash browns, bread and butter and preserves, while Dad sent one of our older brothers to put Gael's horses in the stable and feed them too.

"Warmed and well fed, Bill Gael reclaimed his money and the family went on their way until the next week. We always had plenty of food to share even in the 'hard times' of the depression years," Lloyd informed me.

## Logging Camp

Dad loves the life in lumber camps, the camaraderie and the freedom from domestic life. Mom is left to run the farm and cope alone with their large brood.

But in winter, there is less work to be done although fewer hands to do it. The eldest remaining children assume the tasks of cleaning out the stable and feeding livestock, even so, when the animals are fed and eggs gathered there is still some time to have sleigh-riding fun until supper is ready.

After supper, milking takes less time as only two or three cows are giving milk in winter. The other cows are in calf and not producing. We don't ship cream anymore because the smaller amount of milk and cream is used to feed the family.

If we get our homework done in time, Mom reads aloud to the family. Mostly, it will be a classic like *Uncle Tom's Cabin* or a serial story from the Family Herald and Weekly Star newspaper. One serial story is titled *High Bright Buggy Wheels.* It's about a girl in a Hutterite family in Alberta who longs for colour and beauty in her life where only sombre colours and practical things are allowed. I empathize with that girl.

Other times, our mother sits near the lamp knitting heavy three-ply wool socks for our dad or brothers or else sewing something new for one of the girls to wear to the Christmas concert.

Lloyd sits on the edge of the wood box whittling some creation he's making.

The household isn't always peaceful. Arguments arise and always there is an instigator. Howard often amuses himself by pestering the younger children and Mervyn and June's continual picking and poking at each other becomes irritating.

Mom's remedy for fractious culprits is to send them out to the well, in the cold and dark, for pails of water. By the time they make their way back, icy water slopping against their legs, the offenders are subdued for the rest of the evening.

The frost provides windows with lace curtains. Frost combined with humidity in the house forms intricate raised white patterns on window-panes. How the patterns form, like a blanket of snowflakes over the windows, is a wonder to behold. Cold seeps into the house, around window frames and under the door. Frost makes sharp rifle-crack reports in the frame house as the wood contracts.

On those frigid nights our mother fills a round iron brassier with coals and carries it down to the cellar. She places it in the centre of the earthen floor, away from anything flammable. Heat from the coals will prevent our vital store of vegetables and our precious barrel of apples from freezing during the night. Mom stokes the woodstove and dampers it off so the fire will burn slowly during the night. Even so, the fire will be burned down to ashes by 5 in the morning. A bottle of milk, placed on the table for breakfast, will be frozen.

We huddle in our beds under wool blankets and quilts, even pulling the covers over our heads to keep warm while we sleep. The house is so cold that the urine in the chamber pot under the bed is frozen.

At 6 a.m., the older brothers roll out of bed and get the fire going. They light the coal oil lantern, pull on their coats and boots and head to the stable to feed livestock and milk the cows. Porridge for breakfast is simmering on the back of the stove, the kettle is steaming and the house is warm when they return.

The children bundle up to face the brutally cold trek to school, they hitch up the dog-team and they're off.

Today, Mom sews quilt patches together to make a quilt top. The quilt squares are made from leftover wool overcoat material of basic navy, grey or black. She'll trim it with a red border for colour. On the table she lays out the backing, places quilt batting over it then lastly, lays on the quilt top. Mom pins the layers together and hand-bastes it. In the evening, after the outdoor chores are done, she gets out the quilt frame. The older boys help her set the quilt frame up in the middle of the floor and they help her clamp the quilt in place.

Quilting is a family event. We help arrange chairs around the quilt frame and all are issued with a hank of three-ply red yarn and a darning needle. Our mother instructs, "Now remember, you must put a tie in each corner, and one in the centre of every square, to keep the batting inside from clumping."

Mom demonstrates for the younger ones, pushing the needle down through the quilt top and up through the material again. She clips off an inch of yarn, ties it twice and moves on to the next corner. Each of us suffer a few jabs of our needles but soon get proficient at filling the squares with yarn ties. We all sing together as we work. The more experienced quilters finish a row of squares and roll it under, securing the screws in place again, always keeping a fresh row before them.

The quilt will require another evening's work before the squares are all tied. The older boys fold up the quilt frame – with the quilt attached – and stand it against a far wall until the next night. When the quilting is completed, Mom sews the quilt top to its flannel lining and stitches on a red cotton border. The new quilt will warm one of the children's beds.

On alternate Friday afternoons the United Church minister pays his call. After having supper with the family, the minister conducts an informal worship service. It suffices for the church that is closed for the winter. For our mother, the minister's visit is a respite from isolation. It braces her up mentally and spiritually.

Saturday night arrives. Dad comes home from the logging camp. Mom's face brightens as he comes through the door. They smile to each other but they don't embrace. There is no show affection in front of the children. Dad sends the older boys to brush down and feed the horses while Mom makes him a hot cup of tea and a snack.

Our dad settles in the rocker. He's brought candy for the children. Everyone is happy to see him and hear his tales of the past two weeks. Dad is tired though after the long trip home at the end of a day skidding and hauling logs.

Mervyn and June start their poking and scuffling with each other.

"Be quiet!" Dad says sharply.

A few minutes later, they start up again.

"Stop that!" He orders.

I'm sitting in a corner. I look up from my book and think can't they see where their misbehaviour is leading? June and Mervyn soon shove and poke and tussle with each other again.

Dad is out of his chair in a flash. He cuffs each of them, two or three times. June and Mervyn sniffle quietly. The happy atmosphere is gone.

Sunday morning Dad is bathed and dressed in clean clothing from the skin outward – heavy wool knit underwear, flannel shirt with broad braces holding up thick wool worsted pants. He likes white three-ply wool socks next to his feet. Dad believes white socks are warmer than coloured. Before he leaves, he'll put a pair of grey three-ply socks over them when he pulls on his knee-high deer hide shoe-pacs.

Our dad is lean and sinewy without any fat for insulation. He feels the cold and sitting atop a sleigh piled high with logs, he is very exposed to the wind and cold.

After breakfast he gets out his shaving mirror and strops his straight razor. The house is quiet. The boys are out of the house doing the barn chores. The younger children are cautioned not to run or walk behind him when he is shaving.

Dad's face looks white when his grizzled beard of two weeks is shaved clean. He brushes his teeth - the brush is made from boar bristles. The bristles don't wear. The handle is made of bone. The old toothbrush still looks as good as new.

Mom bustles around making an especially nice noon dinner. Later, Dad sits contentedly rocking in his chair with the two youngest on his lap, having a quiet conversation with our mother.

At 3 p.m., he makes ready to leave for the camp again. He dons his peaked wool cap, the ear-lugs tied on top, for now. To break the wind, the heavy wool coat is covered by a hip-length mackinaw smock; a red handkerchief and a plug of Big Ben chewing tobacco are in the pocket.

He pulls on heavy knitted wool mitts, with leather mitts over them to keep his hands warm and dry while driving the team or levering logs onto the sleigh with a cant hook. The cant hook is also used for levering them into log-piles at river's edge, to await spring breakup.

A quick goodbye, and Dad hitches up beautiful black Duke with his silver mane and tail; and Doc who is black all over, wise, canny and mischievous. They are not only his livelihood but his friends and companions. Our dad is gone again for another two weeks.

My eldest brothers Rea, Carl, Preston, and friend Eric, usually don't come home on Saturday night. They'll take a 5 to 10 mile hike – depending on the location of the logging camp – into Port Loring to a community dance or to visit friends in town. On Sunday, they'll hand wash their own underwear and socks, hang them near the stove to dry, and play cards with other men in the bunkhouse.

In reminiscing about the days when the men went to the logging camps, June recalls what Mom had to cope with when there were three teenage boys in the household, without their father to keep them in line.

June relates this incident: "Mom served the noon meal, and then she left to go to the outhouse. The boys, Gerald, Lloyd and Howard began throwing boiled potatoes at one another. Gerald threw a potato at Lloyd. He ducked. The potato went right through the windowpane behind him. Everyone was shocked! 'What will we tell Mom?' Howard said. 'She'll be so mad!'

"Gerald grabbed up the cat, poured some tea on its tail and threw it out the window. As Mom neared the house, she saw the cat fly through the broken window. 'What happened?' Mom demanded, as she came through the door. Gerald said, 'Oh, I spilled some tea on the cat and it jumped right through the window.' Mom might have been suspicious but she bought the story. She plugged the hole with old rags until she could order a windowpane from the Commanda Store," laughed June.

On alternate Saturday nights when our dad doesn't come home, Mom makes chocolate fudge for us. She probably also makes it to distract herself from her loneliness and need for adult companionship. We watch while the butter, chocolate and brown sugar bubbles. It smells so good! When a drop of the mixture forms a ball in cold water, she beats in vanilla and fresh cream. Mom pours the fudge into a buttered pan to cool.

"Get out the crokinole board and the Snakes and Ladders," Mom instructs the boys. We all have a turn at crokinole. The losers will likely switch to Snakes and Ladders.

While we enjoy the rich fudge, the evening doesn't seem at all dull and long.

The fabled winter of 1944 brings Toronto to a stop but it brings a sleigh rider's paradise to the Peever children in the village of Commanda. Fences are no longer barriers. Snowdrifts cover fences and our sleighs and skis slide right over them.

In the farmyard, we use snowshoes for going out to gather eggs and feed livestock. There is a snowdrift the same height up against the eight-foot high lumber pile. We children dig out a snow house inside the drift, even putting evergreen boughs down for flooring. Sheltered from the wind, the snow house is a cosy place to play.

At school, there is a toboggan run along the ridge above the road. At noon recess one day, four girls are riding the toboggan with their legs outstretched around each other, I'm at the back. Hoogie, a grade nine student on skis overtakes and swerves in to scare us. He misjudges and his skis run over my right shin.

A searing pain goes up my leg. I cry out. I'm unable to stand. Mervyn brings me home on the dog sleigh.

Mom examines the shin. She can feel the fracture. She binds cedar lathes length-wise around the shin to hold the bone immobile. I'm off school and housebound until after Easter.

Mervyn sets about to administer retribution. He is younger but bigger than Hoogie.

Hoogie outruns him but deems it wise not to come back to school again – ever.

Progress overtakes the need for horses to haul sleigh loads of logs to the water's edge to be floated downstream to the mills. Instead, lumber trucks haul the logs to larger sawmills like the Trout Creek Lumber Company. The logging business is changing, there isn't a need for a teamster and our father is getting older.

Half his brood have grown and left home. Four are in the armed forces. Two are studying theology and there are not as many mouths to feed.

Dad takes other jobs like guiding for Alex Smith's city hunters during hunting season. Soon he has groups of hunters staying at our house. Mom cooks for the hunters too. Our superb hunting dogs, Maggie, the red bone hound and her progeny Sport are also assets.

Dad is a gifted storyteller. In the evening, he entertains them with his hunting stories.

Later in the winter Dad sets up a trap line for beaver, muskrat, mink and fox. Lloyd and Howard snare weasels and rabbits too. When they skin their catch, the house reeks from the musk, especially the skunk-like stench of weasel. My dad and brothers stretch the hides by tacking them to wooden frames. The furs bring a nice price. The valuable weasel fur (ermine) provides pocket money for Lloyd and Howard.

In the winter of 1948, Dad, with a younger team of horses, Dan and Maud, works alongside Lloyd, Howard and Mervyn cutting and skidding logs to be sawed into lumber for our new family home. The men stay in the bush at noontime, eating a packed lunch and boiling water for tea over an open fire, just as our dad has done all of his working life.

The new team of horses owes its proficiency to canny old Doc. Dad had teamed the aging Doc with each of the younger horses Maud, Dan and Prince to train them in responding to commands and to work as a team.

Mervyn, at age twenty-one, takes the team into the bush logging for Fred Garten in the winter of 1951. Garten's small operation is in Golden Valley. This is the last time the team is hired out in a logging operation.

When Jim nears what he thinks is his age of seventy, he decides to apply for an Old Age Pension. He has no copy of his birth certificate. In 1952, Annie writes to the little Ottawa Valley church in Fitzroy Harbour, where he was baptised. The copy of his baptismal certificate indicates that he is two years older than he thought.

In the government's good time, a cheque arrives. Jim exclaims "What is this?"

He is amazed to receive two years of back pay. Jim decides that his commercial logging days are over.

The seasons on the farm govern the tempo and events that shape the lives of those who work the land.

# ~Sport the Dog Who Thought He Was People!

Oh joy! No working in the fields this August afternoon. The sky is black and thunder rolls. We scamper across the creek behind the barn to gather branches laden with shiny black choke cherries and head for the barn.

The haymows are stuffed with hay almost to the peak of the barn. With a choke cherry branch clutched in his teeth, Lloyd, the eldest of our band of six, climbs the rungs of the ladder that are fastened to the haymow's framework. Sport, our constant companion follows on his heels. Sport hooks his front paws over the smooth rungs and propels himself upward with his hind legs, using his claws to clutch the rungs. Howard follows close behind, steadying the dog with his chest in the steep climb.

In descending age Mervyn, June, me and Archie follow, our bare feet acting like prehensile toes grasping the ladder's rungs for support, teeth fastened on a cherry branch.

Sport proudly wags his tale and grins in pleasure as he treads unevenly in the soft hay, then seats himself in the midst of his clan.

Settled comfortably on top of the hay near the open four-by-four-foot ventilating door at the barn's peak, we have a bird's eye view of fields and forest. The door is handy as we snack on chokecherries, spitting the pits out of the opening. Sport mouths his share of cherries but opts to swallow the pits.

The steady rain is pelting down, the drumming on the heavy corrugated tin roof just feet above our heads is deafening. Lightning rods on the barn roof protect us as we loll on the soft hay.

Soon it's time for afternoon chores. Our descent is in the same order. Teen-aged Lloyd in the lead, his chest supporting Sport's hind quarters as the dog backs down the ladder. As we descend closer to the barn floor, the younger ones let go the rungs and drop into the waiting arms of Lloyd and Howard. Sport leads the way out of the barn, for he knows it's time to herd the cows home for milking.

Howard saddles up Prince and they're off, Sport loping along beside. The cattle are likely lying sheltered from the rain in a deeply forested glade. They'll be a challenge to find because their stilled cowbells will be silent. Wet branches swipe Howard's legs and the horse's flanks, as they pick their way over the rocky forest floor, slippery with mud. Howard will rely on Sport's sensitive nose to sniff out the cows' hiding place.

Sport's barking rouses the cattle to their feet, setting their bells clattering. He circles the herd and gets them moving homeward.

The cattle rest in the milking ground while the family is at supper.

Sport accompanies us later as we trudge out to do the milking. He knows that the boys will reward him with milk, squirted into his mouth straight from the cow's teats. After the milking is done he'll accompany our dad in driving the cattle back to pasture for the night.

At night, Sport is hooked up to a long chain to prevent the urge of nature from overcoming good sense. A scent of deer or fox, wafted on the breeze, could send him on the chase. Sport's long chain, nevertheless, allows him to guard the house and the baby chicks in their coup beyond the woodpile, from foxes or other vermin.

Under cover of darkness, wartime scarcities sometimes drive "young bucks" from neighbouring villages looking for mischief and excitement. Parking their car on the road, they creep up into the yard in search of scarce gas to siphon from our car's barren gas tank, or to pick up pieces of metal to sell for pocket money.

Sport sets up such a fit of barking that he wakes the household. Our dad fires a rifle shot into the night to warn off the culprits. In the morning the boys laugh to find the gas cap has been taken off our old Whippet, that hasn't held gas in years.

It's hunting season when Lloyd, still in his teens, picks up the powerful 30-30 rifle. With Sport at his heels, Lloyd is tracking a deer trail in the deep bush. Suddenly a huge black bear rears up in front of him.

Since bears don't see distances well, they rely on their efficient nose to sniff prey or danger. This day, the bear is upwind of Lloyd and doesn't smell him or Sport until too late. The startled bear rears to the attack.

In a flash, Sport dashes in and sinks his teeth into the bear's heels. The bear goes down on all fours, spins around and charges Lloyd.

Lloyd backs away and levels the gun but with Sport ragging the bear, Lloyd is afraid of shooting the dog. He holds fire and calls Sport to heel. The bear is just about on him when Lloyd fires at the bear's enormous head. The bear goes down. Lloyd fires another shot into its head for safety.

Lloyd skins the bear, carefully preserving the skin intact over its head and nose. He separates the bear's head from the body, and then rolls the skin around the head to form a bundle.

Sport eats his fill from the carcass.

With Sport trotting at his side, Lloyd trudges home with his heavy bundle slung on his back. Our parents are amazed at the size of the bear skin. They don't reveal their misgivings at his close call. Lloyd finds the biggest cooking pot in the house to boil the bear's head, so that he can remove the flesh and preserve the skull.

The next day, Lloyd scrapes the fat from the underside of the bear's pelt and begins the process of preserving it. He keeps the enormous skull as a trophy. For years we use that bear rug, though it continues to retain a musky bear odour.

"Do you remember the winter when Sport raced the pickup truck?" Mervyn exclaimed, on one of his rare visits home from British Columbia. Sport was pulling all four of us on the sleigh along the 'flat', east of our house. A pick-up truck stopped and offered a ride to the three of you, June, when you were about ten, Thelma at eight and Archie age six. You three sat in the back of the pick-up. I was twelve at the time; I stayed with the sleigh."

"Yes, I remember," June agreed. "When the truck started up, Sport kept pace with it. Then the driver decided to see how fast Sport could run. The driver sped up to 30 miles per hour and Sport kept pace. When he drove faster, Sport, striving to keep up, began to lose ground. The driver purposely drove out of sight. When he let us children off at school, he told us that he was afraid Sport would burst his heart from the effort of trying to keeping up with the truck."

Winter always brings the dogsled and harness for Sport. He doesn't object to the mundane task of hauling cream cans of water from the well to replenish the household supply, but he relishes a Saturday adventure with Lloyd and Howard. They're off to catch minnows.

Running alongside the dogsled loaded with minnow nets, an empty cream can to carry their catch of minnows, and of course food for themselves and for Sport, the teens, Lloyd and Howard, set out on their Saturday adventure. At Commanda Store, they turn south at the junction of the Old Nippissing Road, down Carr's Hill, cross the bridge over Commanda Creek. They pass the sawmill and begin the steep climb uphill toward Booth's farm. The boys then make the turn off onto the Rye Road, but soon turn west to a road, presently overgrown, to Rauche Lake - now renamed Stewart Lake. It's a seven mile trek, made at a stead trot.

Breaking the thin ice at the shoreline, the boys set up their minnow nets, using bits of bread to lure the minnows inside. They make a small fire for warmth and sit with Sport to rest and enjoy the early spring sunshine. While waiting for the nets to fill with minnows, Lloyd finds an interesting piece of cedar lying on the shore. He settles down with his jackknife to create something of beauty from the weathered piece of driftwood.

As they lounge, eating their lunch, the boys plan their next weekend's fishing expedition to Commanda Lake.

Spring has finally arrived! The cows are enjoying the early spring sunshine. They wander from the barnyard into the field to crop tender shoots of grass, poking through the melting snow. But one cow, responding to some primal urge, heads beyond the field into the maple bush. She settles in a brushy thatch to give birth to her calf.

In the farmyard, Sport's sensitive nose picks up the scent of blood and the scent of the still-wet newborn calf. The urgency in his barking draws Annie's attention. From the window she sees Sport straining against on his chain tether and barking toward the maple syrup bush. Pulling on her boots and coat, Annie goes to investigate. Looking toward the maple bush, Annie sees a movement. She spies a flash of red cowhide through the leafless trees, and from experience, guesses what has happened.

Annie is without help. The children are at school and Jim is working in the bush. She'll have to deal with the situation alone. The calf won't last long if hungry wolves or bears pick up its scent, she muses.

Annie unties Sport and stops at the barn to collect a wheelbarrow. With Sport trotting at her side, she pushes the wheelbarrow through the mushy snow, up the incline of the field and into the bush.

The new mother doesn't object at the intrusion until Annie lifts the calf and places it in the wheelbarrow, then as Annie begins to push the barrow toward home, the cow butts it, trying to upset the wheelbarrow. Sport intervenes and attempts to herd the cow out of the way, but the anxious young mother persists in blocking the wheelbarrow.

With an exasperated aarf, Sport takes hold of the cow's ear and hangs on. The cow thus distracted, Annie proceeds unhindered to wheel the calf, bumping over the rough clods of earth, across the field towards the barn.

With the cow and calf safely bedded in a clean stall, Annie calls Sport to her. "Good dog!" She says, patting his head and scratching his ears. Sport writhes with pleasure at her approval and rubs himself against her legs, returning the affection.

Alas, Sport is destined never to grow old. He's devoted to Lloyd. Where ever Lloyd goes, Sport wants to be with him. It is in late March of 1946 that Lloyd tells Sport to stay home, lest Sport be tempted to chase deer – the does being heavy with their spring fawns. Lloyd fastens Sport to his tether before leaving to check his traps, set for mink and muskrat along Peever's Creek.

At daylight the next morning Sport manages to slip out of his collar. His tracks in the light snow show that he's followed Lloyd's trail to the creek. It is on Sport's return, just 500 hundred yards from home that he is struck by a motor vehicle.

June has left home early to light the fire in the box-stove in the Commanda United Church, currently housing Public School students. June finds Sport's body on the side of the road. Back to the house she hurries to alert the family. Lloyd runs to him, hoping for any sign of life, and then Lloyd gently carries Sport's body into the edge of the bush.

Unbelieving, each of us stop on our way to school to view Sport, weeping as we walk. On our return from school we go to view him again, telling ourselves that maybe he is alive – maybe he was just stunned.

Sport's body is still and stiff in death.

We mourn him like a lost brother. Archie, the youngest, says through his sadness, "Sport was family and when he was with us on our excursions, he made us feel brave."

# ~Lillian and the Four Reverends~

Like Hannah in the Old Testament story of Samuel, as each child was born, Annie prayed and offered her child up to the Lord. It seems that God took her at her word. As her children grew, five of her twelve children felt God's call to ministry.

**Lillian**

Lillian was the first to experience that mysterious sense of calling. Given her quiet thoughtful ways, Lillian's choice was not surprising. When she graduated, as was the practice in the 1940s, Lillian was designated a deaconess, not an ordained minister, even though she pastored churches. Lillian married a fellow graduate, Harold Bradley, who did receive ordination and together, they ministered in many churches. Much has already been shared already about Lillian's significant and selfless contributions to her husband's ministry and the communities they served. In this chapter, we explore the roles of four brothers, each of whom served God through sacrifice and dedication.

Lillian was born to Luella Smith our aunt, younger sister of our mother Annie. Lillian's birth out of wedlock was a source of shame in the family and a scandal in the small community of Commanda in the early 1920s. The putative father of the child was the subject of speculation and gossip.

In the summer of 1959, nauseous and weary in early pregnancy with a third child, I was invited to spend a holiday with Aunt Luella at her cottage in Cobourg on the north shore of Lake Ontario. It was there one night after my two little ones were tucked into bed that Luella told me the story of how it came about.

"I don't want you to think too badly of your father," Aunt Luella prefaced her story, and then she related her night of terror. "It was in the winter of 1921 that I was cooking in the logging camp at Pine Lake for my older half-brothers and several other young men. That night they were drinking and they threatened to violate me. I escaped, dressed only in my nightclothes. I ran with desperation, always listening for the sound of pounding footsteps behind me on the dark road.

"The trees crowded the sides of the narrow winding road, casting frightening shadows. I was terrified! The sound of a rifle-crack echoed through the bitter cold. I gasped for breath. I was still alive. It must have been the frost splitting a tree in the forest. Looking over my shoulder, I ran toward Commanda along the narrow old Nine Mile Bush Road from Golden Valley. Such relief as I reached the main road at the cemetery! Ready to drop, I turned west and ran the last mile to your parents' farm."

As Aunt Luella relived that dreadful night 38 years before, her face reflected the horror of her ordeal. She continued her story, "The next morning one of my half-brothers came to take me back. He was carrying a horsewhip. Your father took down his shotgun and ordered him off the property."

In that moment, my father became Luella's shining knight.

That's how Aunt Luella, a tall, raw-boned teen, came to live with my parents, Jim and Annie Peever.

Luella then shared with me her secret of her illicit relationship with our dad. It happened after the death of our two-year-old sister Luella Mabel, whose tragic death overwhelmed my mother with unsupported grief and depression.

Stoic Annie delivered her sister Luella of a baby girl on February 7, 1922.

"I hate this baby!" Luella cried.

"Don't say that! Look at her. She is a beautiful baby," exclaimed Annie.

The baby was given the name Lillian but her birth was never registered. To explain the presence of the baby, our pious and truthful mother repeated the story that our dad and Luella had told her of Luella's violation by a man from a nearby village. Annie wanted to believe them. The three of them, Luella, Jim and Annie entered a tacit, disastrous pact of 'Don't Ask, Don't Tell.' It was disastrous because Jim wasn't held to account for making the teenage Luella, pregnant. Annie's abiding failure to confront troubling issues was to bring her further grief in years to come.

The Salvation Army in Barrie, to which Annie belonged before her marriage, came to the rescue in this dilemma. Aunt Luella, a teen mother with her baby, was found a position as a domestic in the home of Reverend and Mrs. Shorthill of Georgetown, Ontario. Reverend Shorthill was a retired Methodist minister. The couple even arranged for Luella to further her formal education. In the fall of 1926, Luella was ready to enter nurse's training at the Salvation Army's Toronto Grace Hospital.

Luella asked and Annie agreed to raise Lillian as her daughter and Jim travelled to Georgetown to bring Lillian home. "I remember my long ride home with Pa on the train, all the way to the Trout Creek station. I saw some boys in a boat as the train passed a lake. I was three-and-a-half-years old then," Lillian told me this when I asked about her early memories. Aunt Luella had never told Lillian of the circumstances of her birth.

Lillian continued, "When we arrived at the farm, I was taken upstairs to pee. Rea and Carl were just getting up. As they pulled on their pants, the eldest, 11-year-old Rea stuck out a belligerent chin and said to me, 'What are you gawping at?' After that day, Rea and Carl just accepted me as their sister. I was never to be Luella's child again," sighed Lillian as she picked up the story of her beginnings. "It's funny that I don't recall much else before I was five, but I do remember in the spring when I was about five years old and Gerald was about three," said Lillian. "We wandered into the sugar bush above the field where the old well was. We were looking for 'pig's ears', those little red fungi that appear, growing on fallen trees in spring. Gerald was talking a blue streak and we were really travelling, going deeper into the bush. Suddenly I heard a shout; and I have a picture burned into my memory of Ma running up the incline of that field.

She had a switch in her hand and as she ran her clothespin bag was swinging from her neck like a pendulum. Her old felt hat was jammed down on her head," Lillian recalled, shaking her head. "We surely would have been lost in minutes if Ma hadn't caught sight of my little red coat disappearing into the bush. With her switch, she herded us like stray calves on the long walk back to the safety of the farm yard."

Smiling in remembrance, Lillian continued her story. "In the evenings Pa sang and rocked the little ones. Usually there would be three of us in his lap and if one child was feeling sick or fussy, he'd sing silly little ditties. Other times he'd sing hobos' songs like *The Big Rock Candy Mountain*, love ballads or old Irish songs like *The Rose of Tralee* and sometimes they'd be hymns. Ma sat close to the lamplight, mending or knitting at the end of her long day," Lillian's soft voice related. "When we grew older, Ma would read a chapter of a book to us or a serial story from the weekly papers *The Canadian Countryman* or *The Family Herald and Weekly Star*. My favourite place to sit and listen was perched on the wood box behind the big woodstove. It was warm there and I could pet the cat," said Lillian, smiling.

"As we grew old enough to start school, all of us had chores to do after we got home. That was a daily routine. We thought nothing of it, but the chores had to be done before supper. The bigger boys fed the animals in the barn while the younger ones fed the hens, gathered the eggs and carried in wood and water for the next day." Lillian continued, "We girls did the upstairs chores like making the beds and emptying the chamber pots. We did whatever jobs needed finishing at the end of the day, such as scrubbing clothes on the scrub board or putting the last of the wash through the old hand ringer. Sometimes we'd have to finish churning the butter and always there were vegetables to fetch for supper from the garden or from the dark earthen cellar under the trap door in the floor.

"In the cellar there were bins of potatoes, carrots and cabbages, boxes of onions and shelves of fruit and jam. Each year Ma aimed to have 300 quarts of preserves put away to last the family for the winter." She exclaimed, "Best of all, in winter a tall barrel of crisp russet apples stood on the earthen floor. Breathing deeply of their tart aroma could cause a hungry child to tremble with desire," Lillian sighed, breathing in the memory of that wondrous tangy smell. "I would never touch the apple barrel, for those precious apples were the treats rationed out for our school lunches each day."

"In winter, Pa worked in the lumber camps at Loring or Restoule. He usually came home every other weekend. Pa would walk the 20 miles from Loring or, if at the camp in Restoule, he'd walk just five miles. He always brought a bag of 'humbugs' or peppermint candies for the children. Pa probably bought them from Tom Farley's store in Carr just three miles northwest of the long Peever's Hill above the farm." Lillian exclaimed, "Candy was such a treat! Apart from Christmas, it was the only candy we ever got, except when Ma made chocolate fudge. I guess we'd been very good when she made fudge," Lillian opined. "On Sunday afternoon, shaved and freshly bathed, Pa would again set out for the lumber camp," she concluded.

Lillian took a deep breath and recounted another story. "Mervyn was born on the 21st of August, 1930. Preston and I were both eight years old then. That day, Carl, who was fourteen, took all the younger children, including three-year-old Lloyd, on a mile hike to the Sand Hill beside the cemetery to pick blueberries. We were all amazed on our return to find that we had a baby brother with hair so blonde it looked white. The next day, Ma was "lying in" after having given birth. Ma told Preston and me to kill the rooster. She said that I was to make chicken and dumplings for supper. Pa, Rea and Carl were working in the hay field. Well, Preston managed to get the rooster killed and we plucked it while six-year-old Gerald and five-year-old Edna chased each other around the yard flinging handfuls of feathers at each other, laughing and squealing. "Thank goodness that toddlers Lloyd and Howard were having their afternoon nap! About 4 o'clock Ma called from upstairs to remind us to put the rooster on to cook," Lillian grinned sheepishly as she recalled, "We had to tell her that we were scared to take the 'insides' out of the bird. 'In case we break its guts', Preston yelled out. Ma called, 'Bring it here.' We put the rooster in the big bread dish, used for mixing bread for baking, and carried it up to her room. She sat up in bed and took the insides out of the bird and we finally got that rooster on to cook.

"I remember another incident in the fall when I was ten years old," recalled Lillian. "Ma was in the hospital in North Bay. Aunt Luella – we just called her 'Auntie' – travelled from Toronto to North Bay to bring her home from the hospital. They arrived just as I was getting June's bottle ready. June was seven months old. Auntie said, 'Here let me do that.' Standing my ground, I exclaimed, 'You don't know how!' I didn't realize that she was a nurse. I only thought she doesn't have a baby, how can she know? I had no memory of her as my natural mother.

"I'll tell you the story about the bread," laughed Lillian. "I was about eleven or twelve when Ma went away again. It was probably the spring when she went to the Red Cross Outpost in Loring to give birth to you, Thelma. I had to bake bread for the family but the bread must have got 'a chill' and it was slow in rising. By the time it raised enough to bake, everyone had gone to bed. I put the bread in the oven, but I fell asleep sitting by the stove and in my sleep I went upstairs and got into bed. Eventually, Pa woke me up to ask about the bread. He went downstairs and found the fire out and the bread half-baked in the oven. 'Better half-cooked than burned to a crisp' was all Pa said."

"The summer that I was fourteen, Ma let me go and stay with her friend, Mrs. Stanfield, in Golden Valley for a few days. What a luxury to have a holiday in a spacious home and to go on a fishing excursion in their old rowboat on Jack Lake!" smiled Lillian. "One evening Mr. Brunne, the 'honey man' who kept bees and supplied everyone in the area with honey, took Mrs. Stanfield's foster daughter Bella Rayment – a Dr. Bernardo child – and me to a gospel meeting in nearby Arnstein. At the meeting, I heard 'Ye must be born again.' That night in the gospel tent I gave my heart to Jesus. That was an important landmark in my life," stated Lillian.

"Just before Christmas that year our youngest brother Archie was born. How dumb I was... I didn't know Ma was pregnant!" Lillian laughed again, "She must have kept herself well covered by her big apron. She called me to her in the night saying, 'I'm going to have a baby and you must send Preston and Gerald to get Aunt Fanny. Tell them to hurry! '

"I ran to the boys' beds calling, 'Preston! Gerald! Get up quick. Ma is having a baby! Take the dog team and go and get Aunt Fanny.'" Lillian added, "You know that Pa's sister Aunt Fanny and Uncle Bill Hodgins lived in the Thiele's old home. To get there, you had to go down Schermer's Road, cross the bridge over Commanda Creek, go past the Hoffman homestead and turn right just before the old Pilger's homestead. That's where the old road ran.

"It must have been a good moonlight night, for the dogs flew over the snow. It was about seven miles, round trip. Ma told me to put on a pot of water to boil, which I did," stated Lillian. "The boys arrived back an hour and a half later with Aunt Fanny. 'You can go back to bed now Lillian,' said Aunt Fanny. Surprisingly, I fell right back to sleep. In the morning we had our little baby brother Archie," Lillian beamed, as if the miracle of birth had just happened.

"Five-year-old Mervyn was sitting on the floor pulling on his socks near the woodstove when Aunt Fanny brought the baby downstairs. She dipped some warm water from the reservoir attached to the stove, poured it into a basin and bathed the newborn. Standing on tiptoe, Mervyn was able to look with wonder at his new brother," related Lillian.

"Ma called me to her bed again and instructed me to write a letter to Pa. On my way to school, I was to give it to George Smith, the proprietor's son, at the Commanda store. I was to ask George to hand the letter to Pa the next morning when he took a load of groceries in to Charlie Smith's (no relation) logging camp. That logging camp was back of Yerke's on the old Nine Mile Bush Road that is now Bennett's Road," said Lillian.

"When Rea and Carl arrived home from their logging camp for Christmas, they found that there was another baby boy. 'What's his name?' Rea asked Ma. 'His name is Archie', Ma replied.

'Well, you'd better not call him Archibald or I'll drown him in the creek!' Rea threatened in his laconic manner.

'No', said Ma, laughing, 'His name will just be Archie,"' Lillian recounted, laughing at the memory.

She continued, "The following June of 1936, Preston and I wrote our Provincial High School Entrance exams in Loring and it was there I first met Eric Howes. Rea and Eric had worked together at George Ratz's logging camp in Restoule the previous winter when Archie was born, and they became friends.

"One weekend in the winter of '36, Eric and Pa had come home from the logging camp in Port Loring. Rea and Carl were at Tom Hummel's logging camp just beyond Farley's in Carr that winter. As Pa and Eric were getting ready to go back to the camp, Eric sneaked me a hug and a kiss." Lillian sighed, "I will always remember that first kiss!"

Eric was to carry his love for this tall, sweet-natured girl with the soft brown eyes for many years.

"Tell me about Eric," I asked. "My earliest memories of Eric were when he and Rea and Carl set off for Northern Ontario to find work. I think it was the summer of '37. I was about three years old. It must have been quite an occasion because it stands out clearly in my memory. They arrived back a month later with boxes full of blueberries. The three of them had gone up north to Uncle Willie's in Kelso near Iroquois Falls. Rea told me later that they had hoped to get work at the Abitibi paper mill but those were deep depression years and there was no work in the mills. Uncle Willie's sons Jack and Garfield loaned them equipment to cut down trees to sell for firewood. When Rea and Carl earned enough money for train fare, they picked the blueberries and returned home."

"Well," explained Lillian, "Rea and Carl befriended Eric, who had left home following a confrontation with his father. Our mother accepted him into our crowed household, although she kept a concerned eye on his attention to me. Eric remained with us until, along with Rea and Carl; he set out to find more permanent employment away from the seasonal work of the logging camps.

"In January 1938, just before my sixteenth birthday, Aunt Luella came and took me to Toronto," said Lillian. "The next month, I started training at Shaw's Business School. All this was pre-arranged by Auntie and Ma. I knew nothing of their plans. I found out later that they'd planned for me to start business school in September, but there had been an outbreak of polio in Toronto that summer and it was decided to postpone my leaving until January. It must have been a real loss to the family to have the eldest girl leave," said Lillian sadly. "Looking back now, Ma had so much work to do looking after the farm and all those children."

"Within months of my leaving, Carl and Eric found work in Toronto. Rea took a job in the munitions plant in Nobel, near Parry Sound. Eric wanted to continue our close friendship but I felt that God had other plans for my life in mission work. We were both sad in our parting," recalled Lillian. "I missed him so much! I'd write letters to him, then tear them up because I realized that it would only start up the relationship again," sighed Lillian.

"In 1939, war was declared. Rea, Carl and Preston enlisted. Eric was not eligible for the armed forces as he was deaf in one ear, but he met Ethel, who was in the Canadian Women's Army Corp, and they married," Lillian concluded.

Lillian and Eric didn't keep in touch over the years, but suddenly one night in February of 1998, Lillian awakened with the knowledge that Eric was in distress. She prayed earnestly for him. In August of that same year the family gathered to celebrate Lillian's and her husband Harold's golden wedding anniversary. After greeting Lillian, Carl said to her, "Did you know that Eric died?"

With an intake of breath, Lillian named the date in February and Carl confirmed it. Although circumstances and time had separated them, the deep bond remained. Eric passed from this life on the wings of Lillian's prayer.

"I can truly say that God has led me," declared Lillian as she reviewed the events of her life. "I worked as a stenographer in an office in downtown Toronto for more than two years. In 1942, I began three years of study at the Pentecostal Bible College, followed by a year at Missionary Medical School. Each of those experiences prepared me for what was to follow."

While in Bible College, Lillian taught a nine-year-old girl in Sunday school by the name of Eunice Hutchinson.

"She was a bright, intelligent little thing," Lillian remembered. Within the year, Eunice's father died, leaving his wife and six children destitute. Eunice remembers Lillian visiting her home and Lillian taking Eunice on her knee to give her comfort. Eunice Hutchinson attended Lillian's wedding in 1948, little knowing that she would meet and, in 1952, marry Lillian's younger brother Lloyd.

"Harold Bradley, a quiet, serious man, was a classmate but I didn't notice him the first year," Lillian commented. "It was during the summer break when I worked at the Gospel Publishing House that I became aware of Harold. He had gone with another student to Cobalt to do child evangelism. They wrote the Publishing House for supplies and that was the beginning of our acquaintance. After graduating from Bible School, we had little contact with each other - much to Harold's frustration. Harold had gone on to Teacher's College and I went to Missionary Medical School," Lillian related.

"At Missionary Medical School," Lillian continued, "I met my dear, life-long friend Milda Rosenke, and in the fall of 1946, Milda and I went to Elizabeth Bay on the Manitoulin Island to be pastors of the church there. We spent a wonderful year together with the hospitable people of Manitoulin Island. At the same time, Harold taught school in the town of Burwash, south of Sudbury. It was in the winter of 1946/47 that Harold won my heart," Lillian smiled. "We were married in Toronto on August 14, 1948.

"With our few worldly goods and our wedding presents packed in a small trailer attached to Harold's old 1934 Ford, we headed north to Cochrane to begin our mission work," Lillian smiled, remembering their adventure. "In the village of Hunta, 15 miles west of Cochrane, we settled in a little cottage. Harold taught school while I did clerical work. Sundays were busy. On Sunday at 9 a.m., we held Sunday school at Hunta then went on to the small village of Fredrick House to hold Sunday service at 11 a.m., then on to another little settlement four miles beyond for Sunday school at 2 p.m. At the request of the local people, we held an evening gospel service in a school in Cochrane," related Lillian.

"That first fall in Hunta, Harold heard of a former prison camp that was for sale. The camp had been used during the war to house German war prisoners," Lillian stated. "We bought it and every evening after work we went out to the camp and salvaged lumber and nails. An elderly dedicated Christian man came to live with us. To earn his board, he helped in the house and in building the church. When we got home from work, he would have some wonderful food cooking, like baked potatoes and roast beef. By the end of the school year in June, we had enough lumber to begin building a church and parsonage. Those were the beginnings of the Pentecostal Church in Cochrane. On May 24, 1950, we celebrated the church's official opening and dedication," declared Lillian with satisfaction.

During the 50 years that Harold and Lillian were in the ministry, Harold taught school in many remote areas while Lillian tended the sick and provided first aid care to her own family and others. They built churches with their own hands along with the help of parishioners. In thirty towns and villages across the north, the couple preached and taught native people and white alike. Harold and Lillian pastored churches in Ontario, Quebec and the Northwest Territories, in places like Espanola, Restoule, Matheson, Hornepayne, Pagwa River, Wawa, Hay River, Coppermine, Sioux Lookout and Rimouski.

Lillian and Harold's eldest daughter Carol Anne was born December of 1951, while they lived in Hunta. Their son Jim was born three years later in Espanola and the youngest, Janet, was born in Loring in 1955 while they were pastoring and building the parsonage at the Corner Gospel Church in Restoule, Ontario.

"In Matheson, where we pastored from 1957 to 1958, the living quarters were above the church. One night, just before the Sunday evening service, we tucked the children, seven-year-old Carol, four-year-old Jim and three-year-old Janet, into bed," related Lillian. "As the service was in progress, we noticed a flurry of the congregation's attention turning toward the back of the church.

"I turned in my front pew, shocked to see our three little ones coming up the centre aisle," smiled Lillian, shaking her head. "Carol had decided to participate in the evening service. She had tried to dress herself as an adult, with hat and oversized dress. Jim had a shirt pulled over his pyjamas and Janet was still in her sleepers, trailing her favourite blanket. The church people had a good laugh as I ushered them out the door and back to bed," Lillian chuckled.

Lillian ensured that the family ate nutritious meals wherever they settled by growing a vegetable garden, picking and preserving wild raspberries and blueberries, making chili sauce with tomatoes she'd grown and baking her own bread. The family dined on moose meat, beaver and other traditional food shared by the native people.

In the native community of Pagwa River, Harold was both teacher and pastor to the families of one hundred and seventy-five American airmen and to four or five families of weather station personnel, as well as native residents. The town boasted a Hudson's Bay store and a 'free trader's' store, but had no navigable road and no doctor within one hundred miles. The railway was the only link to the outside world. In Pagwa River, they saw native mothers use reindeer moss as diapers for babies. In church, some verses of hymns were sung in English and some in the native language. "We were always particularly vigilant about the children's safety in Pagwa River because of the isolation from a hospital," explained Lillian. "One day, six-year-old Jim announced, 'we're going to build a tree house, can we have the axe?'

"'Yes,' Harold told them, 'but be careful and stay away from the river!' Suddenly we heard screaming. My heart seemed to stop. The children came running up the trail from the bush, crying. What's wrong? I called, as I ran to them. Jim cried out, 'Janet got into a bee's nest and we all got stung!' I put something in their stings, thankful that nothing more serious had happened," Lillian sighed.

In 1963 Lillian had to turn her attention to Luella. Aunt Luella, in Toronto, was terminally ill and the person she longed to be with was her daughter Lillian.

Luella's siblings also gathered at her bedside. Annie with Iva, their youngest sister, and Annie's husband Jim, were gathered at her bedside as Luella lay dying. Luella chose at this time to confess what she'd kept hidden from Annie all those years – that Jim had fathered Lillian. Jim was forced to confess that Luella spoke the truth–he was indeed Lillian's father.

All of my mother's denial and the anger that she had repressed all those years came gushing forth. Bitter words and accusations flowed with her tears.

"Let it go Annie, let it go," said Iva sadly, gently shaking her sister's heaving shoulders.

Finally! Finally, my mother was able to forgive and reconcile with Luella.

The next day our dad spoke with Lillian, in an attempt to justify the affair, saying, "I loved Luella."

"Your both should have been ashamed of yourselves," Lillian rebuked him sternly.

Aunt Luella did become a nurse. She never married. For most of her career she worked for an agency that supplied private nurses to the gentry of old Rosedale in North Toronto. It was while Luella was providing care to the bedridden father of Sir Earnest MacMillan, that she became ill and was diagnosed with pancreatic cancer. A nurse from Luella's nursing registry provided Luella with palliative care in her own home with Luella's sister Aunt Agnes Cooke, Lillian and I assisting in her care.

Although it was a sad time, it gave me satisfaction to assist in her care as she had been my support and advisor when I was a young mother. And throughout her time in Toronto, Luella had provided a second home to the Peever children. For those of us leaving Commanda and making our way to Toronto in search of employment, Aunt Luella – 'Auntie' – made us welcome, mentored each of us and gave pithy advice freely – both sought and unsought. For instance, on the topic of romance, to one sister, Auntie encouraged, "Broaden your horizons! Don't allow your boyfriend to camp on your doorstep all the time!"

To my casual disregard of male attention, 'Auntie' cautioned, "Be careful that you don't go through the woods and pick up a stick on the other side!"

She admonished our brothers, "Now always put your best foot forward!"

Aunt Luella made her peace with God when she entered the Salvation Army School of Nursing. Throughout her life, she was devout, finding inspiration and acceptance in her church and in her profession. Luella Smith is buried in Pine Hills Cemetery, Toronto.

Life came full circle for Luella's daughter Lillian when, in the years 1965 to 1969, she returned with her family to Elizabeth Bay, Manitoulin Island. Harold and Lillian provided gospel services to the people of Elizabeth Bay, Spring Bay and Little Current. During their stay on the Manitoulin, the three children were able to take music lessons. What a cacophony when they all practiced different tunes at once! Music remains a happy part of their life to this day. Carol Anne plays the accordion, Jim plays guitar, while Janet plays the piano. Their family celebrations always feature a songfest.

Harold and Lillian built a cottage on Manitoulin Island where the family returned each summer. Manitoulin Island is the home of 'The Great Spirit Manitou' and their spiritual home. There they felt grounded and refreshed by the beauty and spirit of the place.

Harold and Lillian could not have foreseen that two of their children would one day serve the people of Manitoulin Island.

In August 1998, Lillian and Harold celebrated both their golden wedding anniversary and fifty years of church ministry. Family and friends gathered from across North America to celebrate with them.

In a letter to me three years later, Lillian summarized her life with Harold in missions this way: "We worked hand in hand in all of those places and they were happy years. God gave us three dear children and now it is 2001 and we have just had our fifty-third wedding anniversary. I am seventy-nine and Harold is eighty-five. He is in poor health but I am glad that we still have each other and that I can care for him at home, here in Powassan where we have settled, near to our daughters and to Edna."

Fervently, Lillian wrote, "I can say thanks to the Lord for all His blessings and His leading all these years. Heaven will be the next exciting experience for us. I want the others to know what happened about my birth. I'd like you to write my story and to end it with a verse from my favourite hymn," Lillian penned this verse:

*All the way my Saviour leads me;*
*What have I to ask beside?*
*Can I doubt His tender mercy?*
*Who through life has been my Guide?*
*Heavenly peace, divinest comfort,*
*Here by faith in Him to dwell!*
*For I know what'er befall me,*
*Jesus doeth all things well.'*

On January 24, 2003, Harold Bradley died. Lillian left us suddenly in October the same year.

## Gerald

Gerald, on the other hand, was impulsive and intemperate, physically strong and outgoing with a quick smile and movie star good looks. He inherited his father's gift of voice and music. Gerald loved to sing and play his guitar. But even at the age of sixteen, he could be found in a quiet spot studying his Bible.

As a young man, Gerald followed his older sister Lillian to Toronto and to Bible College and, like many of today's students; he worked evenings and weekends to pay his tuition. Gerald graduated in wartime and answered the call for men to go west to help in the wheat harvest. The farm boy felt right at home in the fields.

The harvest completed, Gerald received an appointment to be the minister of a church near Saskatoon, Saskatchewan. He was a popular and charismatic speaker. It was there that he met and married a fiery redhead. Doris bore him a son but soon she found the role of minister's wife to be irksome. Gerald gave up full-time ministry and they moved to Winnipeg where he found work and only served as a pulpit supply minister to churches in the area. Gerald was passionate about God but more passionate about his wife.

Another son was born. Still Gerald's wife was restless, constantly seeking change and excitement. In 1950 they loaded their belongings in a one-ton truck and travelled east to Commanda.

The family hadn't seen Gerald in nearly ten years, except briefly in 1947 when he returned for his next-older brother Preston's funeral. Gerald, his wife Doris and two little boys Allan and Preston – namesake of his lost brother Preston – settled into the household in Commanda with our parents and siblings Mervyn, Archie and me who still remained at home.

Youngest brother Archie remembers the era this way:

"I was a teenager when Gerald and his family lived at the farm. One day I went with Gerald when he drove to Barrie to trade in the one-ton for a three-ton truck. Gerald intended to work hauling logs and slab wood. We hauled slabs from Charlie Swartz's mill in Commanda to a brick works in Toronto. It was heavy hard work but I enjoyed the change from farm labour.

"Dad used to go with Gerald to load slab wood too, as he knew the location of local mills and I think he liked getting back to the sights and smells of sawmills.

"On Sundays, Gerald served as pulpit supply minister, preaching in local churches. He preached in the dwindling community of Rye, in Golden Valley and Arnstein. Mervyn, Doris and Gerald would often sing as a trio on those occasions.

"During that summer, Gerald was praying that Dad would make a commitment of his life to God and one day Dad witnessed something that changed his life and freed him of his addiction to chewing-tobacco.

"On that particular occasion we drove to a mill site by a little lake in Golden Valley. The slab pile was on marshy ground. As we piled on slabs, the truck sank to the axels in the soft sawdust and black ooze. Gerald calmly finished loading. He knelt at the running board and prayed before he got into the truck.

"Dad had walked up a little hill. He stood in the shade and watched a 'miracle' happen. Gerald started up the truck and it climbed right up out of the bog. Dad told me that he'd said, 'Lord, if you can answer that prayer, you can take away my tobacco habit'.

Dad never bought another plug of Big Ben tobacco but he vigorously chewed gum ever after."

Archie continued, "Gerald found that work with the truck was only seasonal. It couldn't provide an adequate living and Doris became restless. She took off to Toronto in search of excitement. When Doris returned they decided to move west again. In the fall, Gerald sold the truck then piled the family and their belongings into a van he'd purchased. Mervyn went along on their trip out west to help with the move."

Gerald and Doris' marriage continued to deteriorate and after sixteen years together, they went their separate ways. Doris died in middle age.

Gerald moved to Portage La Prairie where he managed the local motor vehicle license bureau. He married again and had about ten happy years with his second wife Freda. Together they performed community service and helped in their local church.

Gerald's sons were scarred by their chaotic home life. In adulthood, both sons had difficulty maintaining close family relationships.

Gerald suffered from heart disease, and after one last heart attack, he died October 19, 1984, at the age of sixty.

God alone will judge if he fulfilled his commission. Gerald is buried in Winnipeg, Manitoba.

### Howard

As a teenager, Howard seemed quite bored and fractious, likely due to his keen intellect, his larger-than-life personality and stature. The summer that Howard was sixteen, he put on such a growth spurt that he reached a height of over six feet. Between meals, the effort of heavy farm work and the demands of his growing body caused him to become lightheaded and to feel faint.

Our mother's solution was to beat several eggs together with lots of sugar and light cream, a pinch of nutmeg and a dash of essence of vanilla. Mid-afternoon, she dispatched me to the distant fields bearing this foamy, golden nourishment for Howard.

He could be irritating at times and at other times exceptionally caring and helpful. Howard seemed very aware of the heavy workload our mother carried after Edna was no longer in the home to help her. If Mom was unwell or away for a few days, Howard would step in to make the meals.

Archie, the youngest of the clan, often tells these memories of Howard; "One day at school when I was about six or seven, I sprained my ankle. The teacher sent me home a little earlier than the rest of the students but I had only walked about one quarter of a mile, as my ankle was too sore and swollen. Howard caught up with me and hoisted me on his back. He carried me to the top of the Sand Hill by the cemetery, set me down for a short rest and then packed me on his back the rest of the two mile-journey home.

"Howard was fourteen or fifteen at the time. He was still living at home because he was able to take his first two years of high school at the Commanda School.

"Howard boarded in Powassan to get his third year of high school, working after school to pay for his board. During the war, he joined the flock of 'A' students who were let out of school early to work on farms in south-western Ontario, harvesting fruit and picking tobacco. Howard worked alongside German prisoners of war, who were also recruited for the harvest.

"Howard took his fourth year of high school in Loring. He had to walk three miles from home to Tom Farley's where he caught the 8 a.m. bus to Loring. On weekends he helped on the farm, including fall butchering of beef and pork. Somehow, he contracted jaundice and became quite ill. Nevertheless, when he learned of Dad's plans for deer hunting, he left his bed. Howard joined the hunt, shot a deer and then returned to his bed and fought off the infection. Such was his determination," exclaimed Archie.

In 1947, after the harvest, Howard left the farm to work in Toronto. As with all of us who arrived in Toronto, Howard stayed with Aunt Luella until he found a job and got established. Howard studied architectural drafting at night school while working in the building industry by day. On Sundays he attended church with Aunt Luella and felt the pull of the Gospel message. In the spring, Aunt Luella introduced him to Rose Grant, a fellow parishioner who ran a boarding house. Howard moved in. At the boarding house Howard met Rose Grant's daughter Wilma. Wilma was attending the Eastern Pentecostal Bible College and in addition, cooking meals for the boarders.

By September of 1948 the two were engaged, just before Howard returned to Commanda. Howard came back home in order to fulfil a promise he'd made to himself, that he would build a modern, comfortable home for our mother.

That fall and winter Howard, his next-eldest brother Lloyd, and our dad felled trees, cut logs and hauled them to the sawmill in Trout Creek to be made into lumber.

In May, 1948, a day after Wilma graduated from Bible College, Wilma and Howard married. They were both twenty-one-years old.

Wilma, a petite city girl, gamely moved to Commanda to be with Howard while he built the house. Wilma, competent and quick, got a job as a clerk in Commanda General Store. They lived in the apartment above the store.

Our dad, Lloyd and next-younger brother Mervyn worked under Howard's direction building the house when not busy with the farm work.

"Don't forget the story of the army worms when you write about the summer of '49," cautions Archie, as he launches into his story. "That was the year when I was thirteen and the whole region was attacked by an infestation of army worms. Mom kept telling me to watch for them when I went out into the fields.

"One day, I was sent to dig potatoes for the noon meal from the potato patch behind the barn. After I filled my pail, I crossed over into the grain field. There I saw a host of army worms stripping the leaves off the oats, leaving bare skeletons of stems.

"When Howard heard the news, he left off building. He walked the path from the barn up through the field leading toward Mud Lake and as he walked, he prayed.

"At harvest time we had perfect crops except between the path and the patch of field where I found the first sign of the army worms," concluded Archie.

By September 1949, the family moved into their two-story, four-bedroom house with its gleaming hardwood floors that Lloyd purchased and installed. In the basement, a giant wood-burning furnace provided warmth. Our mother was pleased and gratified with her spacious new home.

The following month Howard and Wilma left Commanda. Howard entered Bible College. The couple felt the call of God to do mission work. While at college, Howard worked weekends in a butcher shop while Wilma worked full time in clerical work.

After graduation, the couple and their seventeen-month-old daughter Janice took the Canadian National Railways train from Toronto to Edmonton, embarking on the first leg of their journey to join the Sub-Arctic

Mission on the shore of Great Slave Lake. The Mission's purpose was to serve the native people of Canada's far north-west.

From Edmonton, they took a Greyhound bus for their 1000-mile journey to Hay River, Northwest Territories. It was the Mission Centre and home of the director Rev. Ken Goetz.

En route, Howard and Wilma had their first encounter with subarctic conditions. Although it was mid-summer, a cold rain began to fall, turning the one-lane dirt road through the muskeg into slippery mire.

All the men on board – miners and bush workers, and Howard in his city clothes – jumped out to keep the bus from sliding off the road into the bog – all to no avail. The bus driver walked for five hours to the nearest town and returned aboard a caterpillar tractor. The 'Cat' towed the bus to town – and a welcome warm breakfast after a cold night in the bog. Their twenty-four-hour bus ride had turned into a thirty-six-hour endurance test for Howard, Wilma and their young child Janice.

Howard and Wilma spent the summer at the Mission Centre in Hay River enabling the Mission director and his wife to take a furlough.

In September, Howard and Wilma set forth into new territory to establish a gospel mission at Fort Resolution. The village lay one hundred miles distant, angled north-east from Hay River, across at the bottom end of Great Slave Lake.

The Mission Director, the chief of the Chipewyan Indian band and two Indian guides helped load their food supplies for six months. They loaded household goods and gear (all shipped from Edmonton to Hay River) onto the Mission boat. The Mission boat was an old converted fishing scow.

Winds of autumn drove twenty-foot waves at the boat while Wilma prayed and feared for the life of their child. The boat wallowed valiantly but wind and high waves eventually lifted the boat and drove it up onto the shore, narrowly missing hazardous rocks.

The party camped that night on shore and in the morning, the men cut down small trees to make a rolling skid under the boat. The men pried, pushed and rolled the boat back into the water then they were on their way again.

The First Nation village of Fort Resolution had been the site of a World War II army base. It boasted a Hudson's Bay store, an RCMP station and a government-run Tuberculosis Hospital, staffed by the Catholic Sisters of Charity, a Catholic Church and a government-run school.

In Fort Resolution, Howard and Wilma bought a two-room log house from an older army veteran. A lean-to kitchen has been built against the side of the house. The kitchen housed a giant woodstove. Relieved to have their own home at last, they loaded in their supplies and set up housekeeping.

Howard's experience in hunting and fishing while growing up in Commanda served him well. He fished and shot game to feed his family. They'd also need a good supply of wood for winter. He cut and piled firewood for cooking and heating.

Howard purchased and trained a team of five young Husky dogs. The dogs had to be fed too. Howard fished to feed the dogs. His dog team hauled water from Great Slave Lake, the source of all their water to fill forty-five gallon drums. Their water supply sat in those drums outside the kitchen door.

Wilma, city raised, had a greater struggle adapting to the primitive conditions. Her greatest challenge was in mastering the wood-burning stove which she had to use for baking her own bread. She also had to learn to heat water in an old fashioned boiler on the stove for hand-scrubbing laundry. The stove was also the heat source for the whole house.

The family had to rely on canned fruit and vegetables, shipped in twice yearly from Edmonton, except for the summer months when they could enjoy their own homegrown vegetables.

In the house, they started garden plants from seed in containers and then set the plants out after the danger of frost had passed. The plants grew rapidly in the long hours of sunlight as the sun did not set until nearly midnight. Soon the family enjoyed vegetables like lettuce, onions and beets but the slower maturing tomatoes had to be brought indoors in late August to ripen, away from the frost.

At first the adult native people viewed these strange new people from 'outside' with suspicion but the teens and children were eager to hear Bible stories, colourfully illustrated by flannel graph pictures. A classroom in the local school served as a Sunday school room. Wilma played her accordion and the couple sang children's hymns. That was the beginning of their mission work.

Howard integrated with the native men of the community by accompanying them on their hunting expeditions. He must have been a strange sight to them with his blond hair, ice-blue eyes and towering stature.

On the edge of town, their log house lay between the village cemetery and the Indian settlement. The native people didn't like to walk past the cemetery in the dark, but one night there came a knock at their door. An old woman of the village begged Howard, "Come and pray for my son Willie. He is dying."

The doctor was leaving the house as they arrived. The doctor said, "I signed the death certificate and left it on the table. He won't live through the night."

Howard spoke to the semi-comatose man, telling Willie of God's love for him and of Jesus dying for his sins and for bringing healing. Howard prayed aloud for Willie, asking God to forgive his sins and save his soul. He left the house and went on home.

The next day, Howard saw the same man outside his house chopping wood. Willie told him, "I could hear you praying and I prayed too – for forgiveness and I asked God to heal me." He exclaimed, "I woke up this morning feeling like a new person!"

Willie invited Howard to come to his home and to hold worship services for his family and neighbours. Howard and Wilma told them stories from the Gospel and Wilma played her accordion while the two sang hymns. At the people's enthusiastic urging, Wilma played until her arms grew tired. The event marked the beginning of regular adult worship services.

Years later, Howard told his family of another occasion when he was called in the night to the bedside of a native woman in childbirth. Her baby was in a breech position and she was unable to give birth. Howard prayed for the woman. He asked for soap and water to wash his hands then praying for God's help, he gently repositioned the baby and assisted in the delivery. The relieved parents named their newborn son Howard, in his honour.

His experience of assisting in the birthing process on the farm stood him in good stead.

Howard and Wilma became an integral part of the community, ministering to the spiritual needs and helping in times of crisis.

Children's Sunday school, teen club and adult worship services were established and Howard had hauled logs to build a church. But in those five years, another daughter and son had been born to Wilma and Howard. The meagre mission stipend wasn't enough to feed and clothe the children.

Howard felt that he needed to take a job to support the family. The Sub-Arctic Mission found another young couple to take over the Mission at Fort Resolution and Howard moved his family to the town of Yellowknife where he took a job in the gold mine. They moved into a house in the 'old town', in a section where the native people lived. There they established a Mission for the native people of the socially segregated town. Many native men also worked in the gold mine.

Howard's work in the gold mine entailed building wooden supports inside the mine. Howard noted that many safety issues were neglected. He advocated for the miners and organized the first union at the Yellowknife gold mine.

The couple spent five years in Yellowknife working and ministering. During that time another child, Ruth Jean was born. She was less hardy than her three older siblings; therefore, Howard and Wilma decided that after ten years in the Northwest Territories, it was time to leave for a warmer climate.

The family settled in Southern California. Howard obtained carpentry work in a large mine where he again became union representative, respected by both management and workers for his fairness and wisdom in settling labour disputes. Howard continued his ministry to the community as chaplain to prisoners in the local jail and also in hospital chaplaincy. Wilma returned to college and pursued a career in education.

Alas, Howard and Wilma no longer shared a common vision, and after twenty-seven years of marriage, the couple divorced. They eventually found new partners.

When Howard retired, he added visitation and worship at the local senior's residential care centre and nursing home to his ministry schedule. In addition, he served in Presbytery Committee work (denominational administration), solving disputes, providing interim ministers to fill vacancies, helping to select new pastors and personally filling in as pulpit supply.

He remained physically active, maintaining his own property and, for extra income, providing home maintenance for vacation properties in a nearby subdivision. Howard shared many happy years with his second wife June, but near the end of his life, he suffered a series of small strokes that caused brain damage and loss of memory. In October of 1999, his doctor advised Howard that his prognosis meant a gradual mental decline and dementia.

Howard grieved his loss but wrote a letter, with copies informing each of his siblings, commenting, "My reasoning tells me that I had better do what I can, while I can do it." His letter ended, "Not one of us knows what the future holds, but I have faith and assurance enough in God and His blessings of life; and in His presence with me, that I can step out into each new day with faith and joy. "

On the night of February 28, 2005, our brother Lloyd had a dream. Lloyd told his siblings, "In my dream, Howard and I were upstairs in the old house where we grew up. An angel came up and led Howard away. I wasn't surprised when his wife June called the next morning to say that Howard had died. I told her, 'I foresaw it in my dream'."

**Mervyn**

Mervyn was six-feet tall, broad-shouldered and powerfully built, with curly auburn hair, sky-blue eyes and a ready laugh. He sang as he worked and in his leisure time, played his guitar and sang.

In adolescence, Mervyn didn't seem to know his own strength. On the farm, he broke pitchfork and shovel handles lifting loads heavier than the implements were meant to hold. As the eldest of the four youngest siblings, Mervyn was always our protector and defender, quick to react in time of trouble.

Mervyn planned to take over managing the farm from our aging father. In fact, he returned home after a year in Winnipeg with that purpose in mind. It was then that he felt God's call on his life. Serving God in the ministry was meant to be his life's work, not farming.

In Winnipeg, Mervyn had met a sweet-natured young woman and fallen in love with her. He returned to Winnipeg to tell Joyce of his calling and he asked her to be his wife. The two married in 1952, worked and saved money to attend college together. They chose the Apostolic Bible Institute in St. Paul, Minnesota, an evangelical, charismatic college, just over the Canada/USA border from Winnipeg.

Upon graduating, Mervyn and Joyce lived in various towns in northern Saskatchewan and Manitoba, serving in mission work to the Cree people. They also distributed Cree Bibles and song books, provided by the Canadian Bible Society.

From 1961 to 1974, Mervyn, Joyce and their large family lived in Flin Flon, Manitoba. Mervyn worked for Hudson Bay Mining and Smelting Company. Joyce worked alongside Mervyn in establishing both a church and a native Cree mission while she tended their growing family. Mervyn hunted and fished and Joyce tended a big garden in summer to help feed their eight children. Neither was daunted by the severe conditions in winter.

Mervyn was pleased, in 1974, to be hired as a trainman for B.C. Rail. The pay was better, but it meant that the family had to continue their mission work in Williams Lake, British Columbia.

Three years later, in 1977, the railway transferred Mervyn to Prince George, British Columbia. The trains hauled freight from the depot in Prince George to Vancouver. Mervyn's position of brakeman required strength and agility.

Mervyn and Joyce established a Pentecostal church in Prince George called The Voice of Pentecost.

On a fateful day, October 20, 1993, at the age of sixty-three, Mervyn was to experience the supreme test of both his faith and agility. As the heavily loaded, sixty-car train was 20 kilometers south of Prince George, heading toward Williams Lake, the train picked up speed to 64 kilometer per hour. Just then the RCMP alerted the engineer to watch for a lost three-year-old girl who might have wandered onto the tracks. The engineer slowed the train to 19 kilometers per hour and set up the brakes for a quick stop.

Suddenly as they rounded a curve, Mervyn saw a movement 60 metres ahead on the tracks. He watched as the little girl crawled from between the rails and sat on an outside rail tie.

Mervyn lowered himself down the engine's ladder, hovering over the tracks. About 4.5 meters from the child, with a quick prayer for God's help, Mervyn leapt in front of the train. In two strides he reached her, but he slipped on the loose gravel at the side of the tracks. Mervyn felt himself falling; still as he fell, with his long left arm he reached back for her.

Mervyn's hand got a grip on the front of her shirt. He yanked her off the rail as he went down.

The fuel tank at the rear of the train grazed the top of her head as the train screeched by and came to stop 25 metres past where the little girl had sat.

Later, Mervyn recounting the incident to his siblings said, "She was howling from fright and at the sting from the nick on her head. I tried to comfort her but she cried, 'I want my mommy!!' "At the next crossing, an RCMP officer boarded the train and took the child to be reunited with her distraught mother. Her parents took little Keeley to hospital for stitches to the top of her head.

"At a reception in my honour a few weeks later, I met Shirley Campbell, Kelley's mother. Keeley clung to her mother and cried out, 'That man hurt me!'" Mervyn smiled ruefully.

"I couldn't get any rest or sleep for weeks after it happened. News reporters called me day and night and I had to get up early in the morning and go to work," Mervyn complained.

The story of Mervyn's train rescue was reported on television and written up in newspapers across the country. Vancouver Sun's October 22, 1993 headline by Pete McMartin and Rosetta Cannata reads: **PRINCE GEORGE** *Rail brakeman who saved girl from train dislikes hero label.*

His story was also published in the November, 1994 issue of *Reader's Digest*, titled "LEAP of FAITH."

The Governor General of Canada, Raymond Hnatyshyn presented Mervyn with the Medal of Bravery for "an exemplary act of bravery in perilous circumstances." The Governor General wasn't aware that Mervyn, in his youth, had gained plenty of practice while rescuing his younger siblings from various perils.

In retirement, Mervyn and Joyce enjoyed travelling across Canada, visiting their grown children and their grandchildren. He remained strong and vigorous. Mervyn even spent one summer in the Yukon helping his eldest son Curtis in his construction business. Mervyn and Joyce didn't retire from church work. Mervyn continued to be the pastor of their church.

Mervyn was never happier than when he was outdoors hunting or fishing. On March 1, 2003, Mervyn and his ten-year-old grandson Sammy set off for a day of ice fishing on nearby Raven Lake. They caught two fish and enjoyed the day together, but as five o'clock rolled around, Mervyn announced that it was time to gather up their fishing gear and head for home.

Mervyn advised, "Sammy, you start off ahead while I wind up the fishing lines and then I'll catch up with you."

Mervyn didn't catch up.

Sammy looked back and saw his grandfather lying on the ice. Frightened, he ran back. He found Mervyn face down on the ice. Sammy called out to him and shook him but Mervyn didn't respond.

Sammy ran. He ran past their truck on shore. He ran down the dark, snowy road. He ran and ran. After five miles the child was exhausted. He climbed up onto a snow bank to rest.

At home, Joyce worried, where were Mervyn and Sammy? It was hours past the time that they should be home. Joyce phoned her youngest son Fred and asked him to drive out to Raven Lake in search of the two.

In the pitch dark, Fred and his friend drove the road to Raven Lake, watching for any sign of his dad and Sammy. Suddenly the headlights picked up a silver flash. Fred stopped his truck. There, lying on the snow bank was Sammy. He was near death from hypothermia. It was the silver stripe on the pant leg of Sammy's snowmobile suit that saved his life. Fred sped home with him. Joyce put Sammy into a tub of warm water.

The traumatized child told them, "Grandpa is lying on the ice. He wouldn't wake up." The two young men threw a tarpaulin in the back of their pickup truck, knowing what they'd find. His son took Mervyn's lifeless body to the hospital to be pronounced.

Mervyn died Saturday, March 1, 2003 at the age of seventy-three.

Weeks later Joyce wrote to family members, "He was to preach at church the next morning. I found his notes for the next day at the end of the bed, and as I read them, the presence of the Lord surrounded me. Mervyn's theme was 'The King of Glory – Psalm 24: 7-10.'". It reads *Lift up your heads, you gates, lift yourselves up, you everlasting doors, that the king of Glory may come in ---.*

She continued, "Then two separate nights, as I lay awake thinking of my husband's passing, God gave me the same vision both times. I saw Mervyn preaching in church, walking, his hands uplifted exalting the Lord; and he stepped forward – and over the line. He stood in God's presence enveloped in a glorious light...."

**Archie**

Archie, the youngest son and the youngest of the family is tall and lanky, but smaller boned than most of his brothers. Archie is a quiet, introspective man with a surprisingly resonant voice.

In his first year at Powassan High School an astute teacher, who directed the annual high school pageants, appointed Archie the announcer and master of ceremonies because of his gift of public speaking. Archie, like his brothers, also has a fine singing voice.

Archie was the last child left at home. All his siblings had left the farm to find work or further their education. Archie assumed that it was his duty to help his aging parents manage the farm.

When he felt the call of God to the ministry, he was conflicted and felt pulled in two directions.

After harvest in the fall, pragmatically Archie reasoned that if he was to attend college, he'd need to earn the money for his education. He'd have to get a job in Huntsville where he knew work was available.

Reminiscing with me about this troubled phase of his life, Archie said, "I had no money to get to Huntsville, so I had to hitchhike. I went down the hill from our house and stood by the side of the road. But no car would stop for me. My heart was heavy because I felt that I was abandoning Mom and Dad in their old age; so I took my bundle and walked back up to the house and announced, 'I'm not going!"

"Mom said, 'You're afraid!'

"I said, "I'm not afraid but how will you manage without me?

"She sat me down and told me this story: 'A few years ago when I was staying at Luella's cottage recuperating from surgery, I attended a nearby church camp meeting. I was praying and God impressed on me that I hadn't committed everything to Him. I responded, 'But I have, Lord!'

'The "Still Small Voice" said everything? And Archie too?'

'That was a hard question because you were very sick when you were little and you were my last baby. Obediently, I said, 'Yes Lord, and Archie too.'

'Now you go on Archie. We'll be all right for the winter."'

"I went back down to the road and the next car that came along stopped and I was on my way. In the spring I came back home and planted the crops then I cut pulpwood. With the team of horses I hauled the pulpwood out to the road. Edna's husband Les Bain helped me load it on his truck. We hauled it to the Trout Creek railway station and filled an open boxcar. That boxcar load of pulpwood was enough to pay for my first-year tuition at Eastern Pentecostal Bible College.

"After graduation in 1960 I came home to Commanda. I cut and sold pulpwood to pay off a $100.00 loan for an old 1950 Chevrolet car. Then I left for my assigned mission in Nakina, a forest industry town about 80 miles due east of Armstrong and 240 miles north of Thunder Bay.

"The town of Armstrong is famed as the coldest spot in Ontario. I spent a cold and lonely winter working in the bush cutting pulpwood for

Abitibi Pulp and Paper Company. My coworkers included new immigrants from Finland as well as town locals and native men from nearby Arowland Reserve.

"Many winter mornings we were unable to use the horses to haul felled logs. Animal Welfare laws prohibited working horses when the temperature fell to forty degrees below Fahrenheit. Breathing in air at that temperature would freeze the horses' lungs. They remained stabled until about noon when the temperature rose sufficiently.

"No such laws existed for the workmen."

In the spring of 1961 Archie married his sweetheart Kathryn Sleep, a piano teacher and a fellow graduate of Eastern Pentecostal Bible College. The couple set about building a house and then a church with the help of community members and volunteers from congregations further south. Their denominational governing body provided funding for building materials.

Church members included native Ojibwa, long-time residents and Finnish new-Canadians. The congregation sang hymns, some verses in Finnish, some verses in English and some from the Cree hymnbook – the Cree language is familiar enough that Ojibwa residents could understand it.

Archie continued to tell the story of his life in ministry, "When I first arrived in Nakina I knocked on peoples' doors, introduced myself and asked if I could come in. Not everyone welcomed me but one day I visited an old Indian woman who lived in a boxcar beside the railroad tracks. She invited me in and we talked. She showed me a Cree hymnbook. The words were written phonetically and also in Cree writing. The old woman showed me the hymn, *Jesus Loves Me* and taught me to sing it in Cree."

"The natives gave me the Ojibwa name, *Taby Sem Aga*. To me it sounded like Tabway Semaga – it meant, *Jesus Loves Me*.

"I had a new name!" laughed Archie.

He continued his story, "When my new bride Kathy arrived, she accompanied me on my visits. Kathy brought along her accordion. The people loved to hear her play.

"One day we were invited to the home of an old woman who wasn't well. The woman was lying on a pallet on the floor. Her son Rich told us that his mother was one hundred years old. He asked us to pray for her. He said that she was blind but that the light hurt her eyes. I prayed and asked God to ease her pain and; when it came her time to leave this earth, that she might go in peace and comfort.

"Several bed spaces along the floor a man lying on a mat asked, 'You pray for me?' I asked of his problem. He answered, 'Can't walk'.

"Six months later I saw the old woman's son Rich on the street and greeted him. Rich was a commercial fisherman who hauled in his catch from nearby lakes, brought it to Nakina and shipped it south, packed in ice. Another man standing with him pointed at me, speaking in Ojibwa.

"Rich said, 'He knows you.'

"Surprised, I asked, 'What did he say?' Rich answered, He said, 'I can walk.'

"God honoured their great faith and took pity on many of those people, healing their painful bodies," said Archie. He continued, "I also was a volunteer ambulance driver. We'd pick up a patient and meet another ambulance at the halfway point, dispatched from Thunder Bay.

"I felt that it was another way to serve the Lord."

The Peever residence soon served as an unofficial hostel for native men or those who were in peril of freezing to death outdoors – men recently released from jail or those needing to sleep off a Saturday night binge.

Kathy joined her husband in telling the story of their mission at Nakina, saying; "Sometimes we housed as many as ten people at a time. Archie counselled them and prayed with them for their addiction. Our house was within walking distance of the railway station. Natives and transients would come to our door in search of a meal or a place to sleep. If I was alone in the house with our little children, I would not ask them in. I gave them a plate of food and invited them to sit on the doorstep."

"In Nakina we were poor too," Archie added.

Archie declared, "I had great respect though for the native men. They worked alongside of me in the bush and when a forest fire broke out near Geraldton, an hour's drive from Nakina, the men from nearby Aroland Reserve piled onto the bus – which the Department of Lands and Forests had sent for us. They worked hard. Those Aroland people are hard working, honourable men."

In the winter of 1965 Kathy was in crisis. Six months into her second pregnancy she developed placenta previa, a condition that put her unborn baby at risk. In the Thunder Bay hospital, a four hour drive away; Kathy was placed on bed rest. But after a month her water broke.

Archie had just returned from visiting her on the weekend when early Monday morning he got a call from Kathy, imploring him to come back. Archie quickly notified his boss of the problem and some of the neighbours. Laden with anxiety, he faced a four hour trip back to the Thunder Bay Hospital.

In the meantime Rev. Spillner, administrative director of their denomination's northern district, called in at Nakina for a report on how the mission was going.

Archie's house was empty.

Rev. Spillner knocked on the door of a parishioner and heard of the emergency. Rev. Spillner called all available members to the church to pray. He read scripture; and all the people, Finnish, English and Ojibwa alike sang hymns and prayed earnestly for Kathy and her baby.

Archie said, "When I arrived at the hospital I found that Kathy's amniotic sac had closed up two hours earlier and the crisis was passed. God surely answered our prayers!"

Kathy added, "I carried the baby for one more month and then the doctor performed a C-section."

Filled with emotion Archie declared, "We had our precious little Becky!"

Archie continued to tell of the next change in their lives, "A year later the Abitibi Company cut back on their operations in Nakina and cut wages. As a result the Finns left town in search of better work, as did many local residents. There was little work for the people of the town.

In 1966 we took our two little children and also left Nakina," he said sadly. "A young minister, born on the Six Nations Reserve near Brantford came to replace us, although the population of the town had dwindled severely."

From Nakina, Archie and Kathy moved about 30 miles due south to the town of Long Lac where they built another house, funded by their denomination. There was no need to build a church in that town. In an amazing ecumenical arrangement four Protestant denominations: Lutheran, Brethren, Anglican and Pentecostal shared the use of one church building. Each denomination led one Sunday service per month.

When the Anglican minister was unavailable on his allotted Sunday, Archie preached the sermon following the Anglican lectionary. Kathy played the organ for hymns from the Anglican hymnbook. As no other denomination in town provided a Sunday evening service, Archie held a service Sunday evening; and Kathy played the organ. They also opened their home for mid-week Bible study sessions.

All denominations were pleased when Archie and Kathy offered to provide an ecumenical Sunday school for all the children of the town and in summer Kathy organized Vacation Bible School for the children.

In 1969 a third child Mark, was born to them. Archie supported the family by grading plywood for a mill and later took a job with the Canadian National Railroad. He delivered heavy goods like stoves and refrigerators from the CNR warehouse to customers. Kathy contributed to the household income by teaching piano to children of the town.

Again their home became a haven for anyone in need of shelter. Kathy broke into the conversation with the story of Louri, an elderly Finnish man who'd also moved from Nakina to Long Lac. Kathy recounted, "In Finland, Louri built violins but in Nakina he worked in the bush and he attended our church. When he moved to Long Lac Louri lived alone in a little shack.

One day Louri became ill so I said to him, "You'd better come and stay with us until you feel better."

Archie interjected, "He spoke little English and he was very shy but one evening after bathing our toddler Mark, Kathy wrapped him in a towel and sat him on Louri's knee. Louri was thrilled. He had never held a baby before but he and Mark became great friends."

Kathy picked up her story again, "Louri lived with us for about a year and then he had a stroke. He was admitted to the hospital in Thunder Bay. We took our three children and their ukuleles on that 4 hour drive to

Thunder Bay Hospital. We found Louri curled in a fetal position and unable to speak but he perked up when our children played their ukuleles and sang to him.
Mark couldn't really play yet but he copied what Steven and Becky did.

"When Louri was ready for discharge we took him home with us for another five months, but he soon needed a nursing home," concluded Kathy.

Archie added, "Before Louri left our home for the last time he gave Kathy his beloved violin."

After eight years CNR closed their warehouse. Archie was again out of work.

Good educational opportunities for their children were the priority when they made their next move. The family moved about three hundred miles south-east to Iroquois Falls. There Archie took a job with the town water plant. He studied and qualified for the position of stationary engineer. Archie also served as the plant's Health and Safety Coordinator and was called upon to provide counselling to employees in crisis.

Archie built yet another house; this time with their own funds.

Kathy set up her piano classes, giving piano lessons to her own children, as well as children of the town. Many of Kathy's students competed in the annual Kiwanis Festivals. Stephen, Rebecca and Mark attended local schools. Each of the three graduated high school, winning Ontario Scholarships. All three graduated from university and established themselves in their own professions and married.

In Iroquois Falls Archie and Kathy again chose an ecumenical worship setting. In addition Archie provided pulpit supply to the Pentecostal church in nearby Matheson. He preached for Sunday services in both the local hospital and nursing home and he visited the sick.

The churches of Iroquois Falls sponsor a unique event during three nights of the Christmas season. In the centre of town church members, in costume, create a live tableau of the Bethlehem Story, replete with live animals (horses replace camels in the minus 20 degree F. temperatures). Archie and Kathy always participate.

Hardy citizens of the town all turn out to see the narrated tableau before enjoying a massed choir in one of the Protestant churches, a

Christmas homily in the Catholic Church, followed by hot chocolate and desserts in a third church.

Tragedy struck on February 11, 1997.

While driving in Ottawa Rebecca (Becky) hit an icy patch of road, slued into oncoming traffic and was killed instantly. Becky's two-year-old son Caleb strapped in his car seat in the back was unhurt but in shock. The bewildered child repeated constantly "car go boom!"

Marielle, Becky's husband's mother moved into Claude's home to care for the children Caleb and eleven-year-old Justin.

Grief overwhelmed Archie and Kathy. They moved through the days as if in a bad dream. Kathy stopped teaching piano. But Archie had the structure of a job that forced him to maintain a work routine.

For two years grief and mourning drained their energy but gradually they began to recover. Archie and Kathy turned their attention and energy to their ten grandchildren. During summer and Christmas holidays their home is bursting with activity and joyous sounds of happy children.

In Iroquois Falls they again provided care and hospitality to elderly neighbours Lou, a retired United Brethren minister, and his wife Norma.

Norma had suffered a brain aneurism. Surgery was unsuccessful. She was thought to be in a vegetative state. But when Kathy visited Norma and sang familiar hymns to her Norma wept. Kathy realized that Norma was aware, so she took her accordion into the hospital room. One day while Kathy worked the bellows, Norma reached out to play the hymn, Amazing Grace.

The nurses took note. They were motivated to provide rehabilitative care until Norma's condition improved enough to be transferred to a nursing home. In the meantime Kathy and Archie took Lou, her ailing husband, into their home for a year until he joined his wife in the nursing home.

Clearly, Archie and Kathy minister to others through their hospitality.

In retirement Archie, at age seventy-seven keeps fit by jogging a mile to the local hospital where he daily visits the sick. On Sundays he conducts services at both the hospital and nursing home. Archie is frequently sought out by bereaved families to conduct funeral services for their loved ones.

Often he also is asked to conduct funerals for Peever cousins, the descendants of our dad's older brother Willie (William Alexander) Peever who abandoned the farm at Mud Lake and moved to Iroquois Falls in 1920. Willy and Alvina had twelve sons and one daughter. There are many of their descendents in the Iroquois Falls area.

Archie confided, "Conducting funerals is the most difficult duty that I'm asked to do." He said, "It evokes the pain of our own loss."

It seems that God in his wisdom uses Archie's experience of heart-break and unspeakable grief to bring solace and comfort to others who are grieving.

## The Pivotal Role of the Wives in Ministry

The wives of Howard, Mervyn and Archie played a pivotal role in the effectiveness of their ministries. They bore and raised their children in challenging conditions while aiding and supporting their husbands in God's work.

Lillian their older sister, had led the way for her siblings in preparing for serving God through mission work and although she was not formally ordained, Lillian was equally capable in the pulpit, teaching Sunday school and playing hymns in worship services.

Lillian lifted building materials and assisted her husband Reverend Harold Bradley in the physical labour of building churches while bearing and tending to their children. And in her quiet, sweet way Lillian was the family business manager and organizer – the glue that kept family and church relations working.

The four brothers Gerald, Howard, Mervyn and Archie ordained to God's service; and Lillian, carried the message of God's love and care to people in all circumstances, sometimes in Canada's remote, frigid places. They shared God's message regardless of social status or religious traditions. The Four Reverends, Lillian and her husband Harold were like Jesus as He walked this earth encountering people along the road of life. They shared people's loads and brought them Jesus' message of hope and reconciliation.

# ~Memories of Our Father ~

## *June's Memories*

Our dad was born April 12, 1883, although he always thought that he had been born April 28, 1882. His birth records show that he was born in Fitzroy Township in 1883 but the family didn't discover that fact until after his death and they had always celebrated his birthday on April 28th. His gravestone shows his date of birth as April 28, 1882.

When I was born in 1932, Dad was already fifty years old. Thelma and Archie were born after me. Mom at fourteen years his junior, was more than forty years old when her childbearing finally finished.

I remember our dad as a man of few words. In temperament he was like two sides of a coin – one side quick tempered, stern and gruff, the other side amiable and perceptive. If he was in a bad mood we knew that we had better be on our best behaviour, or else!

### The Entertainer

Some early memories of Dad were of him rocking two or three of us on his lap, sitting in front of the big woodstove while Mom and Lillian and Edna cleared the supper table and washed up the dishes. Sometimes he would entertain us with Irish ditties like '*Who Threw Their Over-alls in Mrs.*

*Murphy's Chowder?'* or an Irish jig, improvising words with a "traddle-diddle-daddle-diddle-daddle-dee-dum" while keeping time with his foot.

Before the era of television folks entertained each other with stories and music. On a Saturday night visiting relatives or neighbours would often urge Dad to entertain them with a "step dance".

He would play his mouth organ while step dancing to the tune and sometimes he would dance "The Peg Leg" as if one leg was wooden.

Dad was a great storyteller and if men were present he would entertain them with hunting stories. He was known as an outstanding hunter and during hunting season he would be employed to guide groups of hunters who came from the city.

## The Bear

One of my early memories is of an event when I was about four years old. I asked to go with dad when he drove the cattle out to pasture one summer evening. He drove the cattle up the logging road toward Bill's Field. Bordering Mud Lake, the abandoned farm was about a mile north of ours. There area had plenty of food and water for the cows.

We had only gone a short way up the bush road when the cows stampeded helter-skelter off the trail, scattering in all directions into the woods. The cowbells on their necks made an awful racket as they ran. Dad ran after them, shouting to herd the cows back to the trail, while I stood alone, terrified and crying.

Leaving the cattle to find their own way to pasture, Dad returned to the trail where I stood wailing. He put an arm around me and pulled me close for a minute then took my hand and we walked back home.

The cows had likely picked up the scent of a bear close by and they bolted. The din the cowbells made would have sent the bear running. From time to time, however, the cows would come tearing home from pasture with claw marks on their hind quarters.

## Berry Picking

Another memory I have of our childhood days was when Dad would organize a berry-picking outing to Bill's Field. The abandoned farm fields grew wild strawberries and blackberries in season. We'd pack sandwiches and a jar of milk. We four youngest would grab our straw hats and berry pails and Dad would take a 'tea pail' and his gun. The gun was for protection from the bears who also knew where to forage for berries.

After a morning of picking he'd fill the tea pail from nearby Mud Lake, make a campfire and boil water for tea. We'd have lunch and tea cooled with milk. A real picnic!

In strawberry season at the end of June Dad would sometimes row us across Mud Lake to a mossy hillside where in a good year we would fill our pails before heading home. There would always be a stern reminder to sit very still as we crossed the lake.

## The Bull

One summer day when our dad was leading the big Herford bull out to tether it to the big elm tree near the creek, the bull suddenly charged at him. Dad quickly flung the chain around the tree to control the bull but as the chain went around the large hook on the end hit him in the forehead. It caused a deep gash. He was bleeding profusely and when Mom caught sight of him she fainted.

We children who witnessed it all were filled with shock and dread. He had to be taken to the doctor twenty miles away in Powassan for stitches in his head.

## Painting

An incident comes to mind about my painting mishap when I was fifteen. Our mother had gone to a church Ladies Aid meeting in her old home town of Golden Valley. She always enjoyed reuniting with her girlhood friends and visiting for a few days with her brother Alex Smith and his wife Susan, our dad's sister.

I decided to surprise her by painting the stairwell. It was a difficult chore that needed doing. Four steps up from the main room was a landing then a sharp turn up a steep staircase to the second floor. Above that landing I set up a couple of boards to stand on. I placed them over a four inch ridge bordering the stairwell. I balanced the pail of paint beside me. Dad was having his afternoon nap on the couch at the foot of the stairs. I was working along fine until the board holding the pail of paint slid off the ridge. The pail went bouncing down the stairs and across the landing, spewing paint onto the floor below and spattering his bald head. I thought that Dad would scold me for making such a mess but he just laughed as he wiped his bald head and helped me clean it up.

## *Archie's Memories*

### The Young Buck

"One day when I was about twelve years old, Dad complained of an aching back so he decided to leave the farm work for the day. He took an Aspirin and after a while felt some better. To my surprise Dad said, 'How would you like to come and see if we can pick some strawberries?'

"He fetched a six-quart basket and curiously dumped about a cup of salt into it and, as was his habit when heading into the bush, Dad tucked his 30-30 rifle into the crook of his right arm.

"We walked around the end of Mud Lake and up onto the rocks on the other side looking for berries nestled where moss gathers in the low dips in the rocks. No berries were to be found. Then Dad did a surprising thing. He walked down to a marshy spot at the lake's edge and trampled the salt onto the mud. It was then that I realized that he'd brought the salt to make a 'salt-lick 'for the deer.

"There was no conversation as Dad walked soundlessly, scanning the terrain along the secondary trail from Mud Lake to near where it intersects the highway opposite Schermer's Road.

"I was trailing along behind him when crack went a dry branch as I stepped on it. 'Be quiet you!' Dad hissed as he swung his head around to me. Just then, pointing I whispered, 'There's a deer.' In one motion Dad shouldered his gun as he swung back and fired as the startled deer leapt up. The young buck went down.

"Dad walked over to the deer and with his jackknife slit the belly and gutted it and then he said to me said to me, 'Can you shinny up that tree?' It was a sapling and up I went. He asked me to bend it down and I did. Next, Dad separated the top branches carefully until he had three strands. These he plaited into a rope, and tied it securely around the deer's neck. 'Can you help me boost it up?' said Dad. The deer was raised with its hind feet just a foot off the ground in order to drain its blood.

"'We'll go on home now,' he said. 'The young lads can come and carry it home.'

He was referring to our older brothers Lloyd and Howard. You know our dad was about sixty-four years old then.

"Fresh meat was always a necessity. In summer without refrigeration a butchered pig or cow wouldn't keep but our large family could eat a small deer within a week. At that time of year Dad would never shoot a doe as it might be caring for a fawn.

"Years later I was walking with my son Steven in the bush when he was a boy. He made a crashing noise behind me. I turned back in annoyance and suddenly I had a flashback of Dad's brusque 'Be quiet you!' I stopped on the trail and quietly asked my son to listen to the sounds in the forest. I said, "Do you hear that rustling in the leaves? Now let's walk quietly and listen for the birds singing and other sounds of the forest creatures.

"Recently I was talking with my son Steven about this event and he said to me, 'So, that was what caused the changed look on your face! I wondered about that.'"

**The Sleigh Ride**

"The mid-winter wind whistling from the northwest down Peever's Hill formed a wind tunnel through the exposed quarter-mile of flat straight road. We kids had to face that wind tunnel on the last lap of the long walk home from school. One frigid day I looked up to see Dad with the horses and sleigh coming to meet me. He bundled me into the sleigh without a word, taking off his warm mitts and pulling them over my frozen hands."

**Maud, the Mare**

"Carl brought home three yearling colts before he left for the war overseas in 1941. Dad had the two males gelded and "broken" for harness. The strawberry-blonde mare, however, he kept as a pet. Maud followed him around the farm while Dad fed her treats from his pockets. He never bred her.

"You see, Dad had owned a young mare when he was sixteen. She was his pet and his pride but she died giving birth. Dad was so angry with his father for breeding her that he left home, living and working in lumber camps for several years. He said an old Indian took him under his wing and taught him many things.

"One day when Dad was away Howard harnessed Maud and drove her around the barnyard until she was comfortable in harness. Howard was about sixteen at the time. Howard also accustomed Maud to the saddle.

"One Saturday Howard rode Maud to the Commanda Store to pick up the mail and some groceries. They were just beyond Peevers Creek on the way home when a young driver of one of Jack Odorizzi's Lumber Company's trucks swerved toward the horse intending to scare Howard. As the driver swerved away again, the end of the long lumber table of the truck caught Maud's flank, slicing her entire hip open to the bone. Howard managed to lead the horse home.

"Dad was grim. He called Dr. Rook the veterinary from North Bay to come. After the veterinary cleaned and stitched the massive wound he fashioned a sling under Maud's belly and attached it to a beam in the ceiling of stable to support her. Dad thoroughly cleaned her stall, put down fresh straw and then disinfectant was poured in the stall.

"Maud could not lie down for fear of opening up her wound. We children visited her but were not allowed beyond the stable door.

"Dad phoned Jack Odorizzi, his old friend and lumbering colleague to inform him of the terrible incident. Mr. Odorizzi came to the farm to see the horse. He was sad and horrified by Maud's injuries. Mr. Odorizzi immediately fired the driver. He monitored the horse's recovery and paid for her expenses.

"Maud recovered without infection or complication. She did, however, have a massive scar across her entire hip."

## *Thelma's Stories*

My earliest memories are of the way Dad smelled, the musky mix of his body odour and chewing tobacco as he rocked June, Archie and me in the rocking chair.

### Pneumonia

"The winter that I was six our dad had to come home from the logging camp because he had pneumonia. In the days before penicillin, pneumonia was a serious illness. He had to stay in bed.

"Each day when I returned home from school I would carry up my little red chair from our children's table and chair set to his room. I'd sit and read him stories from the first-grade primer. Mercifully, that was before the days of those insipid stories of Dick and Jane! He always appeared interested in the stories. It was companionable but strangely there was no conversation between us.

"I don't ever remember our dad asking us how our day went the way present-day parents do. He would direct us to do certain chores and certainly he would caution us about matters of safety. I never knew him to demonstrate affection either. Perhaps that was the way that fathers were expected to behave in those days.

### A Summer Storm

"Raspberries were our dad's favourite fruit. When raspberries were available Mom would bake shortcake. She'd slit the cake horizontally, lightly crush the berries with sugar and spread them on the first layer, heap berries over the second layer and serve with fresh cream.

"In raspberry season after the noon dishes were cleared away, I'd often take a berry can and go foraging for berries. One day when I was about twelve years old, storm clouds gathered so I left off picking and headed for home. The sky opened up just as I started across the field about a quarter of a mile from home.

"The rain coming down in torrents soon turned the field into a quagmire. I was sinking to my knees with every step and I was quickly tiring; as the lightning sizzled overhead. From the barn Dad saw my plight. He came across the field, grasped me under the arm and together we struggled our way to safety through the mud."

**Runaway Horses!**

"In the fall of 1952, before I left to find work in Toronto I helped our dad harvest the potatoes and other root vegetables. With the team of horses he'd plow the furrows to uncover the potatoes as I walked behind collecting them. That summer he'd suffered a ruptured appendix and the ploughing seemed almost too much for him. Archie was still in high school at that time.

"The following summer when I was nineteen, I left a very good job in Toronto to return home to help with the farm work as I was worried about our dad. He was seventy-one years old by then. Together Archie and I mowed and coiled the hay, making it ready to be pitched onto the hay wagon and stored in the barn for winter. Lloyd and Rea took their holidays and came home to help with the haying too.

"One day Dad hitched the horses to the hay wagon and took the steep lane down the hill, intending to cross over the highway to the field on the other side. On the hill he lost control of the horses as the wagon rolled forward against their heels. The horses bolted, tearing down the hill and across the road at great speed.

The noise caught my attention and I watched helplessly from the window as I saw the front wagon wheels hit the far bank of the creek. The back of the wagon bucked into the air, pitching him directly over the wagon and onto his head. As in slow motion I saw his head hit the ground and his body fold over to one side. The pitchfork also flew into the air and came down inches from his chest.

"I yelled to my brothers. They ran down the hill and carried our unconscious father home. They drove him to the North Bay hospital about 50 miles away where he laid for two weeks with his head and neck sandbagged in one position.

"Rea and Lloyd had to return to their jobs but our neighbour Frank Pilger came and helped Archie and me to complete the harvest.

"When Dad returned home, he was no longer able to turn his head without turning his entire body. The accident marked the beginning of his decline into dementia.

"In 1967 Mom had a stroke and required long-term care at Eastholme in Powassan. Our dad refused to live with another family member or to stay in care with his wife. He was obstinate and delusional. Though Dad attempted to care for himself, he was eventually admitted to Nippissing Manor, the refurbished former home built in 1934 to house the Dionne Quintuplets.

"On December 1, 1969 Rea collected both our mother and father from Eastholme and Nippissing Manor respectively and took them to their own home in Commanda to celebrate their 55th wedding anniversary together. Mom managed to bake a cake in her own oven for the occasion. The next day, December 2, 1969, Dad at the age of eighty-seven, collapsed and died.

Mom died June 10, 1971. Jim and Annie Peever are buried beside their little daughter Luella Mabel in Commanda Cemetery."

# ~Memories of Edna~

Edna dared to be unconventional. Who else would be seen standing at her open window with a sling shot, shooting pebbles at squirrels who invaded her several birdfeeders? In winter her feeders, each stocked with specialized seed, attracted colourful birds like rose- breasted pine grosbeaks and giant palliated woodpeckers. In summer, families of humming birds enjoyed her feeders filled with nectar and her fragrant garden of flowers.

Edna preferred to be outdoors enjoying nature to worrying about dust collecting on furniture indoors. She'd had enough of housework while helping to raise her younger siblings. When the weather drove her indoors she preferred to read and she was knowledgeable on a wide variety of topics.

Edna enlisted in the Air force at eighteen. The tall willowy blonde who loved to sing *Somewhere over the Rainbow* and the latest Frank Sinatra tunes had successfully rebuffed all suitors. Edna would get to fly "over the rainbow" of her dreams at the Fingal, Ontario, Royal Canadian Bombing and Gunnery School. Fingal was the training centre for Canadian and Allied airmen. As a "parachute rigger" she would sometimes accompany trainees on flights as they took their jumps. She would participate with the investigating team when a parachute failed to open, causing a fatality. Her five-foot-ten stature earned her the nickname Big Ed.

Air Force life opened up the wide world for her and finally the companionship and social life she craved. It was, however, in coming home on leave that she met her future husband, airman navigator Leslie Bain of Loring, as they got off the train together at the Trout Creek station.

After the war they married and eventually settled in Port Loring with their little daughter Arlene. Edna became a widow at the age of 38 when Les was killed in a tragic accident in the winter of 1963. Their daughter Arlene was sixteen when she lost her father.

Edna picked up the pieces of her life; and the following September Edna entered high school in Loring. She started in grade nine, sitting in class with fourteen year olds. She was an adult student before Adult Education was thought of. When Edna had sufficient credits she enrolled at George Brown College in Toronto the very first year that it opened.

Edna became a Child Care Worker. She found work at Hagersville in the first treatment centre in Ontario to pioneer work with emotionally troubled teens.

In retirement Edna returned to her home area and built her house in Powassan.

Edna could indulge her love of learning and, as a Master Gardener; she could share her knowledge with others through the horticultural society. It was in Powassan that she met Alex Holtforster. After twenty years of widowhood, Edna married a man who shared her passion for growing things, her passion for learning and her passion for spiritual things. Together they studied, discussed and argued points of view. Together they served their church and community.

Alex died October 2003. Edna died October 2004.

# ~What Became of Commanda Area Churches and Schools~

Churches were erected to serve the spiritual needs of the influx of settlers to the Commanda area in the 1800s. Churches, as they still do today, also served people's social needs. Commanda had three churches: St. John's Alsace, Roman Catholic: first built in 1878, Presbyterian: built in 1883 and Methodist: built in 1896.

**Saint John's, Alsace Church**

Saint John's, Alsace church could be accessed by turning north off the trunk road, now Highway 522, onto the Alsace Road at the east end of Commanda village just beyond Lewis and Florence Evers (nee Grabouski)'s convenience-style store and gas pumps. The Alsace Road, twisted and turned over steep hills and valleys north-east toward Powassan. It ran parallel, but north of the old Barrett Road. From the north end, Alsace Road connected to the present day 534 Highway by a tote road running south from the settlement of Christian Valley. The church ministered to faithful parishioners in the triangle between the two main trunk roads.

The church served a mix of settlers of German and Prussian, Polish, Italian and Irish ancestry, people with names like Straus, Hummel, Holtforster, Reichstein, Haverlock, Grabouski, Odrowski, Gael and Kelly. They struggled to morning mass through snow-clogged roads in winter, muddy bogs in spring and fall, all on empty stomachs. The Latin liturgy was common to all.

Philip and his wife Mariann Beaupre Straus moved from the German settlement of County Waterloo to Alsace in 1878, after having lost two children, age eight years and another age three months, to typhoid fever. They also lost a third child to an unknown cause. Soon after arriving in Alsace, they lost a baby son, Pius Straus, at age two and one-half years. He was one of the earliest recorded deaths in Commanda. The Church and the solace of their faith sustained them. Death and heartbreak dogged the couple, as ten years later, in 1888-89, Philip and Mariann lost six more children to the diphtheria epidemic that swept through the area. Philip, himself succumbed to the disease on January, 13, 1889.

Philip was the grandfather of Alsace Church historian Gladys (Weiler) Piper. At age ninety, her uncle Francis Straus still lives to tell of those tragic early times.

The original St John's Church, built in 1878, was surrounded by Saint John's Cemetery. But when the old church was dismantled in 1935, parishioners installed a plaque to mark the historic site. The old church stood across the road from the present church, which was erected in 1909.

In that early struggling community, a church hall that was near the site of the existing church, served the social needs of the settlement. Along with most of the settlers, the hall is long gone.

Presently, St John's church is open only during the summer, serving descendents of early settlers and summer residents. In winter, if the roads are clear of snow, local area residents make a nostalgic return to celebrate Christmas Eve mass in the beautiful church of their childhood. During the year residents attend St. Joseph's Church, Powassan.

One March school morning in the mid-1940s, full of the excitement and the energy of early spring, the younger Peever kids kept walking. They didn't stop at the public school, but kept on walking until they turned up Alsace Road, on their way to meet schoolmates Norma and Eugene Reichstein. There in front of St. John's church, they met Norma and Eugene.

"Look!" exclaimed Norma, pointing, "That's Annie Spetz." A slight woman clad in black, her head wrapped in a black headscarf, slipped from the church and disappeared into the dark, still-naked stand of trees.

"Who's Annie Spetz?" asked June.

"She's a saint," answered Norma reverently. "When she dies, she'll go straight to heaven! Annie goes to mass every morning. And, she has even been to Rome and had an audience with the Pope!"

Wow! Rome! I thought. How could someone afford to travel so far away?

Annie travelled far away indeed. She trained as a nurse in Toronto and nursed in the Crimean War. Immigration records also show that during the First World War, in March, 1918, at age forty-four, she crossed into the USA and nursed there.

Annie's parents, Joseph and Mary (Cluthe) Spetz were both children of German immigrants who settled in Berlin (now Kitchener), Waterloo County. Joseph and Mary married in 1871 in Berlin and travelled to Alsace in 1878 when Annie was four years old. Annie was the eldest of four siblings. Annie's brother Wilhelm also was a person of note. He established himself in Powassan and served as an optician and a watchmaker, a Notary Public and Justice of the Peace. Wilhelm, like his sister, never married.

When Annie retired from nursing, she returned to Alsace and to her home in the woods near St. John's Church. She lived alone, without running water or electricity, until just a year before her death.

Lisa Fry remembers Annie skiing through the woods to visit Lisa's parents, Otto and Heddy Schermer of Commanda. Lisa recalls, "Annie had the longest skis that I have ever seen!"

Annie was born January, 22, 1874 and died 1974. Through her nursing skills she served God in healing suffering humanity, both far away and near to home. Even while in Rome she remembered the children of Alsace Separate School. Annie brought each of them a blessed religious medal. Annie is buried with her parents in Mount Hope Cemetery, Kitchener, Ontario. After her death, Annie's late sister Matilda's family, living in New York State, sold Annie's home to out-of area people for a hunting camp.

## S.S. # 2 Alsace Separate School

A new school was to be built to replace the old log Gerber School, built in the early 1800s. In 1907 the Alsace Separate School came about due to a disagreement about where a new school should be built to serve children in the Barrett Road-Alsace area. As a result of the disagreement, Roman Catholic parents voted to build a separate school on the Alsace Road to serve Catholic children from the Barrett Road-Alsace Road catchment area. Consequently, the Gerber School closed that year.

Alsace Separate school, located on the west side of St. John's Church (toward Commanda), opened with an enrolment of fifty children. Historian Gladys Piper states that teachers boarded nearby at the home of Anthony Grabowski or with the Schemelefske household.

Over time, settlers' descendants drifted away from the area. The school closed in 1956 with an enrolment of only seven pupils. The remaining students, Peters and Haverlock children transferred to Commanda Public School. The former Alsace Separate School is now a summer residence.

## Trinity Lutheran Church

Built in 1883, Trinity Lutheran was originally the Presbyterian Church building. The Presbyterian Church was situated on the Nippissing Road just a short distance south of its present site. German speaking Lutherans rented the Presbyterian Church for their services.

Trinity Lutheran Church historian, Lisa Fry (nee Schermer) recalls that the Lutheran minister, who serviced the whole Lutheran circuit, had to travel the early Colonization Roads, one of which was called the Great North Road. That optimistic-sounding road was, in fact, a bumpy one-lane wagon road leading north from Parry Sound north through Dunchurch. The minister's journey began at Magnetawan. The road north from there joined up with the Great North Road. As he continued north, the pastor ministered in homes along the way. Branching off the North

Road near Loring, he took a trail running through an area called Hardscrabble. It was aptly named as such because the land was so poor and stony that those unfortunate settlers barely eked out an existence and when the Canadian west opened for settlement, most from that area abandoned the unwelcoming soil, gathered their meagre belongings and went west.

The pastor wound his way on those rudimentary roads to his Loring area Mills Township flock south to forty-nine members at Arnstein, including the Ziehm family - whose name was eventually anglicised to Simms. From Arnstein, the minister took the North Road again, curving around to behind Golden Valley. From Golden Valley, he took the Nine Mile Bush tote road, exiting at Commanda Cemetery, where he turned right onto the trunk road leading to his Commanda pastorate.

Leaving Commanda, the Lutheran minister connected with the Nipisssing Road south, up steep Carr's Hill and on past Tom Booth's to the Rye church. Finishing his circuit, he continued heading south on the Nippissing Road back to Magnetawan. It should be noted that the south end of Nippissing Road was called the Rousseau Road because it ended at Lake Rousseau.

It took the minister one month to cover his circuit of parishioners. Each church, therefore, had a monthly service. To be constantly travelling the rudimentary roads and connecting tote roads of the era, the minister had to be a hardy, dedicated individual.

Church historian, Lisa Fry states that church records in Commanda show the Lutheran pastor held services in people's homes from 1880 to 1883 but when the Presbyterian Church was built in 1883, Lutherans rented the church for their services.

In 1925, due to the merger of Presbyterian, Methodist and Congregational denominations into The United Church of Canada, the Lutherans in Commanda purchased the vacant Presbyterian Church. In 1926, they moved the church north from the brow of Carr's Hill, less than quarter of a mile, to where it is still situated on the south of junction of the Old Nippissing Road and Highway 522, closer to Commanda General Store - now the Commanda Museum.

The first trustees of the newly named Trinity Lutheran Church were Oscar Haufe, Thomas Booth and William Hoffman. The minister in 1925 was Pastor Gans and there were fifty-one church members. Family names of other church members were Evers, Hanselman, Gherke, Pietschmann (later changed to Peachmann), Richert, Ricker, Rausche, Thiel, Grimm, Baumann, and Coch (later changed to Cook), Fry, Meschewski, Schweitzer and Gerber.

Today, descendents of some of those original members still live in the area and attend the church. Eileen Eckensviller (nee Booth) and now, her grown children serve as church custodians. The church also renews itself when new people move into the area, although theirs is still a circuit charge serving those of the Lutheran faith tradition in the area.

Trinity Lutheran celebrated its one hundred and twenty-fifth anniversary in 2008. On Sunday February 26, 2006, the congregation was inspired to present Lisa Fry with a plaque in recognition of her sixty-nine years as organist. Since 1936 Lisa Fry nee Schermer has been the organist. Lisa, at age eighty-seven, admits, "I felt really nervous, when at ten years old, I started playing the hymns by ear."

Lisa Fry continues to play the organ for the services. She has played the organ at Trinity Lutheran Church for seventy-seven years. Lisa is about to be inducted into the North Bay Hall of Fame for her services.

## Commanda United Church

The little white frame church at the junction of the Old Nippissing Road and the trunk road –now Highway 522 – was established in 1896 as Commanda Methodist Church. In 1925 it became the United Church. The church became a member of the United Church's Nippissing Pastoral Charge, encompassing the villages of Nippissing, Restoule, Commanda and Carr. Services were held in Carr School until the early 1960s when Carr United Church was built. It closed in 1986.

The Commanda United Church had seating for seventy people. Throughout its lifetime, the church was heated by an iron box-stove and lit by hanging oil lamps. A weathered horse shed - an open-sided structure attached along the south side of the church, provided shelter for about a dozen teams of horses. It was torn down when the church was temporarily adapted, in January 1944, to serve as the school when the public school burned down in October 1943.

The United Church minister's manse was in Nippissing and his circuit brought him to Commanda on alternate weeks. Some years, services were held on Sunday afternoon, other years, services took place on a Friday night.

Organists in the 1940s to 1950s were Gladys Schwarze (nee Watt) wife of Ben Schwarze, Mrs Andy Booth and Mr. Charlie Hoffman.

Ministers who served the Nippissing circuit numbered twelve in all, from 1925 to 1962, when the church closed its doors. Most of the ministers stayed in their post for three years or less. In winter, travelling over snowy, often unplowed roads on the circuit would not have been a joy, especially at night. Since few people ever attended Commanda Church on a winter's night, ministers held a service in the Peever's home.

One winter day in 1944, Rev. H. E. Beare arrived late afternoon at the Peever's. He appeared to be feeling tired, so our mother Annie invited him to rest on the couch in a quiet corner. He was in for a rude awakening.

About 5 o'clock, when I, a ten-year-old arrived home from school to the darkened room. I dropped my books on the table and plopped myself down on the couch – right onto the mid-section of the sleeping Reverend! With a startled whoof, his head and feet came up in the air simultaneously. Mortified and speechless, I backed away, while Mom, feeling embarrassed, apologized for her daughter's misstep.

Rev. Beare served during the height of the war years when most families were worried about their sons fighting overseas, or for their own relatives still living in Europe, being bombed amid the conflict.

While Lisa Schermer was the school teacher she invited the minister, when he made his rounds, to provide an hour of religious education to the students. The students appreciated the gospel stories presented by the warm and kindly Rev. Beare.

The next minister to arrive was Reverend John Crook. He and his wife had been missionaries with the China Inland Mission. They had to flee and return to Canada when Japan invaded China. The couple were not young, but they had a baby boy. The strong and intrepid-appearing Mrs. Crook and her baby often accompanied her husband on his ministerial rounds. Mr Crook served from 1945 to 1947. His sermons were lively and interesting and attracted more people to the church, especially when he spiced his sermons with a "Magic Lantern" show of life in China.

Before the era of local movie houses, years before the era of television, Mr. Crook's slides and stories of the Chinese people opened up a mysterious outside world and culture to the people of Commanda. When, during religious education period, he showed his Magic Lantern pictures to the children at Commanda Public School they were entranced, but also educated about a broader world. He taught the children how to sing Yes Jesus Loves Me in Chinese.

Mr. Crook was still the minister when our sister Edna married Leslie Bain, her wartime sweetheart, on Christmas Eve 1946.

In preparation, early that day, Mervyn lit the box stove in the centre of the sanctuary. Edna and her younger siblings decorated the church in ribbons and bows and set up a festive tree for the occasion. Tall candles stood ready to be lighted for the evening service.

The ceremony began; the organ played and Edna's sister-in-law-to-be, Mrs. Ruth Bain sang beautifully as the bridal party stood at the altar but alas, the crowded church became too warm. A helpful brother opened the church door; in trotted a mangy dog, sniffing around the feet of the bridal couple.

Jim Peever, standing ready to give away the bride, tried surreptitiously, to kick the dog away, forgetting that the congregation behind him had a full view of his footwork. When his duty was done, Jim turned and escorted the dog outside. Many had to suppress nervous titters.

The wedding ceremony proceeded and a festive Christmas Eve reception awaited everyone at the Commanda Hall.

Reverend P. Donald Cameron served after Mr. Crook moved on. Mr. Cameron was partial to using large and obscure words in his sermons. He frequently urged his congregation to practice "self-abnegation."

Due to improved roads, the Commanda United Church enjoyed services every Sunday afternoon. On a sultry summer Sunday afternoon, as the minister's voice seemed to drone on about one of St. Paul's Epistles, bored children couldn't help observing half-dead flies buzzing at the window panes, and they envied the birds singing and flitting among the cool, shady trees outside the windows.

In September of 1952, Reverend Cameron was still the minister when our third sister, June Peever married Robert Newby of Toronto, in the Commanda United Church. The couple held their wedding dance in Port Loring Community Hall, where all her friends and their parents from high school days could attend. Friends and acquaintances from all along the school bus route from Commanda to Golden Valley, Arnstein and Loring attended. In the evening, as was the custom, the bride's family served food and refreshments to all who attended.

From about 1930 until 1952, our mother Annie Peever served as secretary-treasurer for Commanda United Church. In the early years, the younger children accompanied her when she visited members and adherents for the annual Every Member Canvas to raise offerings.

Records, provided by the archivist at the Head Office of the United Church of Canada, show that the last board meeting of Commanda United Church was held in 1962.

Our brother, Lloyd Peever was still living with his family on the Peever farm in 1963, when his young children spotted the curious sight of the church riding on the flatbed of a truck. It bobbed along Highway 522, past their house, en route to Farley's Corners then it turned onto Highway 524, on its way to Restoule.

Jerry Hamilton of Restoule purchased the church, and after adding another story and renovating it, he settled into his deconsecrated home.

### The Corner Gospel Church

In 1953 the Corner Gospel Church was erected at the junctions of Highways 524 and 534, Commanda Lake Road and Pilger Road. The church was built on land donated by Everett Preston of Carr – now amalgamated into the village of Restoule.

I was the first bride in the new church. The first minister, Reverend Victor Hillis preformed the ceremony of my marriage to Arthur James on August 2, 1954. Later that same year, Reverend Hillis resigned.

Reverend Harold Bradley and his wife, our sister Lillian, accepted the call to the fledgling church. Harold immediately set about, with the help of the men of the church, to attach a manse to the back of the church, both for convenience and economy of heating.

Lillian provided meals for the workmen while tending their two toddlers, three-year-old Carol and one-year-old Jimmy. That winter, she was about six months pregnant with a third child, when suddenly, Lillian began feeling unwell. She took the children and went to our mother's in Commanda. But she began to hemorrhage. Lillian remained on bed rest in the Peever home until she was stable, while our mother Annie cared for the children.

About a month later, in early March 1955, Lillian went into early labour. Harold drove her to the Red Cross outpost in Port Loring. There, in the midst of an electrical blackout, she delivered a tiny baby girl. Its three pound little body was blue and unresponsive. Minutes later, the electricity came back on and another tiny baby girl was born; this time pink and responsive, weighing four pounds.

Harold built a small casket for his stillborn infant daughter. A small, sad group of men, Rev. Harold Bradley, Jim Peever, youngest brother Archie, with the minister from Arnstein officiating, gathered at the Commanda Cemetery. Archie and Dad dug a little grave in the Peever plot and Harold laid her gently beside the grave of our little sister Luella Mabel. The Arnstein minister gave the message of committal.

As soon as Lillian and her "preemie" baby Janet were strong enough, they returned home to the manse. Lillian's early Missionary Medical School training, and her good sense, stood her in good stead. In a corner of the bedroom, she crafted a special nursery for her premature baby. Lillian set up a heat lamp over the tiny bassinette to maintain a constant warm temperature and to ward off the chill of March. She prayed for the life of her baby and she wore a mask while feeding and tending her.

Nobody else was allowed into the room. Women of the church brought food and casseroles for the family and peeped through a small crack at the bedroom door to view the tiny babe. Baby Janet grew strong and thrived as did the congregation.

Several years later, when the church was well established and building projects completed, Reverend Harold and Lillian Bradley moved on to other mission projects.

But twenty years later, in April, 1975, Janet Bradley, by this time, herself a nurse, married Peter Fathers of Toronto, in the larger Carr United Church. The Carr women catered her reception in their church basement reception room.

Fifty years after the first Corner Gospel Church was built, a larger, modern church was erected on a piece of farmland, once owned by Manson Kidd. A summer resident, an architect, living along the shores of Commanda Lake, learned of plans to build a new church. He designed it at no cost. Rev. Bryan Warner, the son of a builder, skilfully oversaw the construction of the graceful church. The church stands across the road from the original, on the north side of Highway 524. The new church accommodates members from the entire Nippissing Township. People are attracted by the lively music and by activities for all ages.

On September 2003, a community-wide celebration marked the Corner Gospel Church's fiftieth anniversary. In their memory, marking the fiftieth anniversary of the church, the children of James and Annie Peever donated a five-octave set of English hand bells. Their parents' names are engraved inside each handle. The bells ring out the message of God's love and the bells mark the area where the Peevers once worshipped; toiled and tilled the land.

An interdenominational choral group, calling themselves The Four Corners Gospel Singers meets at the church. The group performs for social events and for churches in the area.

While the Corner Gospel Church is a central place of worship in the community, the social hub in Commanda remains the Commanda Hall. The hall is now used as a community centre for arts and exercise groups, and always, for lively community dances.

## The Commanda Public School S.S. #1 Gurd and Pringle

A log school already existed in Commanda when the family of William F. Peever arrived in the spring of 1889. Situated close to Dell Watt's farm on the Nippissing Road, a mile north of the thriving village of Commanda, it meant a two-mile trudge for the Peever children along the rutted wagon road to the village of Commanda, and then a trek, one further mile north on the Nippissing Road.

Jim Peever didn't make that hike. He had a grade three education before leaving the Ottawa Valley and happily deemed himself old enough to help clear the land on the family's new homestead. Jim read well and could quickly calculate numbers in his head. As an adult, he'd look at a log and rapidly calculate the board feet of lumber that it would produce. But his younger siblings Frances (Fanny), Robert (Bob), Isabelle and Susan did attend the log school, built circa late 1870s.

The old log schoolhouse was still standing in the spring of 1945, when teacher Lisa Schermer, who always strove to bring her lessons alive, organized a historical trip to the original log school. She'd sent home a note to parents, requesting that their children should come on a Saturday morning, dressed in hairstyle and clothing of that early pioneer era.

Mervyn and June Peever were allowed to take the morning off from Saturday chores, dressed up in period clothing to attend the excursion. Our mother Annie reasoned that they would soon be graduating from public school and thus it was their last chance for an outing with their classmates. Youngest children, Archie and I were disappointed to be kept at home helping with farm chores. We never got to visit the old log school.

A new one-room Commanda School was built on the Nippissing Road in 1900. It sat at the top of the "Round Hill", a short distance north of the Commanda Store. In winter, the Round Hill was a delight to sleigh-ride down. On the south side, the hill fell away toward the United Church and Commanda Store. On the north side, students could zoom down a steep curve to the stone bridge at the bottom.

Down in the valley, Dell Watt's farm was on the right side of the Nippissing Road. His children Ivan and Mona Watt attended the school.

The farm on the left was Herman Gehrke's. His sons Albert, Arnold and Wallace also attended new school. From the bridge, the road northeast climbed steeply again to the Ricker, Culham and Silas farms whose children all attended the school.

The south-facing white frame school had four steep, wide steps up to the door.

The sunny front steps were a great place for the littlest ones to congregate in the morning before school, or to play on when they finished their seat work, before the rowdy older children were dismissed at noon.

In the school, the desks were arranged row by row, from grades one up to grades nine and ten. Fewer children attended those higher grades. One row was sufficient for those two higher grades. Student population ranged from thirty to forty.

The teacher went row by row assigning seatwork for each subject, then calling each grade to the front of the room to review assigned work and to teach new material from the blackboard. Each child had a turn at reading aloud from the standard Ontario Reader. Children learned early to work independently. It was a serious offence to disrupt the classroom by talking.

The frame brick-red woodshed faced the school's entrance, though far enough back to drive a team of horses with a wagon load of firewood to the shed. In the fall there was always a supply of large sticks of wood to feed into the heat-shield-encased box-stove for the school year. In the large woodshed there was still space for several dog teams to be bedded down awaiting the trip home.

Two Shetland ponies belonging to classmates Evelyn and Don Booth were also stabled in the woodshed. The sure-footed ponies were ideal for carrying the children three miles north, down the long steep Carr's Hill to Commanda school, and back up at the end of the day to their farm on a flat mesa-like piece of land at the top.

In a corner of the yard behind the school, a hand operated water pump supplied sweet, ice-cold water. A spacious schoolyard and playing field lay to the east of the school. In the early 1940s, each school was populous enough to field a baseball team. Rivalry ran high. The Commanda school ball team took on teams from Carr, Restoule and Trout

Creek schools. Ball teams were usually transported by a parent, who volunteered to load the players into the high-boxed back of his farm truck. Nobody thought of liability insurance in those days.

The beautiful white Commanda School burned to the ground in the fall of 1943. School reconvened in the United Church for a semester, in January 1944. But by September 1944, the community had a new, more modern one-room school. As families grew smaller and people left the area to find work in cities, local one-room schools closed.

Lloyd and Eunice Peever's two oldest, Alex and Cathy, attended Commanda Public School until 1962 when the family left Commanda and farm life.

Commanda School closed in 1969 and students were bussed to Trout Creek. The era of local one-room schools came to an end.

The school on the hill became a residence. Jim Peever's granddaughter Janet Bradley Fathers and her husband Peter purchased the converted school from its original owner. They enlarged and renovated their home on the hill, and lived there for nearly twenty years. During that time, Janet commuted from her home to the North Bay General Hospital where she served as Emergency Department head nurse. Peter taught in the consolidated Port Loring and Nippissing School systems.

# ~What Became of the Horses~

Jim Peever acquired his first team of horses in the spring of 1915, a few months after Jim and Annie married in December 1914 and settled on the farm across from his parent's homestead. Doc and his teammate were Jim Peever's first horses. A few years later Doc's teammate died.

Doc, a large black horse, was of exceptional intelligence but full of mischief. His antics made Jim laugh but could sorely try his patience. Jim soon found a mate to balance Doc's quixotic nature.

Duke, a black Percheron with a majestic silver mane and tail became Doc's steadying influence and lifelong teammate. They shared a stall and manger in the stable, and in the bush, laboured together skidding and hauling heavy sleigh-loads of logs. In summer they pulled a plow and other farm equipment.

On a Saturday night Jim liked to entertain visitors with stories of Doc's tricks. He related an incident from the 1930s this way: "One winter Sunday our team and sleigh caught up with Bill Hoffman and his family on their way to Sunday service at the Commanda Lutheran Church." He interjected, "You remember, in those days, Bill Hoffman had a farm down past Schermer's farm on Schermer's Road."

The visitor, nodding assent, Jim continued, "Our team caught up with Bill's sleigh, but the road was too narrow to pass and Doc wasn't willing to let another team be in the lead. He stretched his neck forward and, with his teeth, lifted the tailgate out of the sleigh in front of him and dropped it on the road. Doc then proceeded to climb into the back of the sleigh – to the alarm of the Hoffman family. 'Whoa! Whoa,' I yelled, sawing on the reigns. I stopped our team and replaced Hoffman's tailgate and apologized for their fright. When the road widened enough, Bill Hoffman was relieved to pull over and let my crazy horse and sleigh pass," Jim chuckled, gratified that his friend was enjoying his story.

Another of Jim's stories about Doc went like this: "The following summer, I decided to get some fresh meat for the family. I rode Doc bareback up the Nine Mile Bush Road to a marsh beyond Yerke's farm. At the edge of the marsh, I tied Doc to a tree and then I walked along a big pine log further into the marsh to reach a small tree that seemed like the ideal spot for a look-out. With a rifle in the crook of my arm, I climbed the tree and waited for a deer to wander into the marsh to feed. The next thing I see is Doc walking along the same pine log into the marsh – he'd managed to use his teeth to untie his tether.

"'Get back! Get back!' I hissed at him but Doc kept on coming. He reached my tree, grasped the trunk in his teeth and shook it. I had to climb down and give up the idea of getting a deer that day!"

Jim laughed, enjoying his audience and his own storytelling as he launched into another tale, "Doc was a very intelligent horse. He was always careful about crossing bridges. Doc would stop at a bridge, test the planks for stability with a front foot before proceeding across but one night, on the way home from Commanda Doc refused to cross the white bridge over Commanda Creek. He pounded the planks with his foot but wouldn't budge. Finally, I got out of the sleigh to investigate. There sprawled across the bridge lay a man who'd had too much to drink, likely at Evers' Hotel in Commanda. He would have frozen to death if we hadn't come along and we would have run over him with the sleigh if Doc hadn't stopped and refused to cross the bridge. Either way, the guy would have been dead. I heaved him into the back of the sleigh and took him home to his family. Whether they were happy to see him was not my concern," Jim chuckled.

Eighty years later Jim's son Lloyd, reminiscing day about the horses with his younger siblings one day, told another story about Doc and his antics: "I was five or six years old and it was around my birthday in March when our dad took me along with our older brothers Rea, Carl, Preston and Gerald, on an ice-fishing excursion to Commanda Lake in Restoule.

"Dad loaded hay and oats into the sleigh for the horses and he added a tea pail, a lunch bag full of pork sandwiches, spread with hot mustard, and more sandwiches made with carrot marmalade. When we arrived at the shoreline of Commanda Lake, 'The Old Man' unhitched Duke and

Doc from the sleigh and tied them to nearby trees and he put down feed for them. We went about 500 yards out onto the ice and set up our ice-fishing camp. At noon, we went back to the sleigh to get our lunch, only to find that Doc had untied his tether. We found he'd gotten into our lunch bag too. Doc had sampled our pork and mustard sandwiches, but, fortunately, he didn't like the mustard. The sandwiches were covered with horse-slobber but we were hungry, so we ate them anyway," laughed Lloyd.

Lloyd continued his story about the horses, "In 1939, when Carl decided to enlist in the army, he brought us those three yearling horses, Dan, Prince and Maud. He knew that our team of Duke and Doc was getting old. Carl wanted to be sure that the family would be provided for while he was away at war.

"Dad used Doc to teach each of the young horses how to follow commands. He'd hitch Doc up with young Dan and work them together until Dan learned how to follow commands and pull farm machinery. Later, he'd hitch Prince up with Doc and repeat the process. Dad didn't train Maud to the harness yet. He still kept her as a pet.

"Doc was getting old though, so when Dad had trained the two young horses, he put Doc out to pasture and teamed the young ones up with Duke. But by the early spring of 1943, it was clear that Doc was too old and feeble to go on. 'The Old Man' couldn't bear to put him down. He handed me the 30-30 rifle asked me to do the job. The trees weren't leafed out yet when I took Doc up into the maple bush behind the barn and shot him. I left his body for the wild animals to feed on.

"I was sixteen at the time," Lloyd remembered sadly.

Youngest brother Archie broke in, "I remember when that happened. I was about eight years old. Mervyn and I were at the well getting pails of water for Mom when we saw the horse fall, even before we heard the rifle shot. That's when I learned about the speed of sound. Though we knew that it was necessary, we all felt like a member of the family had died. "

Archie added, "At the battlefront in Holland, Rea read in his letter from home that Doc was gone. Rea wrote back, 'I used get so mad at Doc sometimes when I was driving the horse that I'd threaten to kill him.

But I shed a tear when I read that Doc had been put down.'"

Lloyd continued, "Duke grieved for his teammate Doc. He gave up the will to live. He'd throw himself against the side of his stall until he was all beaten up. Duke wouldn't eat and he became just skin and bones.

"It happened in the summer that Maud was injured by the lumber truck driver. When Maud was able to leave her stall and walk again, Dad and I built a barbed wire fence enclosure in the farmyard over at the old Peever homestead. We electrified it, using batteries for power. We put Maud in there to recover from the terrible injury to her hip and we put Duke in the enclosure with her for company.

"Maud used to play tricks on Duke. She'd bump Duke up against the electric fence just to see him jump and squeal from the electric shock," Lloyd laughed. Sobering, he said, "by fall, there was no hope for Duke. I had to put him down too. Duke and Doc were The Old Man's companions. He couldn't do it," Lloyd concluded, heaving a big sigh at the memory. His siblings nodded, remembering their sadness when it happened.

June interrupted to bring in a happier memory, "Do you remember when we were kids and we'd play in the barn on rainy days? The horses didn't have to work then either, so sometimes we'd go into the feed alley in the stable where we could safely reach across their manger to pat the horses' faces and rub their ears?

"One day I brought Dan a handful of oats. I didn't know enough to feed him from the palm of my hand. I held out the fistful of oats and he took my whole hand in his mouth. It scared me. I could feel his teeth! I pulled my hand back quickly," June recounted her eyes still wide with the memory of her scare.

I replied, "You were lucky! Dan was notorious for biting. The other two horses, Prince and Maud liked to be petted, but Dan would take only so much and then he'd nip your hand."

I added, "Maud was a brat. When we'd lead her out to the creek for water, you'd have to watch out for her. She liked to step on our feet. Fortunately, the ground was muddy and soft around the creek and the foot she stepped on sank down into the mud, instead of being crushed. I'd yell at her and pound on her ribs but she wouldn't budge, until finally,

I'd get my shoulder under her belly and heave her off balance."

Archie nodded, and broke into his story of Maud, "After all of you had left the farm, I was pretty much looking after the farm for Mom and Dad. As usual in the winter, one day after I got off the high school bus, I went and let the horses out for a run and a drink from the creek while I drove the cows into the stable and fed them. When I was done feeding the cattle, I called the horses in to feed them too. Dan and Prince came but Maud didn't. I thought to myself, well you can just stay out until after supper!

"After supper, it was dark of course when I left the house to go and milk the cows but as soon as the door slammed, Maud whinnied – a sound of distress. I followed the sound down to the creek. There she was with her foot wedged between two large stones! She whickered out a welcome when I got to her. Maud was sure glad to see me but I had a struggle to get her foot unwedged. That was one time when she had to suffer because of her bratty reputation!" Archie exclaimed with a smile.

Lloyd added, laughing, "Dan and Maud were bigger than Prince and they bossed him around too when they were in the pasture together."

Archie interjected, "Dan was the horse that used to try my patience! He was big and strong, but slow and oh so lazy. He was smart enough though, that when Dad picked up the lines and barked a command, Dan danced into position, head up and alert, on his best behaviour. Dan had stamina too. Mervyn used to work Prince and Maud on alternate days with Dan. During seeding time and harvest, Sunday was the only day that Dan had off. Archie added, "Before Mervyn went west he took over the heavy farm work from Dad, as he was getting older too.

Archie again picked up the story of Dan, "One fall; a few years after Mervyn went away, another farmer came looking for a horse to buy. Dad decided that we didn't need all three horses. He agreed to part with Dan. The trouble was that Dan had a crooked hoof on one back foot. It was like an ingrown toenail that got inflamed from time to time. But, Dad thought that as long as Dan was shod, he'd be okay. Dad was to regret that decision. The man came back in the spring to say that Dan didn't last the winter. Poor old Dan! He didn't get the care that we gave him and without his lifelong teammates, I guess that he just gave up," Archie said with regret.

Changing the subject, Archie exclaimed, "Prince was my favourite horse! He was a lovely chestnut and he had a white star in his forehead. Prince was smaller, but intelligent, quick and agile. He had the build of a quarter-horse and was perfect to ride. After Howard grew up and left the farm, the job of rounding up the cows for milking, fell to me. As you remember, in the heat of the summer, the creek in the pasture always dried up. We herded the cattle up the logging road toward Mud Lake, where they'd find water at the lake's outlet stream."

Archie confided, "I was always afraid of getting lost in the bush. I got lost in the bush once when I was about twelve years old and afterward, I was afraid in unknown terrain. But when I rode Prince to hunt the cattle from wherever they'd wandered, I felt confident that if I didn't know the way home, I could just give Prince "his head" and he'd drive the cattle home.

"One time though Prince miss-stepped on the rocky ground and crushed my leg against a tree. The pain was so extreme that I fell out of the saddle. I couldn't stand on that leg. I called Prince and he came to me and stood patiently while I clambered back up into the saddle. Prince was a great horse!" Archie said fondly.

Archie continued soberly, "The horses always liked to get out of the stable for a run and for a roll in the grass. One fall day, Dad let the horses out. He decided to drive them down the lane and across the road into the field by the balsams – Dad was deaf by this time. He picked up a long strip of bark and shook it at the horses to chase them across the road. Dad didn't hear the car coming. I yelled 'No!!' But it was too late. Maud got across but a car hit Prince. It broke his hind leg. Prince hobble off the road and stood in the field trembling from shock, shards of bone protruding from his dangling broken leg. We both felt sick for his pain.

"Dad went up to the house and got his big 30-30 rifle. By the time he returned, an Ontario Provincial Police officer had arrived on the scene. Dad handed the officer his rifle and asked him to shoot the horse. None of us wanted to shoot poor Prince! The young officer didn't want to do it either. He protested that he didn't know how to aim a rifle. Both Dad and I told him, 'Just aim at his head.'

"That was a sad, sad day," said Archie, as we all wiped away tears.

Lloyd commented, "Maud was still on the farm when Eunice and I bought it from "The Old Man" in 1957 but Maud was mostly retired because, by that time we used the tractor for the farm work. In winter Dad still liked to hitch her up and skid enough logs out of the bush for firewood though. Maud lived for about another ten years, although she was getting frail.

"Howard was visiting from California in the fall of 1968 when Maud got down in the horse pasture and couldn't get up. Howard worked to encourage her. Maud remembered her old friend and she tried her best. Howard got his shoulders under her front quarters and heaved. Maud finally made it up on her feet. It wasn't long after though, that Maud died. She was thirty years old.

"That is when the era of our farm horses came to an end," Lloyd concluded with a deep sigh.

For all of us, the memories of our beloved horses were bittersweet.

# ~What Became of the Farm?~

"What became of the farm?" I asked our brother Lloyd.

He answered, "I bought the farm from our dad in 1957. My wife Eunice, our children Alex and Cathy and I shared the farmhouse for a year with Mom and Dad while their cottage was being built."

Mom and Dad chose an acre of land across the road from the entrance to the original Peever homestead. Edna's husband Les Bain and his brothers built them a two-bedroom bungalow with an adjoining utility shed. Les Bain, being an electrician, wired it for them. Mom and Dad moved into their home in the summer of 1958. Mom had her dream home. She said, "I never wanted to climb another stair!"

The bungalow was built on a cement pad, without a basement. Our dad built a root cellar behind the house, dug into the side of a gravelly moraine. In the ancient way of pioneers, he dug into the hillside, reinforced the sides with small cedar logs and built the roof with split cedar rails. There our parents stored vegetables from their garden and Mom's preserves, safe from the winter frost. Mom was so proud of what our dad had built! Dad turned his energy into growing a thriving garden and maintaining an ample woodpile. He kept himself occupied splitting wood for the stove that heated their cottage and cooked their food.

Mom finally had time for a social life. She enjoyed the women's meetings at the original Corner Gospel Church where they both attended. Ten years later, in October 1968, Mom had a stroke that ended the period of their lives in the cottage.

Lloyd and Eunice had worked the farm. Eunice, born and raised in Toronto adjusted capably to farming life. She bore three more children, Bruce, Laurel and Eric those ten years. Lloyd and Eunice participated in the social life of the community; and Eunice played the piano for the church services at Carr United Church.

Small farms in the gravelly soil of Parry Sound District never provided enough income to sustain a family. The men always had to find work outside of the farm. Most men worked in the logging industry. The wives and children had the responsibility of maintaining the farm while the men were absent.

Years later in the comfort of their winter home in Florida, Eunice reminisced with me about some of their experiences on the farm; she related this story of coping with an emergency while Lloyd was away. "Four-year-old Bruce burst into the house calling urgently 'Mom come to the barn. We need you! ' I scooped him up and ran.

"From the top of the haymow I heard eight-year-old Alex call out, 'Hurry up Mom, I can't hold her any longer!'

"Scrambling up the ladder to Alex's side, I could see that he was holding for dear life onto his six-year-old sister Cathy's hand. She was dangling in the open space between the barn wall and bales of hay piled three stories high."

"Reaching down I got a good grip on Cathy's arm and pulled her to safety. I can't bear to think what would have happened if she had slipped from Alex's grip!" Eunice exclaimed.

Lloyd and a partner were occupied during the summer retrieving valuable hardwood logs from the bottom of lakes in the region. In years past the logs had slipped out of their booms while in transport to local sawmills. They became 'water-logged' and sank. Lloyd, as a licensed scuba diver, located logs on the lake bottom. He would attach the log to a hydraulic hoist and signal his partner on the barge to haul the log up. They sold the logs to lumber companies but Lloyd and Eunice were barely subsisting financially.

During the winter, Lloyd studied and obtained his certification as a licensed stationary engineer. In 1969, Lloyd sold the farm and took a stationary engineering job in New Hamburg (near Kitchener).

Eunice picked up her story again, "I stayed in Commanda while Lloyd rented a house and made arrangements to move the family. In the last week before Christmas, I played for the Christmas cantata at the Carr

United Church. The next day we packed a rented van with our possessions. We added a butchered beef and a Christmas tree. Lloyd drove the van while I followed in the car loaded with our five children, a dog and houseplants. I had just about reached our rented house in New Hamburg when I was stopped by an OPP officer. He looked into our crowded old car, asked me where we were going, just shook him head and said 'drive carefully'," laughed Eunice.

Lloyd and Eunice soon bought a home near Kitchener where Lloyd had a successful career as a stationary engineer with Schneider's Meats.

The era of the Peevers of Commanda ended in a similar, though more modern journey than our arriving founding forbearers experienced.

Lloyd broke in to tell his memories of what happened next, "I sold the farm to a Toronto woman who gave it to her son. He, along with his "Hippie" friends occupied the farmhouse. They had no idea how to cope with maintaining a house or farm. Those hippies had not the foresight to cut and store wood for the winter. When winter came, the hapless occupants tore up the hardwood floors and support beams of the house and burned them to keep warm. An unattended child, playing with matches, burned down the barn.

"The woman's son sold the house to an equally unreliable friend, who failed to pay the mortgage. I was forced to repossess the farm," Lloyd said with disgust.

"The farm was finally sold to Jack Bennett, the son of our old neighbours Albert, grandson of Tom Bennett senior.

"Jack Bennett used the large field bordering the road along "the flat" for pasturing deer. Jack had a business raising deer for supplying venison to trendy Toronto restaurants. Jack has since died, the rest of the farm lies fallow and the farmhouse was left in disrepair. That is what happened to the farm."

Nature is reclaiming the land where three generations of Peevers poured out their sweat and dedication. The rocky terrain of Commanda no longer produces hay or the cattle that eat it. Instead, men make their living from the very rocks that were their forefather's nemeses. Quarries dot the landscapes, producing crushed rock for road building.

In retirement Lloyd is able to spend more time in wood carving and fashioning sculptures.

In June of 2008, the Ayer News ran an article and photograph by Ron Carson of Lloyd with some of his creative work, titled: "The Life and Times of Lloyd Peever BALTIMORE ORIOLES, CARVINGS AND MUCH, MUCH MORE. A Great Story Teller Long-time New Dundee resident Lloyd Peever displays some of his wood carvings which include elaborate walking sticks, ornamental swords, Indian busts, novelty pipes and figural sculptures. Lloyd spins some great tales from a long and varied life."

# ~Passing on the Faith: The Author's Return to Tralee~

As our plane swoops low, preparing to land at Cork, Ireland we have a bird's eye view of the thumb of land that is the Dingle Peninsula, jutting out into the Atlantic Ocean. I know that at the last knuckle of that thumb is the city of Tralee, our destination. Dingle Peninsula is attached to a fist of land that is County Kerry, Ireland.

A three-hour bus ride from Cork, northwest through rolling green countryside, past sheep grazing on hillsides and peat smoke rising from thatched farm houses, is the picturesque town of Killarney. Killarney was made famous in the ballad *Over in Killarney*, sung by a homesick Irishman. In fact, as the bus slowly winds through narrow streets of the town, houses crowd right up to the sidewalks letting us view up close residents' activities of brushing a fresh coat of paint on a house and pumping gas at a service station.

Sitting at the gate of a charming bed-and-breakfast establishment is a small elderly man in a squashed green fedora, playing an accordion. His ancient knee is pumping in time to the music. What tune is he playing, I wonder?

As we angle west toward the coast, signposts with names like Killorglin and Ballyseedy, tell me that we are passing through the villages of my ancestors, and four miles later, the city of Tralee comes into view. My husband and I cross the plaza from the bus station and head for our hotel. There at the corner, waiting for the light to change, stands a cousin from New Zealand. We embrace and, suddenly I feel that I've come home.

The International Peever/O'Neill reunion in July of 2010 lasts three days. The celebrations of family blood ties are to be held at three local churches, within a few miles of each other and on three consecutive days: at St. John's, Tralee; St. Michael's, Killorglin; and at the Wesleyan Methodist church in the small village of Ballyseedy. The Ballyseedy church is my branch of the Peever family's home church.

On Saturday, the Irish contingent of Peevers provides wonderful meals, hosting two-hundred cousins visiting from Australia, New Zealand, the United States, Canada and England.

Everyone mingles, sharing family photographs, displaying their branches of the family tree, taking lots of photographs and sharing their stories.

At St. John's, Tralee and throughout the days ahead, my husband Art James, utilizing his photo journalist skills, moves unobtrusively among the knots of folks talking and examining sheets hung, displaying the various branches of the Peever family. They excitedly find themselves recorded there by the outstanding Ottawa Peever genealogist and researcher, Lois (Peever) Nuth.

They stand chatting, tall, broad-chested men and slim, fair-complexioned women, betraying their Viking/Norman bloodlines. Their ancestors are the warrior-adventurers who crossed the English Channel from Normandy in 1066 with William the Conqueror. Their names are recorded through the centuries in census and church records.

My husband creates a pictorial record of the reunion that will later be posted on the Peever website, along with photographs taken by New Zealander Kevin Weatherall and others.

Piling into convoys of cars we visit the graves of previous generations, from the 1700s to early 1900s, who are buried in those church yards. The Peevers and O'Neills, having intermarried during all those years, are buried here together. Those Peevers who crossed the Irish Sea, blending their genes with Irish Celts no doubt inherited from them the Celtic gift of music and charm.

When we visit the ancient Dromavalla graveyard, beside the newly built Killorglin church, there stands the gravestone of my great-great-grandfather John Peever, born 1743 and died at the age of ninety-six, in 1839. I pat his gravestone and say, "Hello Grandpa" in a magical moment that makes time stand still!

The Peever and O'Neill families fill the newly erected St. Michael's Church, Killorglin for worship Sunday morning. The church is built on the site of the old railway station, where in the early 1800s, Peevers and O'Neills stood waiting for the train to take them south to Cork. In Cork they boarded ships that carried them to the goldfields of Australia and New Zealand or to North America for the promise of new farmland. Feeling the pain of parting, they stood with their parents, their brothers and sisters or their lovers; each of them knowing that they'd likely never see each other again.

Before the service begins, my husband slips to the front of the church and photographs the worshipers assembled in this beautiful hallowed place.

In a soft Irish brogue the ruddy-cheeked vicar leads as together, we read Psalm One:

> *Happy is the man who does not take the wicked for his guide, nor walk the road that sinners tread nor take his seat among the scornful; the law of the Lord is his delight, the law his meditation night and day.*

Several local Peever members read the lessons and an O'Neill daughter sings a solo, the young woman's beautiful soaring voice filling the sanctuary.

In his sermon, the minister speaks of family traits like the gift of gift of music. He speaks of the gift of faith passing on from generation to generation. The congregation joins in singing the old familiar hymn, *What a Friend We have in Jesus.* The Reverend Cannon Bain Peever of the sprawling Northern Ontario Algoma District assists in serving Communion. His aesthetic but kindly face reflects the solemnity and specialness of ministering to his own kin. We go forward to partake from a common cup.

In closing, as we all sing *God Be with You Till We Meet Again*, my cheeks are wet with tears for God's faithfulness, tears of love for family ties and tears of sadness at soon parting.

In the church hall following the service our Irish cousins lay out a tasty luncheon where again we eat and mingle. A woman approaches me calling me by a name I don't know. As I turn to face her, she apologizes,

"I thought you were Nora O'Neill," she said pointing. I turn to look into the face of my double – same stature, colouring, even our hairstyle. We smile across the crowed space and I think of the power of genes that unite us.

The Ballygarry Hotel and Spa just beyond the boarder of Tralee provides a superb closing banquet, an opportunity to mingle, to know each other better and to say our farewells.

As our plane lifts off over the wide Shannon River, I leave a part of my heart in that green land and with family who continue to live and walk where my great-great-grandfather and his father before him lived and worshiped nearly three hundred years before.

John Peever's Grave

Balleyseedy Church

# ~Recipes from the Peever Kitchen~

## Stuffed Savoury Roasted Pork Side Ribs

For stuffing dice ½ loaf of day old bread

Chop 1 medium sized onion

Chop 1 celery stick - including leaves

Chop 1 tart well washed apple - skin on

Add 1 tsp sage & 1 tsp savoury & ½ tsp salt

Mix all together, add 1 beaten egg,

Pre heat oven to 325 degrees, wash and trim excess fat from a pair of side ribs

Lay 1 side of ribs, meaty side out, on large square of heavy duty tin foil

Form stuffing to fit along the ribs, cover with second side - meaty side out

Rub generously both sides with brown sugar- salt and pepper to taste

With butcher cord, tie in four places, securing rib ends firmly

Wrap snugly with heavy tin foil & place on large cookie sheet

Bake in oven for 2 hours - peel back foil - bake for 15 minutes

Turn over and bake another 15 minutes to brown both sides

Place on platter; remove string, cut in serving sizes

# ~Recipes from the Peever Kitchen~

## Tea Biscuits

2 cups all purpose flour, 4½ tsps baking powder

½ tsp salt, 2 tbsp sugar & 1¼ cup table cream

Mix lightly with a spoon & turn onto a floured board

Knead gently and roll or pat to ½ inch thickness & cut into 4-inch rounds

Bake on cookie sheet at 375 degrees for 12 – 15 minutes